FORMING AND MANAGING
A NON-PROFIT ORGANIZATION IN CANADA

Flora MacLeod

Self-Counsel Press
(*a division of*)
International Self-Counsel Press Ltd.
Canada   U.S.A.

Printed in Canada

First edition: October, 1986
Second edition: December, 1991
Third edition: May, 1995

Canadian Cataloguing in Publication Data

MacLeod, Flora.
Forming and managing a non-profit organization in Canada

(Self-counsel legal series)
ISBN 1-55180-012-8

1. Nonprofit organizations — Canada. 2. Nonprofit organizations — Law and legislation — Canada. I. Title. II. Series.
KE1373.Z82M34 1995   346.71′64   C95-910161-6
KF1388.Z9M34 1995

Self-Counsel Press
(*a division of*)
International Self-Counsel Press Ltd.
Head and Editorial Office
1481 Charlotte Road
North Vancouver, British Columbia V7J 1H1

U.S. Address
1704 N. State Street
Bellingham, Washington 98225

CONTENTS

INTRODUCTION xi

1 SO YOU WANT TO START A NON-PROFIT ORGANIZATION 1
  a. You're part of a tradition 1
  b. You're part of a trend 1
     1. Non-government organizations (NGOs) 1
     2. Volunteer associations or members of the voluntary sector 1
     3. Public interest groups 1
     4. Special interest groups 1
     5. Advocacy groups 1
     6. Private societies 2
  c. You're in good company 2
     1. Volunteer-based 2
     2. Locally based and locally accountable 2
     3. Pioneers of new services 2
     4. Non-bureaucratic 2
     5. Value based 3
  d. Case study: the birth of a non-profit organization 3
     1. The problem 3
     2. Choices 3
     3. Action 3
     4. Results and surprises 4
     5. A checklist for success 4

2 FINDING LIKE-MINDED PEOPLE 5
  a. Assembling your group 5
  b. Deciding what to do and how to do it 5
  c. The core committee 5
  d. Writing a goal statement 6
  e. Choosing a name 6
     Reading and resources 7

3 STRUCTURES AND TOOLS FOR ACTION 8
  a. Forming a board of directors 8
     1. Why a board of directors? 8
     2. The people you need 8
     3. Recruiting new board members 10
     4. Orientation for new board members 11
     5. Why volunteer? 11
  b. What other structures do you need? 12
     1. Officers 12
     2. Executive committee 13
     3. Standing committees 13
     4. Ad hoc committees 13
     5. Task force 13

		6. Committee reports	13
c.	What other tools do you need?		14
		1. An agenda	14
		2. Terms of reference	16
		3. Evaluation	16
		4. Board manual	18
		5. Board record book	19
		6. Organizational calendar	19
		Reading and resources	19
		Courses and workshops	21

4 LAYING THE GROUNDWORK FOR GOOD RECORD KEEPING 22
  a. Written records 22
    1. Taking minutes 22
    2. Keeping a register of members 23
  b. Financial records 23
    1. Opening a bank account 23
    2. Setting up books 24
    3. Appointing an auditor 26
    4. Writing receipts 26
    5. Yearly financial statements 27
  c. The annual report 27
  d. Using records to support funding proposals 30
    1. Background material 30
    2. Support documents for your proposal 30
    3. Other resources 31
    Reading and resources 32

5 HIRING STAFF 33
  a. If you hire staff 33
  b. Who hires? 34
  c. Encourage communication 34

6 FIRST STEPS TO INCORPORATION 36
  a. Why is the government involved? 36
  b. Deciding to incorporate 36
  c. Deciding not to incorporate 38
  d. Steps to incorporation 38
  e. Gathering the documents 39
  f. Reserving a name for your society 39
    1. Representation 39
    2. Acronyms 40
  g. Procedure for reservation 40
    1. British Columbia 41
    2. Alberta 41
    3. Saskatchewan 42
    4. Manitoba 42
    5. Ontario 42

7 CONSTITUTION AND ARTICLES OF INCORPORATION   53
   a. Drafting your constitution   53
   b. Eligibility for registered charitable status   53
       1. Charitable goals   54
       2. No political activity or lobbying   54
       3. Wind-up clause   54
       4. No purpose of gain for members   54
       5. Unalterability clause   55
   c. Sample constitution   55
   d. Variations in provincial requirements   55
       1. British Columbia   55
       2. Alberta   55
       3. Saskatchewan   57
       4. Manitoba   59
       5. Ontario   62

8 FINAL STEPS TO INCORPORATION
(BY-LAWS AND OTHER DOCUMENTS)   71
   a. British Columbia   71
       1. By-laws   71
       2. Comments on the by-laws   72
       3. Preparing your by-laws   81
       4. List of first directors   81
       5. Notice of address   81
       6. Submitting your documents   84
   b. Alberta   88
       1. By-laws   88
       2. Comments on the by-laws   88
       3. Arbitration   91
       4. Custody and use of the society's seal   91
       5. Minute books and records   92
       6. Preparing your by-laws   92
       7. Notice of address   92
       8. Submitting your documents   92
   c. Saskatchewan   95
       1. By-laws   95
       2. The Saskatchewan Non-Profit Corporations Act   95
       3. Preparing your documents   100
       4. Notice of directors   100
       5. Notice of registered office   100
       6. Submitting your documents   100
   d. Manitoba   105
       1. By-laws   105
       2. Submitting your documents   106
   e. Ontario   115
       1. By-laws   115
       2. Submitting your documents   116

9	**MAINTAINING YOUR LEGAL STATUS**		125
	a.	British Columbia	125
		1. Ongoing requirements	125
		2. Registering changes	126
	b.	Alberta	128
		1. Ongoing requirements	128
		2. Registering changes	131
	c.	Saskatchewan	133
		1. Ongoing requirements	133
		2. Registering changes	133
	d.	Manitoba	138
		1. Ongoing requirements	138
		2. Registering changes	138
	e.	Ontario	144
		1. Ongoing requirements	144
		2. Registering changes	144

10	**FEDERAL INCORPORATION**		153
	a.	Obtaining information	153
	b.	Name search and name reservation	153
	c.	Application and by-laws	154
	d.	Staying incorporated	154

11	**REGISTERING AS A CHARITY**		167
	a.	Definition of charitable organization	168
	b.	Steps to registration	169
		1. Applying for registration	169
		2. Completing the application form	169
		3. Collecting the necessary documents	169
	c.	Issuing official receipts	172
	d.	Filing an annual return	173
		1. The Registered Charity Information Return and Public Information Return (Form T3010)	173
		2. Schedules	179
	e.	Keeping books and records	179
	f.	Change of name	180
	g.	Change of address	180
	h.	Ceasing to operate as a charity	180
		Reading and resources	180

12	**THE GOODS AND SERVICES TAX**		184
	a.	Paying the GST on goods and services purchased	184
	b.	Charging customers the GST	184
	c.	Informing customers	186
	d.	To register or not to register	186
	e.	Applying for GST rebates	186
		1. Eligibility for rebates	186
		2. Qualifying as a claimant	186
		3. Filing a return	187

f. Adjusting bookkeeping procedures   187
    Reading and resources   187

13 EARLY DAYS: PUBLICITY AND PUBLIC EDUCATION   192
a. Introducing your society   192
    1. Reaching the public   192
    2. Credibility   192
    3. Clarity of message   192
b. Strategies for gaining support   193
    1. Publicity   193
    2. Education   193
    3. Lobbying and advocacy   193
    4. Local networking   193
    5. Research   193
    6. Requesting help   193
c. Your public relations committee   193
d. Cost   194
e. Networking   194
    Reading and resources   195

14 TRENDS AFFECTING THE VOLUNTARY SECTOR   197
a. Government policy patterns   197
    1. Restraint   197
    2. Privatization   197
    3. Charities and their advocacy role   198
    4. Charitable donations and their impact on government revenue   199
    5. The GST and its impact on non-profit organizations   199
    6. Public gaming   199
b. Organizational management   199
    1. Exploring new structures and styles   199
    2. Sophisticated fundraising   200
    3. Doing more with less   200
    4. Entrepreneurship   200
    5. Using information technology   200
c. Voluntarism   201
    1. Recognizing the economic value of volunteers   201
    2. Participation and empowerment   201
    3. Improving volunteer management   201
d. Voluntary sector   202

FIGURES

#1 Board organization model   9
#2 Committee membership chart   14

SAMPLES

#1	Agenda	15
#2	Terms of reference	17
#3	Register of members	24
#4	Budget	25
#5	Thank-you note	26
#6	Statement of income and expenses	28
#7	Balance sheet	29
#8	Name approval request form (British Columbia)	43
#9	Request for name search and reservation (Saskatchewan)	45
#10	Request for corporate name reservation (Manitoba)	47
#11	Constitution	56
#12	Application under Societies Act (Alberta)	58
#13	Articles of incorporation (Saskatchewan)	60
#14	Articles of incorporation (Manitoba)	63
#15	Application for incorporation (Ontario)	67
#16	By-laws (British Columbia)	73
#17	Constitution title page (British Columbia)	82
#18	List of first directors (British Columbia)	85
#19	Notice of address (British Columbia)	86
#20	Covering Letter (British Columbia)	87
#21	By-laws (Alberta)	89
#22	Notice of address (Alberta)	93
#23	Request for Corporate Services (Alberta)	94
#24	Saskatchewan Non-Profit Corporations Act	96
#25	Notice of Directors (Saskatchewan)	101
#26	Notice of Registered Office (Saskatchewan)	103
#27	By-laws (Manitoba)	107
#28	Transmittal Notice (Manitoba)	114
#29	By-laws of Corporation Without Share Capital (Ontario)	117
#30	Annual Report Notice (British Columbia)	127
#31	Special Resolution Notice (British Columbia)	129
#32	Notice of Change of Directors (British Columbia)	130
#33	Society Annual Return (Alberta)	132
#34	Annual Return (Saskatchewan)	134
#35	Articles of Amendment (Saskatchewan)	136
#36	Annual Return of Information (Manitoba)	139
#37	Articles of Amendment (Manitoba)	141
#38	Notice of Change of Directors (Manitoba)	142
#39	Notice of Change of Registered Office (Manitoba)	143
#40	Initial Notice/Notice of Change (Ontario)	147
#41	Application for Supplementary Letters Patent (Ontario)	149
#42	Application for Change in Location of Records (Ontario)	151
#43	Application for Federal Incorporation	156

#44 Sample By-laws for a Federal Corporation   159
#45 Annual Report (Federal Corporation)   164
#46 Sample Letter   165
#47 Letters Patent   166
#48 Application for Income Tax Registration   170
#49 Registered Charity Information Return and Public Information Return   174
#50 Schedule 1   181
#51 Schedules 2 and 3   183
#52 GST Rebate Application   190

NOTICE TO READERS

INTRODUCTION

This book is intended as a practical guide and source of ideas for those of you active in community groups. In particular, it is designed to help you legally incorporate your organization as a provincial or territorial non-profit society or corporation, and to obtain registration as a charity from the federal government. The terms "society" and "organization" are used interchangeably throughout the book to refer to non-profit community groups that meet to promote some common interest rather than make a profit for individual members.

Depending on which province or territory you live in, registration is carried out under a Society Act or Corporation Act. It is also possible to incorporate federally under the Canada Incorporation Act. Generally, only those organizations which operate on a national basis will choose to incorporate under this act.

This book is directed to those of you who are board members, volunteers, or staff in local, volunteer-based societies concerned with matters such as social service programs, recreation, heritage preservation, education, the environment, the arts, music, and culture.

You can expect to find practical information on forming and operating a board of directors, setting up committees, planning an agenda, maintaining financial records, and incorporating and registering your non-profit society. At the end of most chapters you will find a resource list of suggestions for further reading and sources of inexpensive or free materials.

Finally, the book gives ideas for introducing your society to the community, and for setting up and maintaining good relations with other groups, the media, and with government.

1
SO YOU WANT TO START A NON-PROFIT ORGANIZATION

a. YOU'RE PART OF A TRADITION

Over the centuries, people have gathered together in groups because of the interests or goals they shared. Organized around work, religion, or learning, groups such as guilds, trade associations, lay societies, and universities have become part of our world. Some existed to serve their own membership; others were charities that fed and housed the poor, or founded hospitals and orphanages, providing a basis for the health and social welfare services of today.

But what do these venerable institutions have in common with today's societies and organizations — the local art gallery, environmental groups, or Meals on Wheels? Each of them went through the following stages:

(a) Identification of a need

(b) Agreement by a number of people that a change in the status quo was required

(c) Belief that, collectively, the personal and financial resources to reach agreed-upon goals could be generated

(d) Conviction that a group of people can collaborate to effect a change themselves rather than request action by government or the private sector

b. YOU'RE PART OF A TREND

There are 71 000 registered societies in Canada today. The vast majority of these were formed in the past ten years. Currently about 2 500 charities register each year. These non-profit societies wear one or more of many possible labels:

1. Non-government organizations (NGOs)

This is a label usually applied to national groups like the Elizabeth Fry Society or the Canadian Association for Adult Education. They may be concerned with service or policy but operate under a voluntary board of directors. Many local groups, such as United Way member agencies, Boys' and Girls' Clubs, or Family Service Agencies, are included under this label.

2. Volunteer associations or members of the voluntary sector

This designation describes the relationship between members and their management by an unpaid board of directors.

3. Public interest groups

These include groups with an interest in broad public policy and often an educational role, such as the Canadian Civil Liberties Association or the Consumers Association of Canada.

4. Special interest groups

Special interest groups have defined areas of concern, and usually undertake both public education and advocacy to promote a point of view. Examples are: Mothers Against Drunk Drivers or Canadian Congress for Learning Opportunities for Women.

5. Advocacy groups

These groups represent the interests of defined sectors of society, such as the National Action Committee on the Status of Women.

6. Private societies

Private societies are organized on the impetus of citizens for purposes they themselves define, and are different from public bodies that have statutory duties defined by government. All of the above groups are also private societies.

Why are there so many? Non-profit societies have a traditional role in identifying needs and initiating action to fill gaps in service. This is particularly so in social, recreational, and health services. In this way, they supplement the function of older, more established institutions. In the past, private services have tended to be transferred to public management because of cost or a changing sense of need. For example, a program for parents who have abused their children may be moved from private auspices to the department of social services, where it can be made part of child protection services and expanded to unserved areas.

While the formation of new societies continues, the trend for government to absorb their services is being arrested or even reversed. Increasingly, governments, particularly at the provincial level, are divesting themselves of social services. Some are being picked up by existing agencies, some will be put out for bids or contracted out to new non-profit societies, some will be run on a profit making basis as businesses, and some will simply cease to exist.

Your interest in forming a non-profit society may be directly related to this "privatization" process (see chapter 14 on Trends). If so, pay particular attention to adequate funding, establishing standards of service to clients, good management, program evaluation, and relationship with unions. Also, check the Society Act in your province for special licence requirements for such services as day care or homes for children.

c. YOU'RE IN GOOD COMPANY

It's true that universities, hospitals, foundations, and large agencies are non-profit societies. But most non-profit societies are small, specific in focus, and perform at least two of the following functions:

(a) Service (social, recreational, artistic)

(b) Action (reform, lobbyism, policy development)

(c) Information sharing (hobby groups, collegial associations)

Small, non-profit societies also tend to have the following characteristics in common.

1. Volunteer-based

Even if some staff are paid to provide service or administration, the board of directors is unpaid.

2. Locally based and locally accountable

Even province-wide societies tend to operate in a network of other groups and services, and to recruit their volunteer support from people within a professional, civic, or geographic constituency.

3. Pioneers of new services

They often develop new solutions to previously unrecognized problems. The transition house movement is a good example. Although the first refuges for battered women and their children were opened in Canada only in 1972, now they are operating or being established across the country. Almost all function substantially on grants from government, but are started and run by non-profit societies. They provide a powerful means of citizen participation, education, and influence.

4. Non-bureaucratic

They usually have smaller, more decentralized structures than government agencies, with the potential for greater adaptability and responsiveness.

5. Value based

They are often controversial, innovative, and non-traditional.

But not all community groups become non-profit societies. Groups spring to life for brief periods, particularly those that respond to a crisis (for example, citizens concerned about flood control). These are ad hoc action groups, not necessarily designed to last beyond the problem they organized to meet. Some evolve into more permanent groups; for example, stopping an expressway from destroying a neighbourhood leads to a ratepayer's or neighbourhood association. Others decline and are dormant for a time, capable of re-emerging to meet some future need.

d. CASE STUDY: THE BIRTH OF A NON-PROFIT ORGANIZATION

1. The problem

Suppose you have just learned that an historically important, attractive, and structurally sound building in your town is about to be bulldozed to make way for a shopping centre. In spite of a flurry of protests to city council, it is in fact too late to save it. You and the others who actively or quietly opposed the demolition meet to commiserate and wonder what part of your past will disappear next in the name of progress.

You know there are other structures in town of historical importance. Why not form an historical society? Such a group would be able to survey these structures, decide which are most vulnerable to loss or decay, set priorities, and make proposals for their better use and preservation. Maybe next time you'll be able to redirect that bulldozer.

2. Choices

You and your group will have some choices to make. Do you form a local, independent non-profit society, perhaps affili-

ated with a regional or provincial heritage group? Or do you become a branch of that regional or provincial heritage society?

At this stage, doing your homework is particularly important. Is there already a heritage society active in your area? Has some other group or organization formed a committee devoted to the subject? Nobody wants to use up scarce financial and volunteer resources duplicating services or activities. In the course of making these inquiries, you may discover people interested in joining you. "No, we've never catalogued old buildings in the district. Maybe our library board would like to be involved and lend support."

3. Action

As you begin your work, you become part of the community fabric, finding allies, sources of information, and support. You or other members of your group might begin to —

(a) Attend city council meetings regularly to get notice early of proposed developments

(b) Discover local and regional physical and social planning bodies and make yourself known to them

(c) Get to know local, municipal, provincial, and federal politicians

(d) Find yourself involved in related causes. These might range from flood control to protect the settlers' bridge, to community work service orders where young offenders paint the converted railway station

(e) Liaise with the local real estate board (is the historic Smith house for sale?) and the board of trade (the local craft guild needs a licence to sell goods at the heritage railway station)

(f) Write a column in the community newspaper to inform people of your work, garner interest, and lobby for support and money

(g) Contribute articles to magazines devoted to heritage planning or architectural concerns

(h) Work with a group of seniors who are putting together a catalogue of pioneer homes with anecdotes of pioneer life

The list goes on and on. The number of possible activities is limited only by the numbers in your group, your energy, and your creativity.

4. Results and surprises

Looking back after several years, your fledgling society may find that it has many accomplishments to its credit. It may have saved and renovated historical structures in your community; created a constituency of concerned people with an active interest in local history; been a vehicle for the development of leadership skills (for example, your past president is now on city council); lobbied for and effected reform (for example, procedures for changing zoning regulations); sent delegates to provincial and national conferences; spoken to provincial and national policy; helped to change legislation.

The prospects are limitless and exciting and your success is deserved.

5. A checklist for success

Based on your experience, what advice could you pass on to others? Looking back, you realize that the following steps were important in the establishment and growth of your group. As an individual you:

(a) had a clear idea of the problem and determined whether it was short-term or ongoing,

(b) knew you weren't the only person interested or concerned, and discovered others who cared, and

(c) got together with others for an initial planning meeting.

As a group, you then:

(a) decided on a needs assessment to systematically determine the extent of the problem and to provide a basis for decisions about priorities,

(b) checked out existing resources and other organizations which might already be active on your problem and might be able to support and advise you,

(c) made an informed and politically astute decision about whether or not to become a subcommittee of an existing board, that is, add your problem to the mandate of an existing group or agency,

(d) established your new society within the network of community services, including local, provincial, and federal services, by attending joint meetings of agencies and services and by arranging representation for your group on relevant community boards and committees, and

(e) utilized visits, delegations, press releases, media presentations, briefs, reports, brochures, demonstrations, and research.

This rapid trip from the start of a society to its maturity gives some idea of how important the early planning stages are. The step from "idea" to "organization" is examined in detail in the next chapter.

2
FINDING LIKE-MINDED PEOPLE

If your undertaking is large or long-term, you will be looking for confidantes, allies, and partners who share your goal. While your group may be united in common purpose, individuals may have different ideas about how to achieve that purpose; you may agree on a problem but not what to do about it.

In the early stages, you have two immediate tasks: assembling your group and deciding on a course of action.

a. ASSEMBLING YOUR GROUP

The people who have the same concerns as you may be easy to identify; for example, those who came out to a public meeting on the dumping of industrial waste in your community, or the parents of the other children in a class for the learning disabled.

Or, make a contact list of people who *ought* to share your concern. For example, who should care about starting a sexual assault centre? Your list could include:

(a) people who are directly affected, such as parents, teens, or former victims,

(b) people in professional roles (police, doctors, lawyers, emergency ward staff, counsellors), and

(c) people concerned with social policy, education, and prevention including selected members of government at all levels, the media, and teachers.

b. DECIDING WHAT TO DO AND HOW TO DO IT

Once your group decides to meet, you should be able to clarify the problem or issue and the next steps to be taken. For example, the group concerned with the dumping of industrial waste will want to spell out the reasons why they are against dumping. They will then have to decide whether they wish to "go public" at this stage. They may decide to marshal information, conduct research, seek expert opinion, or exercise political pressure. They may disagree on whether to picket, demonstrate, or take some other form of direct action. Some may want public meetings and information booths; others may want to petition only the industry and levels of government involved.

All of these decisions are part of the process of definition that will eventually articulate the group's goals. Decisions taken also indicate the group's style and method (confrontational, persuasive, educational, and so on). Finally, they give clues to the group's values and philosophy, though these may not be so clearly articulated at this stage. Some groups choose to be explicit about values and list basic assumptions that will guide future decisions. Those individuals who prefer some other solution will probably withdraw at this stage, or, on the other hand, may be willing to suspend their concerns for a trial period.

c. THE CORE COMMITTEE

In the early stages of an organization, numbers are small so keeping in touch and making decisions is easier. Reaching consensus is also more likely. What you have organized is the core committee (also known as the founding committee). As we have already seen, it is the group that decides the central purpose and method of operation. Its primary aim is to define goals and methods sufficiently to attract new members and supporters.

Most core committee members meet regularly and often. They may appoint a permanent chairperson or assign that role on a rotating basis.

Some core committees make decisions only by consensus, some assign members to make decisions in designated areas of responsibility, and some decide that if any two or three members agree, a decision may be made and action taken on behalf of the whole group.

d. WRITING A GOAL STATEMENT

A useful goal statement is a single sentence describing what your group aims to do. For example, the Vulnerable Valley Environmental Society's goal statement is: "To protect Vulnerable Valley and its watershed from damage to its ecological balance or visual beauty."

There may be disagreement among members about the definition of "ecological balance" and "visual beauty." The discussion and resulting decisions will constitute the policy of the group. If the group is to hold together, those policy decisions will fit with the values and philosophies of the group's members.

Note that the Vulnerable Valley Environmental Society decided on "protect" as the key verb, not "educate about," "demonstrate how," "prevent from," or even "preserve from," though all of these goals may be implied by the words "to protect" and may be referred to in the constitution of the society when it is written.

The goal statement of the Vulnerable Valley Environmental Society will prove useful for explaining the purpose of the group to new members, the community, media, funders, government, and industry. The goal statement will probably be found on their posters, brochures, and perhaps letterhead. It will also be an essential part of the application of the group for registered society status.

When your group has met a few times, try the following exercise:

- Ask everyone to write down on a piece of paper one sentence describing the group and its purpose (the reasons for its existence)

- Write each of these on a flip chart

- Find which words everyone agrees on

- Construct your one-sentence goal statement

e. CHOOSING A NAME

Deciding on a legally registered name for your society will be discussed in chapter 6. It will be one of the first decisions your group makes in the process of becoming a society. In the meantime, what your group calls itself will affect who joins. For example, the name Vulnerable Valley Environmental Society defines a geographic area — not as small as Contributory Creek, but not as large as Regional River. And as an environmental society, the group has clearly described its scope and focus.

Some groups work hard to create an acronym such as PACE (Pacific Association for Continuing Education) or CARE (Child Abuse Research and Education). Some society names like Greenpeace or Red Cross have become household words even though they are symbolic rather than directly descriptive. Others, regardless of their legal name, are forever known by their function, such as the crisis centre or the information bureau. Probably the best advice is to keep it short, descriptive, and unique.

In general, the early stages are a time of optimism, cohesion, and high energy. Because they are breaking new ground, members will look to each other for advice, support, and recognition of effort. If the group decides to set up a more formal, long-term organization, then structures to ensure responsible leadership and continuity will be needed.

READING AND RESOURCES

Hill, Karen. *Helping You Helps Me: A Guideline for Self-Help Groups*. Ottawa: Canada Council on Social Development, 1983. 80 pp. Costs $4 plus 40¢ for shipping and handling.

Focuses on getting started and maintaining group momentum; see chapters on problem identification, problem solving, and growth. Brief and in point form. Available from:

Canada Council on Social
  Development
P.O. Box 3505, Station "C"
Ottawa, ON K1Y 4G1
Tel: (613) 728-1865
Fax: (613) 728-9387

Stronger Together: Recruiting and Working with Ethnocultural Volunteers. Central Volunteer Bureau of Ottawa. Carleton, 1990. 30 pp. Free.

Covers benefits, challenges, recruitment, interviewing, and training as well as support and supervision of minority volunteers. Includes a list of Ottawa, Ontario, and federal resources.

Lautenschlager, Janet. *Volunteering: A Traditional Canadian Value*. Voluntary Action Directorate, 1992. 43 pp. Free.

An interesting history of voluntarism in Canada, including chapters on ethnocultural organizations and cultural diversity. Both are available from:

Voluntary Action Programs
Canadian Heritage
Ottawa, ON K1A 0M5
Tel: (613) 996-5977

Schindler-Rainman, Eva. *The Creative Volunteer Community*. Vancouver Volunteer Centre, 1987. 141 pp. Costs $10 plus $1.75 handling.

Includes articles on motivating and recruiting volunteers, community change, and effective boards and meetings. Available from:

Vancouver Volunteer Centre
301 - 3102 Main Street
Vancouver, BC V5T 3G7
Tel: (604) 875-9144

Volunteers Working Together: Skills Program for Management Volunteers. Love Printing, Stittsville, ON, 1986. 124 pp. Costs $10 plus GST and handling.

A participant workbook developed for volunteers in recreation, fitness, and sport, but useful for all types of volunteer programs. The manual provides a step by step approach to topics which measure organizational vitality such as recruitment, training, communication, and negotiation. Part of a series of workbooks available from:

National Office
Skills Program
1600 James Naismith Drive
Gloucester, ON K1B 5N4
Tel: (613) 748-5666
Fax: (613) 748-5706

3
STRUCTURES AND TOOLS
FOR ACTION

The point of forming a non-profit society is to achieve an end: action, information, service. Your group will want to find effective means of making decisions, keeping records, evaluating progress, and providing accountability. The core or founding committee generally forms the base of the first board of the new non-profit society.

a. FORMING A BOARD OF DIRECTORS

1. Why a board of directors?

The board of directors is the main body that carries out the work of your society. The board provides continuity to the organization and helps define responsibility, leadership, and lines of authority. Specifically, the board assigns responsibility for the handling of funds. It also provides a forum for making decisions and settling disputes. And finally, the board sets policy by interpreting the goals, directions, and priorities of the group.

It is important to note that a board of directors is a legal requirement under the provincial legislation by which societies are registered, and under federal policy by which charities are registered and granted tax-exempt status. (Only registered charities may provide a receipt which allows donors to deduct contributions on their income tax returns.)

Some groups which have been accustomed to operating as a collective or at least on a simple consensus basis may opt for minimal structure and assign responsibility for chairing meetings, keeping books, and recording minutes on a rotating basis. A board of directors will still have to be named and a president designated for purposes of records deposited with provincial and federal authorities.

These regulations are not designed to restrict societies but to provide some assurance that they are responsibly run and that the money spent is properly accounted for.

The organizational chart of a transition house society (shown in Figure #1) demonstrates one model of board organization including the respective tasks of various groups and the line of authority when decisions are made. In this case, the executive would probably be made up of the president, vice-president, treasurer, and secretary.

The treasurer heads the finance committee and the vice-president and secretary may head other important committees.

2. The people you need

Generally, people on a new board are:

(a) self-starters who recognized a problem or proposed an idea;

(b) those who have special skills: legal, financial, media;

(c) those who represent a geographic region, an interest group, an area of service, or specific organizations important to the goal of the new society; or

(d) important because of other roles they play, for example, city councillor, clergy, user of the society's service (for example, parent, victim).

FIGURE #1
BOARD ORGANIZATION MODEL

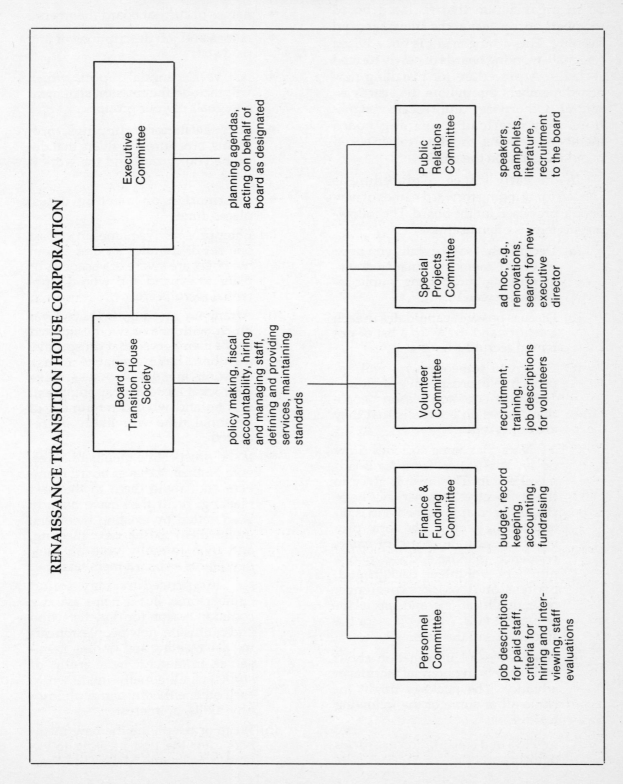

3. Recruiting new board members

You may in the past have been a member of an organization that replaced board members once a year at the annual general meeting. This arrangement is not advised for small, working boards of newly formed societies. A procedure for installing new board members throughout the year is essential. Otherwise, unforeseen resignations may overload remaining board members, leaving too few experienced people to carry on the work.

In the early stages, a procedure is needed for bringing forward names of new people proposed for the board. The following strategy is often useful.

(a) Decide what sort of skills you need in board members (management, accounting, fundraising, public relations, research).

(b) Discuss possible candidates in each category and draw up a list of potential recruits.

(c) Designate someone who will approach the prospective member. The most common reason people don't serve on boards is that they are not asked!

Note that some societies draw up an application form for board membership. This form is given to the prospective member once he or she has been approached and is interested in joining. The form provides an accurate record of name, residence, mailing address, phone numbers, volunteer background, professional work experience, other qualifications, and special interests or skills. Add a place for the signature and the date.

(d) Send copies of information about your society to potential recruits in advance. The package might include all or some of the following features:

- by-laws and constitution or articles of incorporation

- financial statements, including sources of money

- names of current board members

- names and job descriptions of any paid staff

- last year's annual report, which will include the mission statement and goals of your group

- any newsletters, clippings, programs, brochures, or flyers that describe your group and the work it does

- information on meeting dates, places, times

(e) Enter prospective names in at least one set of minutes so that absent members are aware of vacancies or plans to expand and who the potential recruits are.

(f) Arrange a meeting, perhaps over lunch, with one or two designated board members so that prospective members have a chance to ask questions and discuss issues. Make clear what the term of appointment will be and what commitment of personal time will likely be required.

(g) If the prospective members agree, vote on their status as board members and invite them to the next meeting, or, if they have already been vetted by existing members, invite them to the next meeting, and then formally vote on their new status as board members.

This procedure may sound cumbersome, but it helps avoid a common reason for dissatisfaction and confusion: new people appearing at a meeting and finding themselves immersed in a group of strangers, all equally unknown to each other either by name, philosophy, skills, or interests.

(h) Write or telephone the new members after the first meeting to extend a welcome. Make sure their questions are answered promptly and honestly. Boards vary in how they handle the details of getting items on the agenda, writing cheques, or arranging publicity. A chance to clarify such matters will affect the new member's sense of belonging and participation.

Think ahead! Keep a profile on board members so you know who they are, their skills, who they represent, their interests, and the relative balance of men/women, clients/community, and seniors/youth. Determine your needs for nomination to the board well in advance. Keep a recruitment committee active, regularly searching for prospective board members from ranks of committees, general membership, or the community. A board should have a balance of experience between "old" members and energetic "new blood."

4. Orientation for new board members

What do your recruits need to know to be useful, effective members of boards in general? What do they need to know to be members of the board of your society in particular?

There is excellent literature on the subject of training members of established boards. Your local library is an essential resource. Others are the volunteer centre, social service coordinating centre, social planning council, United Way, or community college. Consultation or evening sessions and workshops may be available on such topics as —

- recruitment
- rules of order
- decision-making processes
- conflict resolution
- volunteer recognition
- board development
- standards of volunteer service

If you choose to remain a society with no paid staff, then designate an interested board member to keep an eye on potential training opportunities for both new and current board members.

For new members on a relatively new board, orientation might cover the following topics.

(a) A clear sense of their place in the history of the society. The introduction of new members is a good time to review your society's development and what interim and long-term goals are still to be reached. Informal get-togethers with other board members or staff are essential. New members also need a chance to present themselves and their interests — what they hope to offer and what they hope to gain as board members — in a structured setting, perhaps at a special board meeting.

(b) An opportunity to learn about the work of your society: theories, issues, programs, interests, and services. A personal tour of service agencies or programs is helpful.

(c) Copies of essential documents such as the constitution or articles of incorporation, financial statements, annual reports, and a complete list of the names, addresses, and telephone numbers of other directors, volunteers, and staff. An up-to-date copy of the board manual (discussed later in this chapter) will contain this information.

5. Why volunteer?

So far we have considered what the board member can do for the society. What about the needs of the board member? What does he or she get out of joining your board of directors?

Being a member of a well-functioning board — making an efficient, well-focused contribution of time and energy for a useful civic purpose — is a pleasure. And board membership, as in the corporate world, is a means of exercising leadership, expanding business and social contacts, and working with people from other professional and personal backgrounds you might not otherwise meet.

But starting a non-profit society makes great demands on the time and commitment of volunteers. They are involved in a creative as well as social or organizational venture, with the accompanying stresses and strains of trailblazing. Of course, the sense of accomplishment is great too, but only if the new board has a collective talent for periodically recognizing and celebrating the society's achievements.

The new board should provide the following support for its members:

(a) Periodic review of long-term goals and short-term objectives. Feedback about work completed or not yet completed gives a renewed sense of direction and an opportunity for review.

(b) Acknowledgment of the personal commitment the members have made. Six months on a new board may demand more time and energy than several years on an established board.

(c) The opportunity to be realistic if a personal crisis or heavy professional commitment means a member cannot do justice to the board. Some options include resignation with a clear conscience about the value of work contributed; an invitation to rejoin in another six months or a year; approval of a formal leave of absence, during which the member receives minutes to keep in touch but retires from the committee work and regular meetings.

(d) The opportunity to learn new skills within a "buddy" system. For example, Joan may be a media expert; Peter wants to become more skilled at generating publicity and doing radio and TV work. They can work

as a team until Peter is capable and comfortable on his own, when he can "buddy" somebody else.

(e) The chance to learn and grow. Sponsor board members at workshops and conferences; ask them to attend as board representatives with a responsibility to report back to the board. The member receives recognition by association and also learns about specific issues such as the effect of acid rain, management issues for crisis centres, or new discoveries related to learning disabilities.

(f) Recognition of individual achievements and celebration of the collective goals reached.

People support causes and organizations in a range of ways. Some may be active participants, contributing time, energy, skills, and possibly goods and money. Some may volunteer but do not have money to contribute. Others may offer money, and still others lend their names only to support a group or action. All deserve attention, acknowledgment, and a thank you from the non-profit society that benefits from their help.

b. WHAT OTHER STRUCTURES DO YOU NEED?

1. Officers

Officers of the board are the people who have been elected president, vice-president, secretary, and treasurer. Their various duties are usually spelled out in the by-laws of the society.

The president acts as chairperson of meetings of the board and executive committee. He or she is often the spokesperson for the society and gives leadership to society staff and volunteers.

The vice-president not only acts in the absence of the president, but also usually heads one of the important standing committees of the board, such as personnel.

The secretary keeps minutes of board and executive committee meetings and maintains the registry of members. The secretary may also be responsible for the society's correspondence.

The treasurer has final responsibility for the books, budget, and financial records, and may also chair the finance committee.

The officers work together as a leadership team and facilitate the democratic function of the board and society.

2. Executive committee

The executive committee is made up of the officers and possibly the chairpersons of standing committees of the board. It is responsible for decisions made between board meetings and for other regular tasks delegated to it by the board. Two (or more) of the executive members will have the authority to sign cheques, although decisions about other than routine expenditures will probably be made by the board. The executive committee draws up the agenda for regular board meetings. If the board meets monthly, the executive committee will schedule regular meetings ten days to two weeks in advance of board meetings, allowing sufficient time for materials (including the agenda) to be mailed out and read by the directors.

3. Standing committees

Standing committees are permanent subcommittees of the board. They derive their authority from and report regularly to the board of directors. Generally committees recommend ways the board should act, so they are an important means for delegating and carrying out the work of the society.

Because of the need for clear lines of responsibility about who reports to the board, a member of the board of directors usually chairs the subcommittee. Some subcommittees involve society members other than directors, and others draw on people in the community who may be willing to work with the society as volunteers even though they do not have a direct voice in society policy. Standing committees

must determine how often they plan to meet. An agenda should be prepared for each meeting and minutes kept.

Don't overload any one board member with too much committee work. Some handbooks on effective board management recommend drawing up a simple chart of committees and board members active on committees that quickly displays who is overloaded and who may not be pulling his or her weight (see Figure #2).

4. Ad hoc committees

Modern boards tend to use the ad hoc committee (or task force — see below) in preference to loading standing committees with more work. Ad hoc committees are established by the board when required.

They are short-term and issue specific. An example might be a search committee to find a new executive director or a renovations committee to plan and supervise changes to an art gallery.

5. Task force

A task force implies high profile, goal-oriented activity within a defined period of time and with very specific objectives. A task force is a temporary committee undertaking a task that doesn't fit the mandate of a regular standing committee.

The task force is often investigative or exploratory, resulting in recommendations to the board of directors. The task force then disbands.

Both the ad hoc committee and the task force are short-term commitments. They may in fact prove more satisfying from the volunteer's point of view: the work is clearly defined, a completion date is targeted, and a contribution is made and recognized.

6. Committee reports

The chairperson of a standing or ad hoc committee reports to the board, using minutes of subcommittee meetings as a basic source of information. Regular monthly, interim, or final reports to the board should be

FIGURE #2
COMMITTEE MEMBERSHIP CHART

COMMITTEE ACTIVITY OF DIRECTORS — 199-									
Committee (*Chair)	M.B.	P.B.	P.W.	L.B.	J.G.	G.O.	S.D.	A.R.	W.S.
Executive		X	X			X*			X
Personnel	X						X*		
Finance			X*						X
P.R.					X*	X			
Ad hoc			X				X*		

concise, factual and, if possible, in writing. If you are preparing a report, give the name of the committee, list the committee members and chairperson, briefly restate the mandate, and describe the work to date and recommendations. Remember to date the report. The secretary should file a copy with the board records. Members of the subcommittee should also receive a copy of the report.

The various structures of a non-profit society are designed to support democratic decision making. Members of a new society may be of one mind about goals but have very different points of view about the ways to reach these goals.

Parliamentary procedure sets out ground rules for decision making while still allowing minority opinion to be expressed. Work for consensus or degrees of consensus. But agree on the ground rules of how your meetings are to be run.

c. WHAT OTHER TOOLS DO YOU NEED?

1. An agenda

The agenda is essentially a plan for the work to be conducted at a meeting. It includes regular items, such as adoption of the minutes of the previous meeting and reports from the executive or subcommittees, and other matters for discussion. A good agenda catches the interest of the participants and provides the framework for making decisions and getting work done.

An example is shown in Sample #1. Note that the sample agenda has the following features:

(a) allows for the addition of items, but with the recognition that the meeting time may have to be extended by agreement of the group,

(b) is a "heavy" agenda, with two important, potentially controversial

SAMPLE #1
AGENDA

VULNERABLE VALLEY ENVIRONMENTAL SOCIETY
Board of Directors' Meeting
Wednesday, October 25, 199-
7 - 9 P.M., Elk's Hall
Anyville

AGENDA

Introduction of Mayor John Black	7:00	
Any additional agenda items?	7:05	
1. Adoption or amendments to minutes of September meeting	7:10	
2. Correspondence: letter from National Environmental Society re affiliation — Janet Grey	7:15	Decision
3. Proposed Anyville municipal policy on environmental conservation — Mayor John Black	7:30	Information & discussion
4. Treasurer's report and purchase of advertising space in weekly newspaper — Peter White	7:50	Decision
5. Complaint re M & B Sawmill pollution: presentation and recommendation by Emergency Action Committee — Susan White	8:10	Discussion & policy decision
6. Membership committee report — Hugh Green	8:40	Information
7. Request for speaker from Vulnerable Valley's High School re today's environmental issues — Gloria Ochre	8:45	Decision
8. Booth for Fall Fair — Gloria Ochre	8:55	Decision
9. Next meeting dates	9:00	Please note

items (3 and 5). However, in item 3 the decision may be to defer a vote to a later meeting, or to form a sub-committee to review the policy proposal. It would have to be clear what action the municipal council expects of the society. A comment on the draft proposal? Endorsement? Probably the mayor would leave after the discussion. Item 5 would result in a vote, especially if the emergency action committee believes timing is important,

(c) closes with two "easy" items,

(d) lists estimated time to make everyone aware of the progress of discussion,

(e) lists expected action for each item: information, discussion, decision, or policy decision,

(f) names the people responsible for presentations or chairpersons of standing committees,

(g) provides an invaluable aid to the secretary responsible for compiling minutes of the meeting, and for writing the society's annual report, and

(h) does not use the traditional agenda opening — "business arising from the minutes." However, all unfinished business should be covered, or, if handled by the executive, reported to the meeting and recorded in the minutes.

2. Terms of reference

The board of directors and each committee (whether permanent or short-term, standing or task force) should operate from a written statement describing the goals and tasks to be undertaken. Terms of reference are set or approved by the board and should be reviewed at least yearly.

Terms of reference may vary widely. For example, the transition house society whose organizational chart was shown in Figure #1 has assigned membership concerns to a public relations committee. They are interested in recruitment to the board only, as the society is made up of directors and has no general membership.

Yet in many small societies, recruitment is a major task in itself because of the need to expand board, committee, or general membership as well as any volunteer service function. In the Vulnerable Valley Environmental Society, for example, broad based support is essential. Thus the recruitment work of the membership committee is particularly important.

The terms of reference give a clear idea of the work to be done by any given date, so the time commitment required of the committee members will be easy to determine. See Sample #2 for an example of terms of reference.

3. Evaluation

(a) Overall evaluation

Evaluation of board function and committee performance is usually last on any list, a sort of summary or wind-up. Here, however, it follows directly on the heels of terms of reference. These terms constitute the *work plan* for the society and also stipulate performance goals for its members. Thus, the work plan forms a basis to evaluate the achievement; it is the standard by which progress is measured.

Evaluations should be systematic, continuous, analytical, and co-operative. Outside experts may train you in the methods used to evaluate and analyze results, but decisions about what goals are appropriate and success or failure in meeting them belongs to the non-profit society.

This setting of specific and accurate goals is the basic principle behind *management by objectives*. At least yearly, review board achievement and the movement of the society toward its defined goals. If membership is declining, are people "voting with their feet?"

Membership and board satisfaction or dissatisfaction need to be examined. Is the

SAMPLE #2
TERMS OF REFERENCE

VULNERABLE VALLEY ENVIRONMENTAL SOCIETY

TERMS OF REFERENCE

Name of committee:_____Membership_____

For the year:_____199-/9-_____

Date:_____April 4, 199-_____

Type of committee:

    Standing   (X)   Completion date_____

    Ad hoc   ( )   Completion date_____

    Task force ( )

Chairperson: _____

Committee members: _____ _____

                          _____ _____

                          _____

GOALS

- to continually recruit members to the society
- to collect dues from members yearly
- to provide receipts to members and other donors
- to present a list of people willing to stand for membership on the board of directors as required (at least yearly)

OBJECTIVES FOR 199-/9-

Long term: (by end of fiscal year — March, 199-)

(a) obtain at least 200 new members

(b) establish an awards system to honor individuals or companies demonstrating particular concern for the environment

(c) survey board and membership to determine background, skills, and areas of special interest

Medium term: (by midyear — October 199-)

(a) draft and produce a brochure on the society and its jobs (board to approve draft)

(b) conduct spring and fall orientation sessions for the board, particularly new members

(c) draft criteria for honor awards for board and society members

Immediate: (by June, 199-)

(a) draw up a simple membership card

(b) determine the most cost-effective means of advertising membership in the society

(c) invite the editor of the Anyville Weekly and the graphic arts instructor from Anyville College to join the committee

Report to board: Monthly (X)   Quarterly ( )   Yearly ( )

Budget

society meeting the needs of its volunteers as well as the stated goals? Pay attention to these signs.

- poor attendance
- late arrivals, early departures
- evidence of stress or burnout, isolation or confusion
- complaints
- conflicts (open or underground)

(b) Program evaluation

Just as work plans are the basis for measuring the committee's achievements, so the setting of goals for individual programs provides the basis for program evaluation. Remember, goals must be measurable. How will you know if you have succeeded? What does success mean to you? How can your programs be improved?

Program evaluation may range from a debriefing session for staff, board, and volunteers to a full-blown evaluation using survey data to measure such factors as attitude change or client satisfaction. One useful practice is to carry out assessments of each undertaking or project. After the public meeting, the bake sale, the membership drive, or at the end of a set period of committee work, sit down and write an assessment. Talk with staff, volunteers, clients, and participants. Then record your assessment and include recommendations to improve the process next time around. Some of the by-products of the evaluation planning process might be the following:

- statistical information—Who were the clients? How many? Who did we miss?
- program or project descriptions, including checklists and "how-to" for next time
- cost analyses
- forms devised to make the recording and information gathering easier, quicker, and clearer

- useful material to bring alive the annual report

(c) Staff evaluation

Staff evaluation is also based on goal setting: those agreed on by the worker and supervisor, or those written down and reviewed periodically by the worker as self-evaluation.

The best reason to evaluate is to make the best use of scarce resources and to maximize their impact in achieving your society's goals.

In other words, help yourself do the best job possible. To do that, ask for feedback and take that feedback seriously.

4. Board manual

The board manual is a collection of formal documents of the society: its constitution, by-laws, list of directors, with notations as to when they joined and resigned.

Generally, the board manual is contained in a three-ring binder. Every director should have one, and it should be updated regularly. For instance, if by-laws are amended at an annual general meeting, retype the by-law pages of the manual and distribute them to board members. Include clear instructions about which pages to remove and which to add.

A board manual should be properly labelled with the name of the society. It might also contain the following elements:

(a) goal or mission statement,

(b) constitution,

(c) by-laws,

(d) definition of a "special resolution" as defined in the Society Act of your province (see chapter 8),

(e) basic assumptions (the beliefs and values of the society),

(f) past minutes,

(g) brochures,

(h) list of responsibilities of board members (their job descriptions),

(i) history of the organization,

(j) descriptions of any programs,

(k) organizational chart,

(l) standing committees and their terms of reference,

(m) meeting information: usual day and time; usual length of meeting and place; for example, third Wednesday of each month, 7:00 p.m. to 9:00 p.m., Elk's Hall,

(n) current annual report and any important dates or events,

(o) current financial statements,

(p) job descriptions of paid staff, if any, and

(q) names, addresses, and phone numbers of board and staff.

5. Board record book

At your society's official address (or office, if you have one), you will have a file drawer of records containing correspondence and information on programs, finance, and personnel.

As well, you should have a board record book, which contains selected documents kept in chronological order. It may be used by any board member, but most particularly the president, and it is distinct from the official records of the society (minutes and financial statements) which should be left at the official address of the society.

Clearly label a three-ring binder with the society's name and the period the record covers — usually the calendar or fiscal year.

Keep copies of pertinent agendas, minutes, and a list of committee members for each committee of the board for the executive and the board of directors. Include copies of any important letters and personal notes. Add brochures, flyers (date and identify each one), and dated newspaper clippings. It is easy to give away the last copy of a brochure; this binder is your "originals" file.

The record book will prove an invaluable source of easily located information.

6. Organizational calendar

Another means of displaying deadlines and activating timely reminders is an organizational calendar drawn up at the beginning of the year and added to as required.

Include the following items on your calendar.

(a) Record all dates of regular society meetings, the annual general meeting, and city council or other meetings you may report to.

(b) Record deadlines related to grant proposals, insurance payments, submission of annual reports and financial statements to provincial authorities, reports to federal authorities regarding charity status, and fiscal year-end.

(c) Include events related to fundraising, programs, and seasonal obligations.

(d) Enter any other reminders which may influence how time is spent. Get the sequence right and don't overload busy times, such as pre-Christmas, long weekends, or the income tax deadline.

(e) Post your calendar, or use a permanently displayed board you can write on with chalk or felt tip pen.

READING AND RESOURCES

Chapman, Harold; Holland, Douglas; Kenny, Sean and others. *The Contemporary Director: A handbook for elected officials of co-operatives, credit unions, and other organizations.* Co-operative College of Canada, 1987. 247 pp. $15. Available from:

Canadian Co-operative Association
#400 - 275 Bank Street
Ottawa, ON K2P 2L6
Tel: (613) 238-6711
Fax: (613) 567-0658

Crowe, Roy (ed.) *Resource Kit for Board Action.* 41 pp. $6 plus $1.75 handling.

A collection of resource sheets for board members and administrators to use as an overview to board functioning. Includes sample job description for board members, notes on task group process and leadership strategies.

Crowe, Roy (ed.) *Volunteers: How to Find Them, How to Keep Them: An Action Book.* Second edition, 1990. 94 pp. $10.

A workbook of ideas for volunteer recruitment and the basics of volunteers management. Both books available from:

Vancouver Volunteer Centre
#301 - 3102 Main Street
Vancouver, BC V5T 3G7
Tel: (604) 875-9144

Edmonton Social Planning Council. *Get on Board: A Working Guide to Better Board Development.* 1992. 100 pp. $12.

Focuses on developing organizational skills for board members. Workbook-style exercises on 12 topics including committees, board meetings, and evaluations. Available from:

Edmonton Social Planning Council
#41 - 9912 - 106th Street
Edmonton, AB T5K 1C5
Tel.: (403) 423-2031
Fax: (403) 425-6244

Fels, Lynn. *Getting Started: Establishing a Volunteer Program.* Volunteer Centre of Metropolitan Toronto, 1988. 30 pp. $15 plus $4 shipping and handling.

Includes program design and management of volunteers. Available from:

Volunteer Centre of
  Metropolitan Toronto
#207 - 344 Bloor Street West
Toronto, ON M5S 3A7
Tel: (416) 961-6888
Fax: (416) 961-6859

Graff, Linda. *By Definition: Policies for Volunteer Programs.* Volunteer Ontario, 1993. 91 pp. $13 plus GST and handling.

Described as a manual for executive directors, board members, and managers of volunteers, this book emphasizes policy development, wording of sample policies on many topics, insurance and liability, and management skills and techniques. Available from:

Volunteer Ontario
2 Dunbloor Road, Suite #203
Etobicoke, ON M9A 2E4
Tel.: (416) 236-0588
Fax: (416) 236-0590

MacLeod, Flora. *Motivating and Managing Today's Volunteers.* Self-Counsel Press, 1993. 173 pp. $11.95

Includes choosing the volunteer program manager, planning for a new volunteer program, designing and using forms and records, recruiting, interviewing, training volunteers, and maintaining commitment.

Multiculturalism and Citizenship Canada. *Profiles of Volunteer Activity in Canada.* 1989. Free.

A series of 34 monographs based on the 1987 National Survey of Volunteer Activity. Topics include a profile of volunteers for each province, profiles of youth, seniors, and women volunteers and volunteers in a range of settings such as health, social service, law, arts, religion, and recreation. Available from:

Voluntary Action
Canadian Heritage
Ottawa, ON K1A 0M5
Tel: (819) 994-2255

Paul, Kevin. *Chairing a Meeting with Confidence: An easy guide to rules and procedures.* Self-Counsel Press, 1992. 96 pp. $7.95

Information and ideas on conducting fair, orderly, and efficient meetings.

Ross, David and Richard Shillington. *A Profile of the Canadian Volunteer; a Guide to the 1987 Survey of Volunteer Activity in Canada.* 1989. 30 pp. Available free in English and French from:

National Voluntary Organizations
947 Bronson Avenue
Ottawa, ON K1S 4G8
Tel: (613) 238-1591

Victoria Volunteer Bureau. *Evaluation for Community Service Organizations*. 1991. 71 pp. $15

Evaluation guidelines based on a course book for social work students, but written in nonacademic terms. Discusses reasons for evaluation, type of evaluation (with examples of applications), and steps in the evaluation process. Available from:

Volunteer Victoria
211 - 620 View Street
Victoria, BC V8W 1J6
Tel.: (604) 386-2269
Fax: (604) 386-2279

COURSES AND WORKSHOPS

A range of courses and workshops are available on such subjects as board development, planning and evaluating programs, effective meetings, and evaluation.

An example is the National Certificate Program in Voluntary and Non-Profit Sector Management at Simon Fraser University. For information contact:

Continuing Studies
Simon Fraser University
515 West Hastings Street
Vancouver, BC V6B 5K3
Tel: (604) 291-5087

Another is the York University voluntary sector management program expanded to include management education and applied research. More information is available from:

Faculty of Administrative Studies
York University
4700 Keele Street
North York, ON M3J 1P3
Tel.: (416) 736-5092

Contact continuing education departments of local colleges and universities; volunteer centres and volunteer resources; sports and recreation departments of municipal and provincial governments; and organizations devoted to assisting non-profit societies. For example —

Non-Profit Organizations
947 Bronson Avenue
Ottawa, ON K1S 4G8
Tel: (613) 238-1591
Fax: (613) 238-5257

4

LAYING THE GROUNDWORK FOR
GOOD RECORD KEEPING

A method for keeping financial and written records is essential to the good management of your society and, ultimately, to success in reaching your goals. Records need not be elaborate. They must, however, be attended to regularly; it's time-wasting, discouraging, and of little use to have to reconstruct records at the end of each fiscal year, or years down the road. Not only will your real records be lost, but so will your history and sense of direction.

Good record keeping in a non-profit society increases the efficiency and the effectiveness of the organization in reaching its goals. Accountability to the membership and to government is improved, and the likelihood of financial support from government and the community is enhanced.

a. WRITTEN RECORDS

1. Taking minutes

Minutes are a brief written record of all meetings of the board and subcommittees. In a non-profit society, the secretary is generally appointed as a member of the executive committee and has responsibility for keeping minutes at executive and board meetings. These and other responsibilities may be required to be spelled out in your by-laws (see chapter 8).

For subcommittee meetings, including standing and ad hoc committees and task forces, a member should be assigned to take brief notes. Whatever the setting, committee members should always review, correct, and take ownership of the recorded activities of the previous meeting.

The minutes are both a record and a reminder: minutes of committee meetings help the chairperson make a report to the board and minutes of the board are reviewed by the president in preparing the annual report.

If you are the recorder, begin with the type of meeting (for example, board of directors; task force on fundraising) and record the date, time, and place of meeting, and a list of people present and absent. Indicate who chairs the meeting and who records the minutes.

Summarize reports and discussion; make a clear statement of any motions passed. Include the names of people making motions, seconding, abstaining, and whether the motion passes or fails. Care should be taken about recording the wording of motions accurately. Headings follow the same categories as the agenda, making it easier to look up various points in the past minutes. The minutes should end with a list of unfinished business or items deferred to carry forward as the basis for the next meeting's agenda. Note the time of adjournment.

Ideally, minutes should be typed and distributed to members before the next meeting. If you mail minutes out to members, highlight names of people responsible for action with a coloured pen or print their names in the margin as a reminder. If minutes are not mailed, they should be legibly written and read out at the next meeting.

Keep minutes in chronological order in a file, minute book, or three-ring binder.

Keep separate files or sections in your minute book for general meetings of the society, the annual general meeting, and meetings of the board of directors or important subcommittees.

At the front of your minute book, put the certificate of incorporation in a plastic page protector and keep a copy of the constitution and by-laws next to it for easy reference. Keep a copy of your banking resolution here as well (see the next section on financial records) and make sure it is kept up to date. Minute books for past years should be clearly marked and stored at the society's place of address.

2. Keeping a register of members

The register of members of the society may be either long for an organization with many general members or relatively short if the society is made up only of directors. The secretary of the society is responsible for the register of members, which should be kept at the registered address of the society.

The first names entered on the list will be those of the founding members. Include their current home address and telephone numbers. Leave a place to enter the date members leave the society.

Remember to keep the list current. Note that, in some provinces, it is an offence to fail to keep such a record. In all cases, the list will make running your society easier and more efficient. Sample #3 shows a register of members.

Keep an additional register for the board of directors, recording the date they joined the board and the date they resigned at the end of term, or add several columns to your general register. Note that resignation from the board of directors should be in writing.

In conjunction with the registers, keep a typed set of current address labels. This is especially useful if you mail board or committee minutes each month and if you have access to a photocopier to copy the original list onto a sheet of blank labels.

Remember to keep track of "alumni." People who leave your society may still be interested in your goals and willing to support special projects or funding drives.

b. FINANCIAL RECORDS

The treasurer is responsible for recording and reporting the financial matters of the society. Reporting should be done monthly to the board of directors and at least yearly to the general membership. The treasurer may set up books personally, if skilled in that direction, or appoint a bookkeeper. Because even a simple bookkeeping system should be set up correctly, ask the advice of an accountant in your community. Many are willing to assist in doing this job and providing training to your society's treasurer or bookkeeper.

1. Opening a bank account

This is an important step, even for groups with small budgets, since funds must be properly recorded when both received and spent. Generally, non-profit societies are required to have at least one account with a bank, credit union, or trust company. A resolution must be passed at a meeting of directors to decide at which bank, credit union, or trust company the account will be opened, and who will have cheque signing powers.

Most societies have three or four people listed with the bank as signing officers. The treasurer will be one signing officer, as will one staff person (if applicable), and generally some other members of the executive. Usually, each cheque requires two signatures.

Other organizations authorize one person (usually staff) to sign cheques under a given amount (usually $200), and two people (one staff person, one director) for cheques over that amount.

CENTRETOWN SOCIETY FOR EXCEPTIONAL CHILDREN REGISTER OF MEMBERS				
Date of joining	Full name	Home address	Phone	Date of resignation
Feb. 12, 199-	John A. Brown	123 Field St. Anyville, Alta. A1B 2C3	220-1234	Sept. 30, 199-
Mar. 1, 199-	Alice B. White	456 Garden St. Anyville, Alta. A1B 2C4	220-5678	

Banks or credit unions will provide you with the necessary forms, cheque books, and instructions. Remember to plan ahead for changes in cheque authorizations. The bank will "bounce" a cheque issued several weeks previously if new signing officers have been authorized with the bank in the meantime.

2. Setting up books

This is a catch-all phrase which includes preparation of a yearly budget, daily cash balance record, cash income record, cash expense record, and general ledger accounts.

(a) Budget

The board of directors of the new society should review a draft budget as soon as possible. In the early days the budget may be relatively simple; there will be no complete record of actual expenses until the end of the first year of operation.

Essentially, the budget is a projection of income and expenses and the resulting balance (surplus or deficit) at year's end. It is a financial plan for running the new society. See the sample budget in Sample #4.

Decide if you are to operate on a calendar year basis (begin January 1, end December 31) or on the fiscal year used by government (April 1 to March 31). The trend is to the latter.

Make sure the board of directors discusses the budget before it is formally approved. When approved, make any changes required, remove the word "draft" and enter the date approved at the bottom of the page.

(b) Daily cash balance record

The daily cash balance record is made up of the chequing account and deposit book for the society.

The stub on the cheque book gives you room to record who a cheque is made out to, the date, the amount, and the balance remaining in the account. The monthly bank statement provides a summary of transactions and allows you to check totals.

(c) Cash income record

The cash income record book allows you to enter the date money is received, who it is from, and the amount deposited.

(d) Cash expense record

The cash expense record book allows you to enter the date payment is made, to whom it is made, the cheque number, and the amount.

SAMPLE #4
BUDGET

VULNERABLE VALLEY ENVIRONMENTAL SOCIETY
PROPOSED BUDGET — DRAFT
OCTOBER, 199-

	Actual 1995	Estimated 1996	Proposed 1997
INCOME			
Municipal Grant	$1 500.00	$1 500.00	$1 500.00
Fundraising events	914.47	1 200.00	2 500.00
Donations	1 152.60	1 400.00	2 000.00
Members' fees	230.00	380.00	500.00
Bank interest	104.20	120.00	200.00
Miscellaneous	69.10	—	—
Fee for service (speaker's honorarium)	150.00	—	—
	$4 120.37	$4 600.00	$6 700.00
EXPENSES			
Salaries	1 032.00	1 135.00	2 497.00
Benefits	48.50	56.00	125.00
Travel allowance	210.50	300.00	500.00
Conference registration fees	80.00	150.00	150.00
Office supplies	63.55	100.00	150.00
Postage	280.15	400.00	500.00
Printing expenses	582.97	1 000.00	1 300.00
Telephone and hydro	482.66	500.00	600.00
Rent	600.00	600.00	600.00
Subscriptions and books	74.14	75.00	100.00
Fundraising events costs	116.40	250.00	400.00
Miscellaneous	12.42	—	—
	$3 583.29	$4 566.00	$6 922.00
SUMMARY			
Excess of income over expenses	$537.08	34.00	$(222.00)
Surplus at beginning of year	—	537.08	571.08
	$537.08	$571.08	$349.08

(e) General ledger account

The general ledger account is a book containing pages headed for various categories of assets, liabilities, income, or expenses. For example, one page may be for recording expenses related to a specific program of the society. This account will be properly titled and will show the amount budgeted, the previous month's balance, the monthly total of income and expenses, and the month-end balance. If the program is funded by a grant from government or a foundation, a separate budget and account will have to be kept in any case. If not, it is a useful and quick way of determining if a program is on budget.

In the early days of your organization, with no staff and no funds, except perhaps membership fees, the daily cash balance record will provide sufficient accountability, supplemented by a general ledger account page titled "Membership Registration."

Books and records must be held at the address of the society unless a resolution has been passed to keep them elsewhere. Some accounting companies offer services to non-profit societies at a special rate, including a monthly printout and year-end statement.

3. Appointing an auditor

If you plan to register as a non-profit society, you may be required by provincial legislation to appoint an auditor (see chapter 9). Even in those provinces where an official audit is not required, it is a good idea to have the society's books checked yearly by an independent accountant (one not in some way involved with your society).

The auditor is appointed at the first general meeting of a new society and at the annual general meeting each year. A motion is made, specifying the name of the auditor, and recorded in the minutes.

It is the treasurer's responsibility to keep books in order in preparation for the yearly audit. Remember to make provision in your budget to pay an auditor.

4. Writing receipts

Receipts should be written for membership fees and any donations of money. An official receipt is signed by the treasurer of the society (or other person designated by motion of the board of directors), clearly dated, and stamped with the name and address of the society. You should also indicate the federal tax number. Some societies have receipts printed with name, address, and tax number included, or have an inexpensive rubber stamp made up with the same information.

It is courteous to enclose a letter of thanks with an official receipt to donors, or a slip such as the one shown in Sample #5.

A copy of all receipts issued for donations to the society must also be kept at the office or official address of the society.

SAMPLE #5
THANK-YOU NOTE

CENTRETOWN CRISIS CENTRE
789 Main Street
Centretown, Province
A1B 2C3

THANK YOU

Your contribution to our society is very much appreciated. It is because of your support that we are able to provide information and services to the members of our community who need our assistance.

An official receipt is enclosed for income tax purposes.

_____
President

Telephone:
Crisis line   555-4000
Business line   555-7222

5. Yearly financial statements

At the minimum, a non-profit society must produce a yearly statement of income and expenses (Sample #6) and a balance sheet at the end of the fiscal year (Sample #7). These two documents present the story of the society's activities and programs in financial terms. They show what money came to the society, what was spent, and what other assets or liabilities the society has. Note that two directors must sign these statements prior to submission to federal or provincial authorities or the annual general meeting.

c. THE ANNUAL REPORT

Many societies make their annual report, or an expanded version of it, into a publicity tool providing information on the society's activities during the year. Such a report is of great interest to prospective funders, prospective board or society members, MPs, MLAs, and others who want to know about the society.

Collect annual reports from a range of foundations and societies. They are generally available free on request and are a useful source of information and ideas. For example, the annual report of the major funding foundations in your province will tell you who gets money and how much they get.

The annual report of the provincial office of the ombudsman is essential reading for an advocacy group. Sample cases and measures taken to respond to complaints and resolve problems are very instructive.

The annual report *must* include the names of the executive, board of directors, and staff, and the balance sheet and a statement of income and expenses. It may also include the following:

(a) Message from the president, including the goals the society established in that year, what was achieved, what difficulties were encountered, changes, priorities, policies addressed or implemented, and future directions.

(b) Message from the executive director, including commentary on continuing and new programs, staff changes, volunteer achievements, and significant issues for the coming year.

(c) Treasurer's report, including the relative financial position of the society, major financial decisions the board of directors made during the year, and any comment on the balance sheet or statement of income and expenses.

(d) An auditor's report, usually in the form of a letter from a firm of chartered accountants to the effect that they have examined the balance sheet of the society and any other statements.

The auditors will make it clear that, in their opinion, the financial statements of the society fairly present the financial position of the society at a given date (usually December 31 or March 31, depending on the fiscal year of operation of the society).

The report may also include notes to the financial statements which define accounting policies of the society, any changes in accounting policy, and additional information such as mortgages payable and lease and rental commitments.

(e) If your society is not required to perform (and pay for) a yearly audit, you may still have an accountant's report prepared by an accounting service which will prepare a monthly printout and year-end statement for a minimum charge.

In that case, the financial statements in the annual report will state "Prepared Without Audit" on each page and will be accompanied by a statement from the accounting firm such as the following:

SAMPLE #6
STATEMENT OF INCOME AND EXPENSES

```
VULNERABLE VALLEY ENVIRONMENTAL SOCIETY
     STATEMENT OF INCOME AND EXPENSES
     FOR THE YEAR ENDING MARCH 31, 199-
```

INCOME

Anyville municipal council grant	$2 000.00	
Fundraising events	914.47	
Donations	1 152.60	
Members' fees	230.00	
Bank interest	104.20	
Other miscellaneous income	69.10	
Fee for service (speaker's honorarium)	150.00	$4 620.37

EXPENSES

Salaries (15 hours per week @ $6.50/hour = $419.25/month @ 4 months)	$1 677.00	
Benefits	134.16	
Travel allowance	210.50	
Conference registration fees	80.00	
Office supplies	63.55	
Postage	280.15	
Printing expenses	582.97	
Telephone and hydro	482.66	
Rent	600.00	
Subscriptions and books	75.14	
Fundraising events costs	116.40	
Miscellaneous	12.42	4 314.95

SURPLUS FOR THE YEAR	$305.42

ACCEPTED ON BEHALF OF THE BOARD OF DIRECTORS

Peter White _____Treasurer

Gloria Ochre _____President

SAMPLE #7
BALANCE SHEET

VULNERABLE VALLEY ENVIRONMENTAL SOCIETY
BALANCE SHEET
AS AT MARCH 31, 199-

ASSETS

Current assets		
Cash		$528.75
Shares (credit union)		26.80
Accounts receivable		5.10
Prepaid expenses		68.50
TOTAL CURRENT		$629.15
Fixed assets		
Furniture and fixtures at cost		682.00
TOTAL ASSETS		$1 311.15

LIABILITIES AND NET WORTH

Current liabilities		
Accounts payable		$51.80
Net worth at March 31, 199-	723.27	
Surplus for the year	536.08	
Net worth at March 31, 199-	1 259.35	$1 259.35
TOTAL LIABILITIES AND NET WORTH		$1 311.15

ACCEPTED ON BEHALF OF THE BOARD OF DIRECTORS

Peter White _____ Treasurer

Gloria Ochre _____ President

We have prepared the accompanying balance sheet as at March 31, 199- and the statements of surplus, income, and changes in financial position for the year then ended from the records of Centretown Crisis Centre Society and from other information supplied to us by the company. In order to prepare these financial statements, we made a review consisting primarily of enquiry, comparison, and discussion of such information. However, in accordance with the terms of our engagement, we have not performed an audit, and consequently do not express an opinion on these financial statements.

Centretown, Province
April 12, 199-

Black and White
Chartered Accountants

(f) Information on programs, special projects, or activities, highlighted with examples, descriptions, or photographs.

d. USING RECORDS TO SUPPORT FUNDING PROPOSALS

Many non-profit organizations, at some point in their existence, will decide to write a funding proposal. Organized record keeping will make this task much easier. The basic financial and reporting information already described in this chapter is essential to grant applications.

1. Background material

Long before you come to write a funding application, begin collecting information on the sources of funds available to your organization — prospective funders, potential amounts, application deadlines and so on. This material might be organized into the following categories.

(a) Foundations

- Annual report (include record of grants given)
- Criteria and deadlines
- Contact person

(b) Federal/provincial government ministries and departments in your area of interest

- Applicants' guide
- List of projects funded
- Criteria and deadlines
- Contact person (local if possible)

(c) Municipalities

- List of previous grants
- Criteria
- Report of planning departments
- Contact person

(d) Corporations

- Information on corporate and employee funds designated for charity
- Criteria and sorts of projects funded
- Contact person

(e) Service clubs, churches, unions

- Information on funds small and large which may be tapped
- Criteria
- Contact person

(f) Other societies or organizations like yours

- Annual reports

2. Support documents for your proposal

Your funding proposal should include the following:

(a) Budget

The budget (and, if your society is more than one year old, balance sheet and statement of income and expenses) is a useful support document to an application. Even if the amount of money requested is small, the proper presentation and effort at accountability are important.

(b) Annual report

The annual report allows the prospective funder an overview of the society, indicates who has supported you already, and provides an idea of how the new money requested will extend or expand the work of the society. It will present the goals of your society in action. If the report demonstrates a strong volunteer base, the prospective funder knows that money donated goes directly to service.

(c) Up-to-date list of directors of the board

This list should accompany funding proposals to add credibility and reassure funders of the presence of a community base to your society. Add addresses, telephone numbers, and profession or place of work, if relevant, to indicate broad board representation.

(d) Material on your society's work in the community

Brochures, flyers, and copies of newspaper articles on your society's work in the community all help to present your organization as active, organized, and part of the community.

(e) An information kit on your society

The material listed above can be organized into a kit to accompany your proposal. A kit helps inform funders as well as prospective board members and others interested in your work. Use a coloured folder, clearly labelled, with two inside pockets that contain a separate page for each of the following items:

- a paragraph on the history of your society

- a brief statement of goals, basic assumptions, and principles

- a statement on the magnitude of the problem your society is trying to solve, for example, pollution in the Regional River, or destruction of potential heritage sites and houses

- definitions, if necessary, or a glossary of terms, to help update and inform the reader

- examples of support from community agencies or others — it is possible to solicit letters of support, depending on your goals; point out the diversity of your board members or how the type of representation on your board indicates acknowledgment and support from municipalities, churches, or other societies or agencies

- information on the funding base of your society — a large membership may be a highlight; financial support from businesses, large corporations, churches, or government adds to the credibility of your society

- a statement of need — indicate what services the government provides, what other private societies already do, what the gaps are

- an open letter requesting financial support

- a copy of the last annual report

- brochures describing programs

- flyers about special events or copies of relevant clippings

The information kit can serve not only the purposes of your funding committee but also assist the public relations committee in broadcasting your message to the community (see chapter 13 on publicity and public education).

3. Other resources

Local community colleges or universities may have courses in grant proposal writing or fundraising procedures. Inquire at adult education or extension departments. Social planning councils, interagency councils, and the local United Way are other good sources of information about training and assistance.

There is also more and more literature on the subject of writing effective grant proposals (see the **Reading and Resources** section below and chapter 3).

READING AND RESOURCES

Flanagan, Joan. "Raising Money from Members: Who Needs What You Do?" *Grantsmanship Center News*, Los Angeles, September/December 1984.

Techniques for expanding membership, mail solicitation for membership, the pros and cons of dues, sliding scales and variations, and pledges and fees for service.

The *Grantsmanship Center News* will probably be available at your local library. It is a useful periodical with information for non-profits, big and small, and American trends in the non-profit field.

Granger, Alix. *Financial Management for Non-Profit Community Groups*. Vancouver Volunteer Centre, 1984. $7.50 plus $1.75 postage and handling.

A guide to systems used in non-profit societies to ensure that funds are used effectively. The board of directors' role in financial management, planning the budget, regular financial reporting, the annual audit, bookkeeping and cash management systems are some of the topics included. Available from:

Vancouver Volunteer Centre
Suite 301, 3102 Main Street
Vancouver, BC V5T 3G7
Tel: (604) 875-9144

Haller, L. *Financial Resources Management for Non-Profit Organizations*. Englewood Cliffs, N.J.: Prentice-Hall, Inc., 1982. 192 pp. About $12.95 in Canada.

Practical guidelines to understanding resource needs, translating them into useful budgets, and controlling financial expenditures. Topics addressed include how to plan activities before seeking funds, how to handle the funds obtained, common financial problems in non-profit organizations, and how to deal with accountants.

The Public Legal Education Society. *Volunteers and the Law*. Vancouver: Peoples' Law School, 1988. 39 pp. $5 plus 50¢ per copy for mailing.

Useful sections on volunteer and agency liability and insurance. Available from:

The Public Legal Education Society
Suite 150 - 900 Howe Street
Vancouver, BC V6Z 2M4
Tel: (604) 688-2565

Young, Joyce. *Fundraising for Non-Profit Groups: How to Get Money from Corporations, Foundations and Government*. Vancouver: International Self-Counsel Press, 1989. 161 pp. $8.95.

A useful guide on how to approach potential major funders, as well as a source of ideas for community fundraising.

5
HIRING STAFF

a. IF YOU HIRE STAFF

The transition from fledgling society to the hiring of one or two paid staff may take years or may be the first order of priority for the new society. In either case, careful planning must precede hiring.

Given the effort required of a volunteer board to write proposals and pursue funding possibilities, there is often relief but not much energy once funding is at last secured. But that's only the beginning! A personnel committee should be set up prior to money being received. Your organization needs to consider the following points.

(a) Don't hire until after your society has been registered as a society in your province. It is at this point only that the society is a legal entity.

(b) Is the job short-term? If the task that someone is hired to complete is short-term and specific, with an end in sight, then project funding or employment grants from the federal government may suffice. Remember that the latter are very minimal wages, and that the society will have to cover any benefits or supplement to wages that are considered necessary. The society should make it clear to the short-term employee whether or not the grant is renewable and whether or not employment ends with the termination of the grant.

(c) Is the job really long-term? If you need to hire an executive director, co-ordinator, manager, or secretary — core staff — then short-term, one-time grants will lead to grief. Seed funding, which keeps the essential operation in action, needs a reliable and long-term source.

A personnel committee will be needed to put into writing the personnel policies and practices of your society. These need not be elaborate, but should not be overlooked, even for short-term work. Any paid co-ordinator or director should be a member of the personnel committee.

The committee's tasks include:

(a) Written job descriptions defining the expectations of the employer and including responsibilities to be undertaken, who the person reports to, and minimum qualifications

(b) Drawing up of a sample contract or letter of understanding which makes it clear which job the person has, for how long, at what salary, dates of probation period (if any), and evaluation.

(c) Developing policy related to the following:

- probation period

- hours of work

- salary range and increments

- benefits (unemployment insurance and Canada Pension Plan)

- statutory holidays

- vacation with pay

- terms of termination (resignation or dismissal) and notice required from staff and from the society

- grievances, appeals, and complaints

- layoffs
- overtime
- absences (sick leave, maternity leave, compassionate leave)
- outside work
- job expenses
- staff development
- performance evaluation

(d) Policy covering how new vacancies are dealt with; for example, will they be posted first for those already employed? Do volunteers have priority?

(e) Development of a personnel practices manual for staff, to include all written policy, salary scales, job descriptions, and statement of staff and board accountability. The Ministry of Labour in your province will have information on any provincial employment standards act with minimum requirements related to statutory holidays, layoffs, vacation with pay, and so on.

b. WHO HIRES?

The board may delegate this decision to (or request a recommendation from) the personnel committee or a special committee of the board. If you hire several staff members, it is good practice to hire the co-ordinator or executive director first. The board hires this person; the executive director then hires other staff. However, he or she may well ask a panel of the board or other staff to assist in hiring. The board is responsible for the work performance evaluation of the executive director.

The committee, or whoever is responsible for hiring staff, has the following specific duties:

(a) advertising the job or jobs

(b) screening applicants

(c) interviewing, selection, and appointment

(d) setting up books for salary payment — Revenue Canada will provide information as to requirements for deduction of unemployment insurance, Canada Pension Plan, and income tax (make sure income tax is deducted from paycheques or individual directors may be liable)

(e) orientation of new staff to the society and to the job

(f) evaluation of work performance

The decision to hire staff adds to the legal responsibilities of the directors of a society. Depending on your provincial legislation, board members may have personal or individual liability for any unpaid staff wages if the society runs out of money.

c. ENCOURAGE COMMUNICATION

The decision to hire staff marks a shift in role for the volunteer board of directors. Because the working board now passes over some of its functions and responsibilities, it is vital to be clear just what jobs remain with volunteer board members and which now fit into the job description of the staff member. Write it down; discuss, revise, and frequently review the division of labour. There will be some overlap, and good communication is therefore essential to make sure everyone pulls in the same direction and has the same priorities; don't duplicate each other's efforts.

The staff person (or executive director in a larger society) acts as staff to the board of directors and attends board and executive meetings. The board hears reports on staff activities at every meeting.

Don't let a gap grow between board members and individual staff. Unless the society is very large, it is to everyone's advantage to be well-acquainted with each other. While the formal business usually takes place at board or committee meetings, social events that involve all of the staff, board members, and other key volunteers help to break down barriers of communication.

All concerned are working, in different ways, toward the same ends.

For a more detailed guide to finding, interviewing, and hiring employees, see *A Small Business Guide to Employee Selection*, another title in the Self-Counsel Series.

6

FIRST STEPS TO INCORPORATION

Your organization might function for years without making application to the provincial or federal government for incorporation as a society. During this time, though, it will not be a non-profit society in the official sense. If you want to make sure that your society's name is not adopted by some other group, and if you want to be able to provide tax-deductible receipts to donors who make charitable gifts to your society, then your group should consider both registration as a society (incorporation) and registration as a charity (described in chapter 11). The full process will take about six months. It need not be particularly complicated or expensive, but will require at least one person to pay close attention to requirements and details.

Note that incorporating your group and registering as a charity are two separate choices. You may do one without the other — or you may do both. This chapter and the following four chapters describe in detail the incorporation process. Chapter 11 deals with registering as a charity.

Incorporation can be accomplished in about a month. Costs vary from $90 in Saskatchewan to $217 in Ontario. See the **Reading and Resources** section at the end of this chapter for a province-by-province list of addresses for the incorporation forms and material you will need.

a. WHY IS THE GOVERNMENT INVOLVED?

There are two important trends in Canada today: an increase in the number of non-profit societies, and an increase in the transfer of services to non-government organizations, many of which are also non-profit societies.

To impose some order on this growth and to ensure, at least minimally, proper administration of charitable dollars, many provincial governments have revised their Society Acts or similar statutes. The federal government has recently revised and improved Revenue Canada's response to non-government, non-profit groups in Canada (see chapter 11).

Both levels of government have a system for checking proper certification and registration of non-profit societies while still allowing freedom to pursue societal goals. Primarily, the government wishes to ensure the democratic functioning of societies and the responsible management of money donated from the community or granted from any level of government.

b. DECIDING TO INCORPORATE

The process of incorporating your organization can be started at any time in the life of an organization. The society will then have legal status and will continue under its name, independent of who the individual members happen to be, and whether or not they remain members of the organization. Incorporation means creating an ongoing legal entity; it also means that the society accepts certain public responsibilities and gains some distinct advantages. There are several reasons why incorporation is a good idea.

(a) *Facilitating the search for funding:* Most foundations and government sources of funding for societies and their programs require that a society be incorporated.

(b) *Securing your society's name:* A registered society has a name unique to itself; it cannot then be used by any other group in your province or territory.

(c) *Responsibility and accountability:* The requirements of incorporation add to an image of stability and responsibility for the society. A balance sheet, submitted yearly, is also public. The requirement of an annual meeting with proper notification of members adds to the accountability of the society and its executive. In the past, follow-up from the provincial government on societies that have been lax in meeting incorporation requirements has not been particularly stringent. It is, however, entirely possible to lose certification as a registered society if requirements are not met (see chapter 9 on maintaining your legal status).

(d) *Limited liability for directors:* Liability (financial obligation) for debts incurred by a properly constituted and operating society rests with the society and not with individual board members. Incorporation therefore limits, but does not eliminate, the personal liability of members for the debts of the organization. Similarly, only the society may be sued for actions undertaken in the name of the society or for accidents or injuries. (However, it is advisable for a society that operates a facility or vehicle to obtain liability insurance.)

Note that there may be exceptions to this in some provinces. For example, the Society Act of British Columbia states in section 24(8):

> Where a society has less than three members for more than six months, each director is personally liable for payment of every debt of the society incurred after the expiration of the six months and for so long as the number of members continues to be less than three.

In Manitoba, the Manitoba Corporations Act for non-profit societies states that the directors have personal liability under certain unusual circumstances. They may be liable for up to six months' wages payable to employees for services performed for the corporation while they were directors.

(e) *Holding title to property and contracting:* An incorporated society may hold title to property, contract in its own name, and initiate legal action.

(f) *Contracting with employees:* Contracts with employees may be drawn up in the name of the society and signed by board members on behalf of the society rather than as individuals.

(g) *Borrowing money:* Procedures set out in most Society Acts require that borrowing of money and related procedures be carefully prescribed and specifically addressed in a society's by-laws. Generally, a bank will not lend money to an unregistered group unless individual members guarantee the loan.

(h) *Order and board procedure:* Setting up proper documentation and good businesslike practices is more likely to receive attention in the course of incorporation. The goals of the society will be clearly stated, books and bank account opened, details about membership and voting rights discussed and decided on, and a name for the society established.

(i) *Beginning a history of your society:* Public record is established from the point of incorporation, which includes the constitution, by-laws, and board members. An annual report is filed each year listing changes in board membership and other details of historical significance.

(j) *Facilitating registration as a charity:* Incorporation is not required for registration with the federal government as a charitable organization, but certainly assists the application.

(k) *Eligibility for tax benefits as a registered charity:* Specifically, GST rebates are available. Non-profit corporations do not pay taxes.

c. DECIDING NOT TO INCORPORATE

On the other hand, there are reasons why you may not choose to incorporate as a society:

(a) *Not appropriate:* Another form of incorporation may be more suitable to your group. For example, a company is also a legal entity but with the main purpose of making money (a profit) and paying dividends to its shareholders by selling goods or services.

A co-operative may decide on incorporation, but its main purpose is to serve its own members who benefit from reduced rates for clothing, food, housing, etc. It is not "non-profit" in the same sense, and will incorporate under a different act.

Remember, a non-profit society does not make money for its members; it is organized and operated for the benefit of the public at large or for people the society serves.

(b) *Time and money:* Drawing up a constitution and by-laws and carrying on correspondence with the Registrar of Companies is time-consuming. Cost is not high, but may be appreciable to a small voluntary organization. Is it worth your while? Ask yourself:

- Could you operate just as effectively under the wing of an already incorporated society?

- Will your new society likely be long-lived?

- Will it apply for funding from a source which requires incorporation?

- Might it hire staff, make contracts, or incur debts?

(c) *Stage of life in an organization:* Your group may define itself as an "action" group, more goal-focused and freewheeling than other groups. If you are concerned with the installation of traffic lights at specific school crossings, then incorporation isn't for you.

Or your group may decide to operate under the auspices of an already established society with similar goals which has an interest in your involvement, perhaps as a task force of the existing board of directors.

Or if the pace of development is not rapid, you may simply leave incorporation until some later time and focus instead on such matters as public education, or building up membership.

(d) *Restrictions and requirements:* There are often a range of limitations on a non-profit society; for example, it cannot issue diplomas, cannot be primarily concerned with profit for members, and cannot have more non-voting than voting members. Restrictions vary among provinces and are discussed in later chapters.

Requirements both to register and to retain incorporation status may not interest you when your group is just getting started. Annual meetings, annual reports, and keeping books and minutes may seem like unnecessary obstacles. Remember, it is always possible to apply for incorporation status later in the life of your group when it becomes desirable.

d. STEPS TO INCORPORATION

The steps toward incorporation are generally the same no matter whether you incorporate federally or in one of the provinces. Generally, you have to do the following:

(a) gather the necessary documents and resource information,

(b) reserve a name for your society,

(c) prepare a constitution and by-laws (articles of incorporation), and

(d) complete and submit the necessary forms, including payments.

This chapter and the next detail the steps of incorporation and specify differences among the provinces. Chapter 10 provides details for incorporating federally.

e. GATHERING THE DOCUMENTS

Write for information on incorporation of a non-profit society in your province or territory (for addresses see the **Reading and Resources** section at the end of this chapter). Request the necessary forms, documents, and information on fees and name reservation, and a copy of the act defining the procedures for incorporation of a non-profit society.

Inquire what other resources are available to you as you begin the task of incorporation. For example, your provincial law society or society for public legal education may have simple forms or guidebooks specific to your province. There may be night classes (free or at minimal cost) on incorporation and the successful operation of non-profit societies. Local community colleges often run such courses or may begin to on request.

Some law societies have an information line to answer questions about incorporation or the free services of a lawyer to read over your documents prior to submission.

f. RESERVING A NAME FOR YOUR SOCIETY

What's in a name? A great deal in some cases! It may be important to you (or an already established society) not to lose a society name which has built up credibility in the community. Names that are too similar to each other create confusion so be sure the name you choose is not already in use in your province. In the end, this is the responsibility of the Registrar of Companies, but to save time and disappointment check telephone directories, agency listings, or relevant hobby and sport magazines.

Contact any society with a similar name to request permission for approval of the name of your new society. Note that in some provinces the Registrar decides the degree of similarity for you, with or without the other society's permission. Distinction is better!

You should reduce any possibility of confusion related to —

- the purpose of your society,

- its geographic location,

- who your society represents (for instance, you must not suggest a connection to government or the Royal Family), and

- who has endorsed your society.

A suggestion is to include a descriptive word and a distinctive word. The name "Vulnerable Valley Environmental Society" is relatively clear as to location and purpose. "Vulnerable Valley" is distinctive, and "Environmental" is descriptive of its work. The "Vulnerable Valley Environmental Association" would also be acceptable.

Also include a legal description or corporate designation as part of the name, for example, association, club, or society.

1. Representation

The Ashford City Heritage Society would require the approval in writing of the city or municipal council to use "city" in its name. The name "Ashford Heritage Society" would be acceptable (unless it is already in use) without such approval. In general, avoid the use of the word "city," "municipality," "borough," or "village" in your name unless you plan to request endorsement.

The name "Ashford Heritage Society of Manitoba" means that the society is in the province of Manitoba. However, the name "Manitoba Heritage Society" or "Heritage Society of Manitoba" clearly implies a broader representation. Check with the Registrar's office. You will probably be required to obtain proof that your society represents a majority of people involved in this concern, including a fair representation from all regions of the province. You may also be required to obtain permission from some other government department or ministry. For example, in British Columbia you would check with the Provincial Secretary.

Again, the Registrar will probably prohibit use of names which imply approval or close connection to government, or which may be confused with government boards, bureaus, councils, departments, or branches.

The name "Ashford Heritage Council" (or "Bureau," "Board," etc.) may require the approval of the Ashford Municipal Council or the regional or provincial departments of government concerned with designating or maintaining historical monuments.

2. Acronyms

A name made up of a joined word or initials is called an acronym. An example is "CARE Productions," which stands for Child Abuse, Research and Education Productions of British Columbia. If a name consists of a joined word or initials, set out its full meaning. In some provinces, the acronym may be incorporated into the full registered name of the society.

g. PROCEDURE FOR RESERVATION

To avoid much correspondence to and fro and possibly the need to rewrite required forms and documentation, follow the steps outlined below.

(a) Contact the Registrar early in your incorporation procedure by letter or by telephone to determine the procedure for name search.

(b) Submit two possible names with your preference made clear, if this is allowed. Otherwise, do some homework with telephone directories at your public library and submit one name likely to be acceptable that doesn't belong to any other group, whether already incorporated or not.

(c) Remember that most provinces require a small fee for each name search. (If you are not sure, ask to whom the cheque should be credited.) Increasingly, provinces are pulling out of the name search business, notably Alberta and Ontario, and referring people to private companies that search records for a fee.

(d) Once reserved, inquire how long the name will be reserved pending the arrival of the completed documentation regarding the new society.

(e) Settle on a spelling of all the words in the title, and don't let it vary. If you propose to be the "Cultural and Artistic Society," don't type in "Cultural & Artistic Society." Any such variation could result in your forms being returned. Don't switch from "Incorporated" to "Inc." in the course of completing your various documents. Leave "The" out of the title.

(f) Avoid including punctuation marks such as apostrophes or hyphens that are likely to be left out and make the use of your title inconsistent. The Senior Citizens Club should leave out the usual apostrophe ("Citizens'").

Any inconsistency in the various forms you submit could result in their being returned to you with resulting delay.

1. British Columbia

A copy of a fee schedule and Name Approval Request form (see Sample #8) will be included with the incorporation information you receive from the Registrar of Companies. Incorporation information may also be obtained and submitted via any government agent; the reply will be routed the same way.

Fill in three choices of name in order of preference. Second and third choices are not searched unless the first choice is not available. Keep the yellow copy of the application form for your own records.

The fee for a name search is $30. The application is GST exempt. Send a cheque, bank draft, or money order with the name application request form made payable to the Minister of Finance. Submit fee and completed forms to:

Societies Unit
Registrar of Companies
Ministry of Finance and Corporate
 Relations
940 Blanshard Street
Victoria, BC V8W 3E6
Tel: (604) 356-8673
Fax: (604) 356-8923
1-800-775-1046 (for use in Lower Mainland B.C. only)

Name search and approval takes one or two working days, but you may request priority service of about 24 hours with the prior payment of an additional $100. Once approved, the name will be held for 56 calendar days. This will give you time to submit full documentation for incorporation to the Registrar of Companies. If you have questions about the requirements or procedures, call the Societies Unit for clarification.

2. Alberta

You must contact a private search company (rather than the government) to check on the availability of a name. A list of Alberta search houses is included as part of the Corporate Registry kit. The fee will be about $35 per name searched depending on the search house used. Check terms of payment in advance. Some search houses require a major credit card number before the work is done. Others will accept only cash on pickup or a cheque on invoicing. The name search company will produce a printout within 24 hours, and, if it is available, will reserve the name for you for a period of 90 days. The printout will tell you which society names most similar to yours are already registered. Within the 90 days you must submit your application, by-laws, and other forms to the Registrar, along with all pages of the search report and the reservation notice you received from the search company. The printout is referred to as the NUANS report — New Upgraded Automated Name Search system — which is owned and operated by Consumer and Corporate Affairs Canada.

The name must comply with the regulations set out in the Societies Act and must not be the same or similar to that of any other society in Alberta.

The regulations affect your choice of name in the following areas:

(a) The name of the society *must* contain one of the following words: society, association, club, fellowship, guild, foundation, or institute. If you wish to use a name that does not contain one of these words, you must obtain special permission from the Registrar of Corporations.

(b) The name must specifically describe the activity in which the society is engaged (use "Musical Arts" instead of "Arts"). You must include a distinctive element; a unique word of location which sets your society name apart from others (Anyville Historical Association sets it apart from the Otherville Historical Association). In the interest of being unique, avoid too commonly used names such as Alberta, Western, or Calgary.

(c) You must obtain permission from certain organizations if your society's name suggests association with royalty; a government agency; a university, college, or technical institute; a professional or occupational association; or with any of several other place names listed in the Corporate Registry Instructions.

(d) If you want to use the name of an individual in your society's name, you must have the consent of that person and/or his or her heirs, executors, or guardians.

It is wise to obtain approval for your choice of name in advance of completing and submitting other forms. The Registrar reserves the right to make a final decision about the acceptability of your proposed society name. Submit your request for approval to:

Corporate Registry
8th Floor
John E. Brownlee Building
10365 - 97 Street
Edmonton, AB T5J 3W7
Tel: (403) 427-2311

or

Corporate Registry
3rd Floor
407 - 2nd Street S.W.
Calgary, AB T2P 2Y3
Tel: (403) 297-3442

3. Saskatchewan

Form 27, the Non-Profit Corporations Act Request for Name Search and Name Reservation, is the form provided in the incorporation kit (see Sample #9). This form may also be used for the name change of a presently registered corporation or for amalgamation. Also note that section 3 of Form 27 requires a listing of purposes for the society. (See the **Reading and Resources** section for the address to write to for this form and accompanying kit.)

In Saskatchewan, it is also possible to telephone the Corporations Branch with the proposed name. A name search can be conducted and confirmation received within several days. There is a fee of $20 for each name searched. Fees are made payable to the Minister of Finance.

Do not include the word "The" as the first word of the name. The word "Incorporated" (or its abbreviation "Inc.") must be included at the end of the name.

Names will be reserved for 90 days during which time all documents for incorporation should be submitted. A reply will be telephoned (if requested) or mailed the same day the form is received. The inquiry line is (306) 787-2962. Mail fee and Form 27 to:

Corporations Branch
1871 Smith Street
Regina, SK S4P 3V7

4. Manitoba

You will need Form 25 (see Sample #10), the Request for Corporate Name Reservation, part of the incorporation package available from the Corporations Branch. Only one name is searched at a time; response time is 24 hours. Note that in Manitoba it is the user's responsibility "to ascertain that the name is not confusingly similar" to other associations. Also note that the name for the organization must be concluded with "Incorporated," "Inc.," "Corporation," or "Corp."

The reservation is valid for 90 days only.

Complete two copies of the form and submit with a $30 fee. Cheques should be certified and made payable to the Minister of Finance of Manitoba. Mail the fee and two copies of Form 25 to:

Corporations and Business Names
  Branch
1010 405 Broadway
Winnipeg, MB R3C 3L6
Tel: (204) 945-5999

5. Ontario

Your first step is to check the Yellow Pages under "Searchers of Records." There are at least 70 such companies in

SAMPLE #8
NAME APPROVAL REQUEST FORM (BRITISH COLUMBIA)

Province of British Columbia

Ministry of Finance and Corporate Relations

REGISTRAR OF COMPANIES
CORPORATE AND PERSONAL
PROPERTY REGISTRIES
2ND FLOOR – 940 BLANSHARD STREET
VICTORIA, B.C. V8W 3E6
Fax No.: 356-1428

Phone No.: 356-2893 *or*
Greater Vancouver area only: 775-1044

INSTRUCTIONS: Please retain the yellow copy for your records. The Name Reservation Office will notify you by letter once your request is completed.

SHADED AREAS ARE FOR OFFICE USE ONLY.

Please type or print clearly.

NAME APPROVAL REQUEST

DOCUMENT CONTROL NUMBER	**NR 205148**

Please quote this number on all correspondence

PRIORITY REQUEST – *Additional fee required*

☐ **YES** – This is a priority request and I have enclosed an additional fee for this service.

ROUTING SLIP NO.	DEBIT BCOL ACCOUNT NO.
FOLIO NO.	DEPOSIT ACCOUNT TRANSACTION NO.
GOVT. AGENT TRANSACTION DATE Y M D	DATE RECEIVED Y M D
GOVT. AGENT TRANSACTION NO.	GOVT. AGENT AMOUNT COLLECTED $

APPLICANT SURNAME	FIRST NAME AND INITIALS
GREY	JANET G.

ADDRESS: RR #1 ROAD 7

CITY	PROVINCE	POSTAL CODE
ANYVILLE	B.C.	V0W1C0

APPLICANT PHONE NO.	APPLICANT FAX NO.	CONTACT PERSON NAME
539-1234	539-5678	

Indicate what the name request is for: (In order for this request to be completed, one box must be (✔) ticked)

☐ CORPORATION ☐ PROPRIETORSHIP/PARTNERSHIP ☑ SOCIETY ☐ FINANCIAL INSTITUTION ☐ COOPERATIVE ASSOCIATION

Is this request for an extra provincial registration in B.C.?	☐ YES ☑ NO	IF YES, SUPPLY THE JURISDICTION	NATURE OF BUSINESS

ADDITIONAL INFORMATION

Name Request *(first choice)* PLEASE TYPE OR PRINT CLEARLY

VULNERABLE VALLEY ENVIRONMENTAL SOCIETY

Name Request *(second choice)* PLEASE TYPE OR PRINT CLEARLY

VULNERABLE VALLEY PRESERVATION SOCIETY

Name Request *(third choice)* PLEASE TYPE OR PRINT CLEARLY

FIN 708B Rev. 93 / 4 / 28   WHITE: NAME RESERVATION OFFICE   YELLOW: APPLICANT COPY

43

various locations throughout the province. Request an "Ontario biased" name search report for the name under which you wish to register your organization. Phone to check the cost (two different search houses contacted quoted $50 to $75 respectively). Each company will have access to a computer data base of corporate names, trademarks, and business names in Canada. (The NUANS data base refers to the New Upgraded Automated Name Search system which is owned by Consumer and Corporate Affairs Canada.) They will check if anyone else in the province has your proposed name, check if the name is available, and will return two copies of the cleared search report to you. If the name is not available or is rejected, they will tell you why. You should have a reply in two or three days.

The fee applies to *each* name searched, so to avoid extra cost ask the search house staff for advice on your proposed name; they have a good idea of what has been rejected in the past and why. The name must be both descriptive and distinctive. Note you are not required to have the word "Limited" as part of your name. You may include "Incorporated" or "Inc." to indicate incorporation, but it is not required. You are legally required to include the term "Society," "Association," or "Club."

On acceptance, submit the original copy of the NUANS report, together with your application for incorporation, to the office of the Public Trustee.

This procedure, begun in November, 1989, means that your forms, including the statement of objects, are vetted first by the Office of the Public Trustee before they are submitted to the Companies Branch. If there are problems with the application, the forms will be returned to you for proper completion. Each page will receive a separate stamp indicating that it is acceptable for submission to the Companies Branch. As soon as you receive your approved

forms from the Public Trustee, send them immediately to the Companies Branch who must receive them within 90 days of the reservation of your proposed society name.

Office of the Public Trustee for Ontario
Charities Division
595 Bay Street
Toronto, ON M5G 2M6
Tel: (416) 314-2800
Fax: (416) 314-2716

Companies Branch
Ministry of Consumer and
    Commercial Relations
393 University Avenue, Suite 200
Toronto, ON M5G 2M2
Tel: (416) 314-8880

The Ministry of Consumer and Commercial Relations' information kit suggest the purchase of *Not for Profit*, a handbook available for $5 plus GST from:

Publications Ontario
50 Grosvenor Street
Toronto, ON M7A 1N8
Tel: (416) 326-5300

It stresses that a new name must not be easily confused with existing names of corporations, trademarks, or unincorporated associations so as not to mislead or confuse the public as to the society's purpose and nature, or regarding its relationship to existing corporations.

Check the Corporations Act and Ontario Regulations, section 13, to ensure that the proposed name fits requirements listed there. Your local public library will have the act or will obtain a copy for you.

The Companies Branch has the power to give a society a name different from the one proposed — that is, to make any minor alterations that may be necessary. They may also refuse any name considered to be objectionable on public grounds. Forms and the guide for their use are available in French as well as English.

You will receive a NUANS report in duplicate showing that the name you plan

SAMPLE #9
REQUEST FOR NAME SEARCH AND RESERVATION (SASKATCHEWAN)

Saskatchewan Justice	Request for Name Search and Reservation	Form 27
	The Non-Profit Corporations Act	

Corporations Branch

Name and mailing address of person (or company) requesting the name search:

_____
Contact person

_____
Telephone number where you may be
reached from 8 a.m. to 5 p.m.

1. Type of Search you would prefer:

   ☐ **Saskatchewan Only** - a search of names only registered in Saskatchewan   **$20.00**

   ☐ **Saskatchewan plus** - a search of names registered in Saskatchewan,
   including Canada corporations and registered Trademarks   **$50.00**

   ☐ **Canada-Wide** - a search of names registered anywere in Canada and registered Trademarks   **$60.00**

2. Name(s) you would like to use (in order of preference):

   a) _____

   b) _____

   c) _____

3. Type(s) of activities this corporation intends to do (be specific):

   _____

   _____

4. This name is to be used for:

   ☐ Incorporation   ☐ Amalgamation
   ☐ Name change from: _____
   ☐ Extra-provincial registration from: _____
                                        Name of province or state where incorporated

The above name appears to be available for use and is reserved for the above person (or firm)
for 90 days ending _____, 19 _____.

OR: The above name is not available for the following reason(s):

_____

Department Use Only
Searched by: _____

Request for Name Search and Reservation

FORM 27

INSTRUCTIONS FOR COMPLETION

Before you incorporate your organization, we must do a name search to make sure the name you have selected is not similar to any other registered name.

ITEM 1: There are 3 levels of name searches you may request: a Saskatchewan only search, a Saskatchewan plus search or a Canada-Wide search. Please check the appropriate box.

ITEM 2: Type or print the name(s) you would like searched in your order of preference. Only the first available name will be searched unless you ask for all names listed on the form to be reserved.

ITEM 3: Describe the type of activities your organization will conduct. Please be as specific as possible.

ITEM 4: Check the appropriate box.

CAUTION: If you select a Canada-wide search, you will find out if a similar name or trademark has been registered anywhere in Canada. If you select a Saskatchewan plus search, you will find out if there is a similar federal corporation or trademark. If you don't select either of the above searches, you may find out later that the name you have selected is too similar to a federal corporation or is trademarked. This might result in your having to change the name of your corporation, which could be very expensive for you.

SAMPLE #10
REQUEST FOR CORPORATE NAME RESERVATION (MANITOBA)

Manitoba

The Corporations Act /
Loi sur les corporations
REQUEST FOR CORPORATE NAME RESERVATION
DEMANDE DE RÉSERVATION D'UNE DÉNOMINATION SOCIALE

CAUTION : RESPONSIBILITY FOR CHOICE AND USE OF THE NAME RESTS ENTIRELY WITH THE APPLICANT. READ GUIDELINES ON REVERSE BEFORE ANSWERING ALL QUESTIONS.
ATTENTION: LE CHOIX ET L'UTILISATION DE LA DÉNOMINATION INCOMBENT AU REQUÉRANT. LIRE LES DIRECTIVES QUI FIGURENT AU VERSO AVANT DE RÉPONDRE AUX QUESTIONS

A

Name and address of sender / Nom et adresse de l'expéditeur

Denise Dansante

1879 Reel Road

St. Boniface, Manitoba   R1A 2B3

Contact person / Personne ressource

Denise Dansante

Tel (8:30-4:30) / Tél(8 h 30-16 h 30) :

347-5689

B

1. Proposed name / Dénomination projetée

St. Boniface Folk Dancing Society Inc.

2. Reason for reservation / Motif de la réservation

[X] INCORPORATION / CONSTITUTION EN CORPORATION
[ ] AMALGAMATION / FUSION
[ ] REGISTRATION OF FEDERAL CORPORATION / ENREGISTREMENT D'UNE CORPORATION FÉDÉRALE
[ ] REGISTRATION OF EXTRA- PROVINCIAL CORPORATION / ENREGISTREMENT D'UNE CORPORATION EXTRA-PROVINCIALE
[ ] TRUST AND LOAN CORPORATION / CORPORATIONS DE FIDUCIE ET CORPORATIONS DE PRÊT
[ ] REVIVAL OR RESTORATION / RECONSTITUTION OU RÉTABLISSEMENT
[ ] CONTINUANCE / PROROGATION
[ ] CHANGE OF NAME FROM / CHANGEMENT DE DÉNOMINATION DE _____
CURRENT NAME / DÉNOMINATION ACTUELLE

3. Describe the main type of business to be carried on in Manitoba / Indiquer l'entreprise principale qui sera poursuivie

Promotion of ethnic dance for the cultural etc...

4. How or why name was chosen / Indiquer les raisons du choix de la dénomination

Self-explanatory

5. Note any relevant information (e.g.names of affiliated businesses, consents available from other companies, etc)
Donner tout autre renseignement pertinent (e.g. le nom des entreprises qui appartiennent au même groupe, le consentement d'autres compagnies, etc.)

n/a

C

OFFICE REPLY / RÉPONSE

[ ] **YES,** the name appears to be available and is reserved for you for **90 DAYS** until
OUI, la dénomination semble disponible et elle est réservée pour **90 JOURS** jusqu'au

[ ] **NO,** the name is not available. Please see reasons on reverse.
NON, la dénomination n'est pas disponible pour les motifs indiqués au verso.
REMARKS / REMARQUES _____

DATE/DATE   SIGNATURE/ SIGNATURE   TEL/ TÉL

SAMPLE #10 — Continued

SEND FEE AND TWO COPIES OF THIS FORM TO

CORPORATIONS AND BUSINESS NAMES BRANCH
1010 - 405 BROADWAY
WINNIPEG, MANITOBA, R3C 3L6
(204) 945 - 2500

FAITES PARVENIR LE DROIT ET DEUX COPIES DE LA PRÉSENTE FORMULE À :

CORPORATIONS ET NOMS COMMERCIAUX
405, BROADWAY, BUREAU 1010
WINNIPEG (MANITOBA) R3C 3L6
(204) 945 -2500

GUIDELINES

1. A corporate name reservation request will result in a four page report. The first two pages list names on record in Manitoba. The last two pages will list some trademarks and names in use in other Canadian jurisdictions. It is your responsibility to ensure that the name you choose is not identical or confusingly similar to an existing trademark, business, association or corporation. If anyone complains about your name, and that complaint is held to be valid, it will be your obligation to change your name.

2. You can check for similar names by reading telephone directories, trade publications, magazines, advertisements, and by contacting the corporations branches in other jurisdictions.

3. Reservation of a name is not "protection" or a "guarantee" that your name is automatically available. Use of a name is done at the risk of the user.

4. If the name is not available, a new name must be selected, AND a new Reservation form AND FEE will have to be filed. Careful selection and research of a name may save you time and money.

5. Read the reasons for rejection listed below. These may help in choosing a name.

DIRECTIVES

1. Un rapport de quatre pages vous sera remis après le dépôt de votre demande de réservation d'une dénomination sociale. Les deux premières pages donnent les dénominations enregistrées au Manitoba. Les autres pages donnent certaines marques de commerce et dénominations utilisées ailleurs au Canada. Il vous incombe de veiller à ce que la dénomination choisie ne soit pas identique à une marque de commerce ou à une dénomination existante et qu'elle ne prête pas à confusion avec une telle marque de commerce ou dénomination. Si quelqu'un portait plainte au sujet de votre dénomination et que cette plainte s'avérait fondée, vous devriez alors changer de dénomination.

2. Vous pouvez vérifier s'il existe des dénominations semblables en consultant les annuaires téléphoniques, les publications commerciales, les périodiques, les annonces et en communiquant avec la direction des corporations d'autres administrations.

3. La réservation d'une dénomination ne vous garantit pas que votre dénomination sera automatiquement retenue. L'utilisation de la dénomination se fait au risque de l'utilisateur.

4. Si la dénomination ne peut être retenue, vous devez en choisir une autre et déposer une nouvelle formule de réservation accompagnée du droit prescrit. Vous épargnerez temps et argent en choisissant avec soin votre dénomination.

5. Lisez les motifs de rejet ci-dessous. Cela facilitera le choix d'une dénomination.

REASONS FOR REJECTION OF NAME / MOTIFS DE REJET DE LA DÉNOMINATION

☐ Prohibited / Dénomination interdite.

☐ Consists of general words **or** only describes the nature of business./
Dénomination entièrement formée de termes généraux **ou** ne faisant que décrire la nature de l'entreprise.

☐ Consists of surname or geographical name only /
Dénomination formée uniquement d'un nom de famille ou d'un toponyme.

☐ Too similar to name(s) on attached report /
Dénomination trop semblable à une ou plusieurs des dénominations figurant dans le rapport ci-joint

☐ Obscene or on public grounds objectionable /
Dénomination obscène ou inadmissible pour des raisons d'ordre public.

☐ Distinctive element should be added / Il manque un élément distinctif

☐ Descriptive element should be added / Il manque un élément descriptif

☐ Read remarks on front / Lire les remarques au recto

48

to use for your corporation has been cleared and is not already in use by any other organization. Some search houses will highlight for you on the printout any names of existing corporations that might conflict with your proposed name. One copy of the report will accompany the application for incorporation (see chapter 7).

READING AND RESOURCES

British Columbia

On request, the Ministry of Finance and the Registrar of Companies will send a letter reminding you of the requirement to prepare a constitution and by-laws and to submit two notices (Notice of Address and Notice of First Directors). Copies are provided. Write to:

> Registrar of Companies
> Second floor
> 940 Blanshard Street
> Victoria, BC   V8W 3E6
> Tel: (604) 356-8676
> Fax: (604) 356-1428

Cost:

Name reservation	$30
Incorporation fee	
(payable to Minister of Finance)	$65

Society Guide for British Columbia. Community Legal Assistance Society, May, 1991. $20 plus $2 postage.

An excellent guide to incorporation. Available from:

> World Wide Books and Maps
> 736 Granville Street
> Vancouver, BC   V6Z 1G3
> Tel: (604) 687-3320
> Fax: (604) 687-5925

Society Act. $4.85 Available from:

> Crown Publications Inc.
> 546 Yates Street
> Victoria, BC   V8W 1K8
> Tel: (604) 386-4636
> Fax: (604) 386-0221

Alberta

Societies Act Information. Alberta Consumer and Corporate Affairs. Free.

An excellent kit that includes all necessary forms, examples of how to complete them, sample by-laws, and a checklist guide through the process. Available from:

> Corporate Registry
> Consumer and Corporate Affairs
> Box 1007
> Main Post Office
> Edmonton, AB   T5J 2M1

You can telephone Corporate Link, a quick reference telephone guide:
In Edmonton: 427-2311
In Calgary: 297-3442

Cost:

Incorporation fee	
(payable to Provincial Treasurer)	$50
Name search	about $40

Additional forms are available at regional offices of Alberta Consumer and Corporate Affairs.

Societies Act. $4 and Societies Act Regulations $4. Available by mail from:

> Publications Services
> 11510 Kingsway Avenue
> Edmonton, AB   T5G 0X5
> Tel: (403) 427-4952

> Publication Services
> 455 - 6 Street SW
> Calgary, AB   T2P 4E8
> Tel: (403) 297-6251

Saskatchewan

Incorporation Kit. Available from:

> Corporations Branch
> Second Floor, 1871 Smith Street
> Regina, SK   S4P 3V7
> Tel: (306) 787-2962

Inquiry lines:

Name search and	
registration information:	(306) 787-2962
Non-profit section:	(306) 787-3008

Cost:

Incorporation fee
(payable to Minister of Finance) $50
Fee for each name reserved $20
Publication in Gazette $10

Non-Profit Corporations Act and Regulations.
Act — $24; Regulations — $9.15 plus GST.
Cheques payable to Minister of Finance.

Available from:

> Queen's Printer
> Third Floor, 1874 Scarth Street
> Regina, SK S4P 3V7
> Tel: (306) 787-6894

Manitoba

Forms and instruction sheets from:

> Cooperative, Consumer and
>   Corporate Affairs
> Corporations and Business Names
> Branch
> 1010 - 405 Broadway
> Winnipeg, MB R3C 3L6
> Tel: (204) 945-5999
> Fax: (204) 945-1459

Cost:

Name search and
reservation $30 per name
Fee for incorporation
(without share capital) $70

Payable by certified cheque or money order to Minister of Finance.

Corporation Act. $31.05 plus GST. Available from:

> Queen's Printer
> 200 Vaughan Street
> Winnipeg, MB R3C 1T5
> Tel: (204) 945-3101

Fees payable to Minister of Finance.

Ontario

Forms and a free guide, *Not-For-Profit Incorporator's Handbook,* are available from:

> Companies Branch
> Ministry of Consumer and
>   Commercial Relations
> 393 University Avenue, Suite 200
> Toronto, ON M5G 2M2
> Tel: (416) 314-8880

Cost:

Fee for incorporation
(without share capital,
payable to Minister of Finance) $155
Name search $50 to $75 per name

The Corporations Act and Ontario Regulations. 1990. $19 plus GST.

Contains information on names requirements (see the Regulations section) and copies of all forms.

Not for Profit: Incorporator's Handbook. 1993. 68 pp. Ministry of Consumer and Commercial Relations. $5 plus GST. Both available from:

> Publications Ontario
> 50 Grosvenor Street
> Toronto, ON M7A 1N8
> Tel: (416) 326-5300
> Fax: (416) 326-5317

See also: *A Guide to Incorporating a Nonprofit organization in Ontario.* 1991. 27 pp. $20 plus GST. Available from:

> Lamp Consultants to Non-Profits
> 10 Water Street North
> Kitchener, ON N2H 5A5
> Tel: (519) 578-8040

Quebec

A full instruction kit in French only is available from:

> Directeur
> Direction des Entreprises
> Inspecteur General des Institutions
>   Financieres
> Direction des Entreprises
> 800 Place d'Youville
> Quebec, PQ G1R 4Y5
> Tel: (418) 643-3625

New Brunswick

Non-profit companies are incorporated under the Companies Act. A brochure and forms are available. A copy of the Companies Act may be obtained from:

> Queen's Printer
> P.O. Box 6000
> Fredericton, NB E3B 5H1
> Tel: (506) 453-2520

Cost:
Letters Patent: fee is based on
      real and personal property
      and will be between $50 and $200
Publication fee: $10
Name search:
(via name search services)   about $40

A guide to incorporation is also available and includes samples of four basic forms. It may be obtained from:

> Corporate Branch
> Department of Justice
> P.O. Box 6000
> Fredericton, NB E3B 5H1
> Tel: (506) 453-2703

Nova Scotia

Sample by-laws and constitution are available as well as necessary forms and set of instructions from:

> Department of Justice
> Registry of Joint Stock Companies
> P.O. Box 1529
> 1660 Hollis Street
> Centennial Building
> Halifax, NS B3J 2Y4
> Tel: (902) 424-7770

Fee for name search and filing is $25.

Prince Edward Island

Non-profit companies are formed under the Companies Act (Part II). A copy will be mailed to you upon request. Sample forms are included in the act as appendixes. The fee for incorporation is $125, payable to the Minister of Finance. The application and by-laws must be reviewed by a lawyer resident in the province who gives a written opinion to the effect that the application complies with the Companies Act. There is also a $10 charge for publication in *The Royal Gazette*.

Names can be searched and reserved for 90 days for a fee of $40 by writing to:

> Corporations Division
> Consumer, Corporate and Insurance
> Services, Department of Provincial
> Affairs and Attorney General
> Shaw Building
> 105 Rochford Street
> P.O. Box 2000
> Charlottetown, PE C1A 7N8
> Tel: (902) 368-4550
> Fax: (902) 368-5283

Newfoundland and Labrador

The Corporations Act (Chapter 12) was revised in 1986. You may request a kit be mailed to you including Articles of Incorporation (Form 1), Notice of Registered Office (Form 3), Notice of Directors (Form 6), Schedules A and B for recording of society objects and by-laws and an instruction guide.

Cost:
Reservation of a name for 90 days: $10
Filing: $60

Cheques should be made payable to Newfoundland Exchequer Account. A copy of the act is available from the Queen's Printer at the same address as the Registrar. Write to:

> Department of Justice
> Registrar of Deeds and Companies
> P.O. Box 8700
> Confederation Building
> St. John's, NF A1B 4J6
> Tel: (709) 729-3316
> Fax: (709) 729-0232

Yukon

A full set of forms, sample by-laws, constitution, and completed sample forms are available on request. An excellent checklist of registration information, a copy of the Societies Ordinance, and sample balance sheet and statement of income and expenditures are also available free. There is no charge for name search. Cost of Certificate of Incorporation is $30 and Notice of Incorporation Publication is $20. Write to:

Registrar of Societies
Yukon Justice
Box 2703
Whitehorse, YT   Y1A 2C6
Tel: (403) 667-5314

Northwest Territories

A full set of forms, a copy of the Societies
Act, fee schedule, instructions, and an application are available free on request. Cost
is $50, which includes incorporation and
publishing notice of incorporation.

There isn't any procedure for name
search, but the department will tell you if
any existing society has your proposed
name. Write to:

Registrar of Societies
Department of Justice
Government of the Northwest
  Territories
Yellowknife, NT   X1A 2L9
Tel: (403) 873-7490 or 920-8985
Fax: (403) 873-0243

7

CONSTITUTION AND ARTICLES OF INCORPORATION

A constitution is essentially a statement of purposes listed under the approved name of your society and endorsed by a group of applicants or first directors. In some provinces, it is combined with other information to form the Articles of Incorporation. In all cases, the non-profit society must be clearly described in the constitution as a charitable organization with defined goals and objectives that are distinct from political parties, privately owned clubs, or businesses. These distinctions are required in order to satisfy both provincial and federal requirements.

a. DRAFTING YOUR CONSTITUTION

Your first task is to draft a statement of purpose for your society. It tells what you plan to do. The statement of purpose should — like your goal statement — be phrased in general but descriptive terms. You do not want to place limitations on what your society (given its overall purpose) wants to do by being too specific. Simply phrase each of your purposes in the same style, beginning with "to": for example, "to promote," "to facilitate," "to educate," "to establish," "to assist."

Be sure to read the Society Act (or equivalent) for your province paying close attention to purpose and procedure. If there are variations between draft materials, such as kits, distributed by the province and the contents of the act, the act is the final authority.

Of course, the constitution or the name of your society can be changed later (though there may be a fee) provided proper procedure is followed.

The documents you submit to the provincial government form a permanent record of the society or corporation. They are open to public inspection and may be photocopied or put on microfilm. Use good quality paper (8½" x 11") and type your documents or print them neatly.

Note that in all provinces it is a requirement that business must not be one of the purposes of your society. Societies can carry on a form of business (and increasingly do) provided that the business is incidental to and supportive of the main purposes of such societies, and provided that members of the societies do not personally receive profit from the business. But business as such should not be listed as one of the purposes of the society and if it is a central concern, then incorporation as a company should be considered. Increasingly, societies have added the following simple statement to the list of purposes: "To be carried out on an exclusively charitable basis."

b. ELIGIBILITY FOR REGISTERED CHARITABLE STATUS

If you also plan to apply for registered charitable status from the federal government, your constitution must meet the criteria outlined below. They apply to societies in all provinces and should be considered at the time of registration as a charity with provincial authorities. Also see chapter 11.

1. Charitable goals

Your society must have charitable goals of benefit to the community, not simply its members. For example, a musical group whose sole purpose is enjoyment and participation of its members may not be granted status as a charity.

2. No political activity or lobbying

Political activity or lobbying listed as a purpose will make your society ineligible for registered charitable status.

However, challenges to stringent interpretation of this policy have been made by several national non-government organizations who were threatened with loss of registered tax-exempt status. In May, 1985, the government announced their intention of revising the interpretation of policy to allow charitable institutions to carry out lobbying campaigns on public issues as long as those actions are not actively partisan and directly political, and as long as they are "ancillary and incidental" to their charitable purposes.

3. Wind-up clause

Include a wind-up clause to determine what will be done with the society's assets if it disbands. The wind-up clause is not essential to obtain status as a registered society (with provincial governments), but is necessary to obtain status as a registered charity (with the federal government).

Revenue Canada must be assured that individual members of the society will not benefit on dissolution of the society and disbursement of its assets. The assets of your society may be non-existent, but in some societies they are substantial.

If donors are allowed tax-deductible receipts for contributions, Revenue Canada must be assured that no individual will benefit directly and personally as a result of such tax-deductible donations.

The wind-up clause can follow the list of purposes, and might for example read:

On the winding up or dissolution of this society, funds or assets remaining after all debts have been paid shall be transferred to a charitable institution with purposes similar to those of this society, or, if this cannot be done, to another charitable institution recognized by Revenue Canada as qualified under the provisions of the Income Tax Act of Canada.

For those societies that do not have a specific provision in their own constitution, by-laws, or record of business, the Society Act for your province will contain a clause regarding the disposal of assets on wind-up. Generally, it is stipulated that first, all debts be paid, and that "unless the constitution, by-laws, or resolution of the members provides for the transfer of any remaining money to another charitable institution, then it will be paid to the Minister of Finance."

Even if your society is not concerned about obtaining charitable status, it is a good idea to include a wind-up clause, as most people prefer their assets to go to some non-profit society with similar aims to their own rather than to the general revenue fund of the federal government. Be sure, however, that any non-profit society specifically named is in fact a recognized (accepted by Revenue Canada) charitable organization.

4. No purpose of gain for members

Separate from the wind-up clause, the constitution should also contain a clear statement that no members of the society will receive income of any sort from the society. Board members will not be paid, however, it's possible to be an employee of or under contract to a society and also be a member of that society. However, the distinction is a fine one, and generally societies find it preferable not to hire members, or to have members resign from a society or board before being hired as employees of that society. It is permissible to pay reasonable out-of-pocket expenses for directors and other volunteers.

Revenue Canada requires the following clause in your constitution if you plan to request status as a registered charity:

> The purpose of the society shall be carried out without purpose of gain for its members, and any profits or other accretions to the society shall be used for promoting its purpose.

5. Unalterability clause

Finally, end your constitution with a statement about the unalterability of certain clauses. For example:

> Paragraphs 3 and 4 of this constitution are unalterable in accordance with the Society Act.

Two clauses (the wind-up clause and the non-profit clause) are required for registered charity status. Revenue Canada must be assured that the society will not change the intent of these clauses after registration.

Certain items which might otherwise be by-laws may be of such importance to your group that you choose to make them unalterable. They must then be part of the constitution and specifically declared to be unalterable.

c. SAMPLE CONSTITUTION

Sample #11 shows a sample constitution. This constitution would meet the requirements for registration in British Columbia. It also provides model wording for the completion of application forms for Alberta, Saskatchewan, and Manitoba. Ontario forms have the statements required by Revenue Canada already included.

Revenue Canada summarizes its requirements for the constitution of an organization as follows. Note items (c) and (e) are required for registered charitable status with the federal government.

(a) The name of the organization

(b) The object(s) of the organization

(c) A clause stating that the organization shall be carried on without purpose of gain for its members

and that any profits or other accretions to the organization shall be used in promoting its object(s)

(d) The organizational structure (President or Chairman, Secretary, Treasurer, etc.)

(e) The signatures of at least three of the present officers of the organization

The above items may be contained in the constitution or other documents which describe the organization's purposes and govern its operations, including (depending on the province concerned) Letters Patent, Certificate of Incorporation, Memorandum or Articles of Association, Trust Document, or Constitution.

d. VARIATIONS IN PROVINCIAL REQUIREMENTS

1. British Columbia

The package you receive from the Societies Unit, Registrar of Companies will contain a copy of the Society Act and three sample forms related both to the constitution and bylaws of a new society. (The forms are clearly marked "sample" and need to be retyped on a plain piece of paper.) Variations of bylaw format are discussed in chapter 8. Sample #11 gives a statement of purposes for the Vulnerable Valley Environmental Society.

The by-laws must be followed by the names of at least five applicants for incorporation (full names and home addresses) and one or more witnesses (full names and home addresses). (See format in chapter 8.)

2. Alberta

The form provided is set out as an application for incorporation (see Sample #12).

In item 2 a list of sample objectives is provided. Any objectives that do not apply should have a line drawn through them. Add any additional objectives in the blank space.

At least five members must sign the form and include their full addresses. If

SAMPLE #11
CONSTITUTION

1. The name of the society is

"VULNERABLE VALLEY ENVIRONMENTAL SOCIETY"

2. The purposes of the society are:

• to work to protect Vulnerable Valley and its watershed from damage to its ecological balance and visual beauty

• to provide educational services related to the environmental and safe accessing of wilderness areas

• to promote co-operation amongst levels of government and citizens in planning which will affect the physical environment in Vulnerable Valley

The purposes will be carried out on an exclusively charitable basis.

3. On the winding up or dissolution of this society, funds or assets remaining after all debts have been paid shall be transferred to a charitable institution with purposes similar to those of this society, or, if this cannot be done, to another charitable institution recognized by Revenue Canada as qualified under the provisions of the Income Tax Act of Canada.

4. The purpose of the society shall be carried out without purpose of gain for its members, and any profits or other accretions to the society shall be used for promoting its purpose.

5. Paragraphs 3 and 4 of this constitution are unalterable in accordance with the Society Act.

signatures are hard to read, type the name just under the handwritten names.

3. Saskatchewan

No constitution as such is required under the Non-Profit Corporations Act. Instead, a society is required to file articles of incorporation (see Sample #13). The Request for Name Search and Name Reservation (Form 27) already presented in chapter 6 (see Sample #9) requires a listing of main activities or purposes. Because the society will have already listed its main activities or purposes on Form 27 these are not required to be listed in the articles of incorporation.

(a) Filing the articles

Note the following:

Item 1

Remember to show the society name exactly as approved by the Registrar. This is how it will appear on your Certificate of Incorporation. Do not use "The"; do not use "Association" in one place and "Assoc." in another.

Item 2

Write in the city, town, village, or rural municipality (hamlet). If the registered office of the society is located in a hamlet or other area, then show the name and number of the rural community in which the hamlet is located.

Item 3

Having one class of members is the simplest arrangement. Thus, all members have equal rights and responsibilities. Though you may have regular members and honorary members, if both have the same right to attend meetings, vote, and hold office, then — in spite of titles — your society has in fact one class of members. You will have a second or third class of members if, for example, "honorary" members are exempt from fees, or "associate" members are not entitled to become directors. In this case, Schedule I, Classes of Membership, is incorporated into Form 1. This is a separate piece of paper that names the classes and sets out the rights,

privileges, restrictions, and conditions of each class. The information kit is available on request from the Corporations Branch, Consumer and Commercial Affairs, and contains an example of such a schedule.

Item 4

Usually there is no right to transfer membership interest stipulated for a charitable organization. If there is to be a right of transfer, the conditions of transfer must be set out here.

Item 5

Usually a minimum and a maximum number of directors is designated; for example, a minimum of five and a maximum of 12. The act says there can be no fewer than three directors. Note that duties of directors are specified in the act and directors are responsible for managing the activities and affairs of the corporation in accordance with the act, articles, and any by-laws. Further, no by-laws, article, or resolution of the society relieves the directors of acting in accordance with the act:

> 106.(1) Every director and officer of a corporation, in exercising his powers and discharging his duties, shall:
>
> > (a) act honestly and in good faith with a view to the best interests of the corporation; and
> >
> > (b) exercise the care, diligence, and skill that a reasonably prudent person would exercise in comparable circumstances.
>
> (2) Every director and officer of a corporation shall comply with this act, the regulations, articles, by-laws, and any unanimous member agreement.
>
> (3) ...no provision in a contract, the articles, the by-laws or a resolution relieves a director or officer from the duty to act in accordance with this act or the regulations or relieves him from the liability for a breach thereof.

SAMPLE #12
APPLICATION UNDER SOCIETIES ACT (ALBERTA)

Alberta

CCA-06.003
(Rev. 8/87)

CONSUMER AND
CORPORATE AFFAIRS
Corporate Registry

THE SOCIETIES ACT
APPLICATION

We, the undersigned, hereby declare that we desire to form a society under The Societies Act, R.S.A. 1980, and that:

1. — The name of the society is — Ashford Day Care Society

2. — The objects of the society are —

       DRAW A LINE THROUGH ANY OBJECT THAT DOES NOT APPLY.
       ADD ANY ADDITIONAL OBJECTS IN THE BLANK SPACE.

(a) ~~To provide for the recreation of the members and to promote and afford opportunity for friendly and social activities.~~
(b) ~~To acquire lands, by purchase or otherwise, erect or otherwise provide a building or buildings for social and community purposes.~~
(c) ~~To encourage and promote amateur games and exercises.~~
(d) ~~To provide a meeting place for the consideration and discussion of questions affecting the interests of the community.~~
(e) ~~To carry on a literary and debating club for the discussion of topics of general interest, and to encourage the practice of public speaking among its members.~~
(f) ~~To procure the delivery of lectures on social, educational, political, economic and other subjects, and to give and arrange musical and dramatic entertainments.~~
(g) ~~To establish and maintain a library and reading room.~~
(h) ~~To provide all necessary equipment and furniture for carrying on its various objects.~~
(i) ~~To provide a centre and suitable meeting place for the various activities of the community.~~
(j) ~~Generally to encourage and foster and develop among its members a recognition of the importance of agriculture in the national life.~~
(k) ~~To sell, manage, lease, mortgage, dispose of, or otherwise deal with the property of the society.~~
(l) To provide day care services to children between the ages of two and six years.
(m) To provide a centre for the various activities of the children and their parents.
(n) To generally encourage and foster and develop among the members a recognition of the imprtance of day care in the life of a child and in the lives of his or her parents.

DATED this ......14th.......................... day of ...July.......................... 19 .9.-.

NAME (SIGNATURE) PLEASE PRINT NAME BELOW SIGNATURE	COMPLETE ADDRESS
Betty Able Betty B. Able, Homemaker	49 Elm St., Ashford, AB T0L 1A2
Harry Best Harry R. Best, Carpenter	18 Oak St., Ashford, AB T0L 2B3
Wendy Caring Wendy L. Caring, Lawyer	8 Pine St., Ashford, AB T0L 3C4

NAME (WITNESS)	COMPLETE ADDRESS
Shawn Dependable Shawn M. Dependable, Teacher	52 Oak St., Ashford, AB T0L 2B4

Item 6

Note that a distinction is made between a membership corporation and a charitable organization. The former is supported by its members and donations, and does not solicit donations from the public or receive grants. Its activities are for the benefit of its members (for example, a sports or music club). At wind-up, a membership corporation is not prohibited from distributing any assets to its members (it has the choice of doing so). The charitable corporation is prohibited from benefiting its members.

The purposes of charitable corporations are defined in the Non-Profit Corporations Act. The charitable society:

> (i) carries out activities primarily for the benefit of the public; or

> (ii) solicits or has solicited donations or gifts of money or property from the public; or

> (iii) receives or has received any grant of money or property from a government or government agency in any fiscal year of the corporation that is in excess of 10% of its total income for that fiscal year; or

> (iv) is a registered charity within the meaning of the Income Tax Act and has a registration number (or is proposing to apply to Revenue Canada for a number).

Item 7

Remember that registration as a charity with the federal government will restrict the corporation's activities. Among other things, these activities must be "without purpose of gain for its members" and "on an exclusively charitable basis."

It is important to contact Revenue Canada (see chapter 11) to check that the proper restrictions are built in before the forms are submitted to the Corporations Branch. Amendments cost $20 per item.

Item 8

It must also be clear that, on dissolution of the society, funds or assets will be transferred to a similar charitable institution. This statement is necessary if you wish to be registered as a charitable organization with the federal government. If you do not know which organization should receive assets in the event of dissolution, put "as may be permitted under the act." If your organization wishes, this can be changed at a later date by an amendment to the articles and submission of the proper form.

Item 9

Do not annex already existing by-laws in this section to your articles of incorporation. They will probably conflict with the Non-Profit Corporations Act requirements in some way. Remember, under this act it is advisable not to include by-laws in the articles of incorporation.

However, items may be entered here which limit the power of by-laws that are accepted at (or changed at) annual general meetings. An example would be:

> The by-laws may not require more than a majority of members to constitute a quorum at a meeting of members.

Item 10

It is possible for one of the incorporators (persons who sign the application to incorporate) to be a representative of another organization. For example, the incorporator may be the Saskatchewan Métis Association.

4. Manitoba

The Corporations Act does not require a constitution, but defines what sort of groups may incorporate as non-profit organizations under the act.

The objects of a charitable non-profit organization may be of a patriotic, religious, philanthropic, charitable, educational, agricultural, scientific, literary, historical, artistic, social, professional, fraternal, sporting, or athletic nature. The organization is to be

SAMPLE #13
ARTICLES OF INCORPORATION (SASKATCHEWAN)

Government of Saskatchewan

The Non-profit Corporations Act

Articles of Incorporation

(Section 6)

Form 1

1. Name of corporation: Centretown Society for Exceptional Children Inc.

2. The municipality in which the registered office is to be situated: The City of Centretown

3. The classes of membership: One class

4. Right, if any, to transfer membership interest: N/A

5. Number (or minimum and maximum number) of directors: Minimum of 5
Maximum of 9

6. The corporation is a membership corporation ☐ or a charitable corporation ☒ .

7. Restrictions, if any, on activities the corporation may carry on or on the powers the corporation may exercise:

   The society will fund the education and development of exceptional children lving in Centretown and its surrounds to a radius of 100 km only.

8. Persons to whom remaining property is to be distributed in the course of liquidation and dissolution of the corporation:

   The Association for the Support of exceptional Children in Nearbyville.

9. Other provisions, if any: None

10. Incorporators:

Name in full	Place of residence, giving street and number or R.R. number and post office	Signature
Ivan M. Petit	49 High St., Centretown, SK S1T 2V3	*Ivan Petit*
Joan R. Little	18 Main St., Centretown, SK S4T 5V6	*Joan Little*
Heinz L. Jung	66 Rail Rd., Centretown, SK S7T 8V9	*Heinz Jung*
John A. Brown	123 Red St., Centretown, SK S1T 3L5	*John A. Brown*
Alice B. White	87 Falls St., Centretown, SK S9T 4R9	*Alice B. White*

SAMPLE #13
(Back)

The Non-profit Corporations Act   Form 1

Articles of Incorporation   Instructions

Format:

Documents required to be sent to the Director pursuant to the Act must conform with sections 2 to 5 of the regulations under the Act. Where any provision required to be set out is too long to be set out in the space provided in the form, the form may incorporate the provisions by annexing a schedule in the manner described in section 5 of the regulations.

Item 1:

Set out a proposed corporate name that complies with sections 10 to 12 of the Act and with sections 7 to 9 of the regulations. It would be preferable to clear the proposed name with the corporations branch before submitting the document.

Item 2:

Set out the name of the municipality within Saskatchewan where the registered office is to be situated, for example, City of   Town of   , Village of   , or Rural Municipality of   . Address of registered office will be provided in Notice of Registered Office (Form 3), which must accompany Articles of Incorporation. The procedure for changing the address of the registered office within the municipality is set out in section 19 of the Act whereas the procedure for changing the municipality in which the registered office is situated is set out in section 156 of the Act.

Item 3:

If more than one class of membership, set out the rights, privileges, restrictions and conditions that constitute the membership interests of each class.

Item 4:

If the right to transfer membership interests is permitted, set out a statement to this effect and the conditions of such transfer.

Item 5:

State the number of directors or a minimum and maximum number of directors.

Item 6:

State whether corporation is a membership corporation or a charitable corporation.

Item 7:

If restrictions are to be placed on the activities the corporation may carry on or on the powers the corporation may exercise, set out the restrictions.

Item 8:

Identify to whom any remaining property of the corporation is to be distributed upon its liquidation and dissolution. Sections 184 and 199 of the Act provide for the distribution of the remaining property in the event the articles do not do so.

Item 9:

If any provision that may be set out in the bylaws should preferably be contained in the articles, set out the provision.

Item 10:

Each incorporator must state his name, residential address and affix his signature. If an incorporator is a corporation, the address shall be that of the corporation, and the articles shall be signed by a person authorized by the corporation.

Other Documents:

The Articles must be accompanied by (a) Notice of Registered Office (Form 3); (b) Notice of Directors (Form 6); (c) Request for Name Search and Name Reservation (Form 27) unless name is reserved; and by Petition (Form 1.1) unless there are five or more incorporators.

Completed documents in duplicate and the prescribed fee payable to the Minister of Finance are to be sent to:
Director, Corporations Branch,
2nd Floor,
1871 Smith Street,
Regina, Saskatchewan.
S4P 3V7

operated in the province of Manitoba on a non-profit basis.

Sample #14 shows the form you will need for incorporating as a non-profit society. Submit two copies. Note the following:

Item 1

The name of the corporation must include its legal status; that is, include either "Incorporated," "Incorporee," or "Corporation" or the abbreviation "Inc." or "Corp." Settle on one format, and don't change it while completing the documents.

Item 2

The address of the society must be written in full; include office number if in a multi-office building, and remember the postal code. A box number alone is not acceptable for the registered office.

In rural areas, use the physical location of the registered office along with the mailing address (which may be a post office box number).

Item 3

There cannot be fewer than three directors.

Item 4

In listing the names of first directors, include all given names; use no initials. Also list their full residential addresses (or mailing addresses) plus postal codes (again, a post office box alone is not acceptable). A majority of the directors must be residents of Canada. At least three individuals must be listed as directors.

Item 5

The basic purpose of the corporation must be stated here (usually beginning with "to provide," "to assist," and so on). For example:

> To promote ethnic dance in St. Boniface for the cultural and educational improvement of its members and the community.

Note that the form states: "The undertaking of the corporation is restricted to the following...."

Item 6

To satisfy the requirements of Revenue Canada, the following statement must be entered here as "Other Provisions:"

> Upon dissolution of the corporation, after payment of all debts and liabilities, any remaining property and assets of the corporation shall be transferred to a recognized charitable organization in the community, as determined by the members at dissolution.

Item 7

This statement regarding capital gain to members meets another requirement of Revenue Canada by making it plain that members will not profit from the corporation, but that all profits will go toward promoting its stated purposes.

Item 10

This states that the directors have made sure that the proposed corporate name is unique and is not likely to confuse or mislead.

Item 11

First directors here are called "incorporators." Set out the full names (no initials) and full residential addresses. The incorporators must be the same people as the directors.

5. Ontario

The objects of the new corporation — its purposes — are written as part of Form 2, the Application for Incorporation of a Corporation Without Share Capital (see Sample #15). The instruction sheet for completing the application emphasizes the appearance of documents. They should be typed or hand-printed in block capitals. They *must* be legible and clear enough to photocopy or microfilm.

There are four pages to the application (shortened to two pages for the purposes of our sample only), and they must be submitted in proper order and in duplicate. Applications with missing pages will be returned to you. If a section does not apply, write in "not applicable."

The Corporations Act/
Loi sur les corporations
ARTICLES OF INCORPORATION (without share capital)/
STATUTS CONSTITUTIFS (corporations sans capital-actions)

MANITOBA

Corporation No.
N° de la corporation

1—Name of Corporation / Dénomination sociale

St. Boniface Folk Dance Society Inc.

2—The address in full of the registered office (include postal code) /
Adresse complète du bureau enregistré (inclure le code postal)

1879 Reel Road
St. Boniface, Manitoba
R1A 2B3

3—Number (or minimum and maximum number) of directors /
Nombre (ou nombre minimal et maximal) d'administrateurs

Three and not more than five

4—First directors / Premiers administrateurs

Name in full / Nom complet	Address in full (include postal code) / Adresse complète (inclure le code postal)
Denise Elle Dansante	1879 Reel Road, St. Boniface, Manitoba R1A 2B3
Henri En Pointe	Suite 2, 44 Swan Crt., St. Boniface, Manitoba R1A 3C4
Gilles Marie Pieds	1725 Red River Sq., St. Boniface, Manitoba R1A 2B7

5—The undertaking of the corporation is restricted to the following /
Les activités de la corporation se limitent à ce qui suit

To promote ethnic dance in St. Boniface for the cultural imrpovement of its
members and the community.

FORM 2 /FORMULE 2

2

6—Other provisions, if any / Autres dispositions, s'il y a lieu

> Upon dissolution of the corporation, after payment of all debts and liabilities, any remaining property and assets of the corporation shall be transferred to a recognized charitable organization in the community, as determined by the members at dissolution.

7—The corporation has no authorized capital and shall be carried on without pecuniary gain to its members, and any profits or other accretions to the corporation shall be used in furthering its undertaking. /
La corporation n'a pas de capital autorisé et exercera ses activités sans que ses membres en tirent profit sur le plan pécuniaire; tout bénéfice réalisé par la corporation sera consacré à l'avancement de ses activités.

8—Each first director named herein becomes a member of the corporation upon incorporation. /
Chacun des premiers administrateurs nommés dans les présentes devient membre de la corporation à la constitution de celle-ci.

9—Where the undertaking of the corporation is of a social nature, the address in full of the clubhouse or similar premises that the corporation will maintain. /
Lorsque les activités de la corporation sont à caractère social, indiquer l'adresse au complet du lieu où elle les poursuivra.

1879 Reel Road, St. Boniface, Manitoba R1A 2B3

10—I have satisfied myself that, the proposed name of the corporation is not the same as or similar to the name of any known body corporate, association, partnership, individual or business so as to be likely to confuse or mislead. /
Je me suis assuré que la dénomination sociale projetée n'est ni identique ni semblable à la dénomination d'une personne morale, d'une association, d'une société en nom collectif ou d'une entreprise connue ou au nom d'un particulier connu et qu'elle ne saurait prêter à confusion ni induire en erreur.

11—Incorporators / Fondateurs

Name in full / Nom complet	Address in full (include postal code) / Adresse complète (inclure le code postal)	Signature / Signature
Denise Elle Dansante	1879 Reel Rd., St. Boniface, Manitoba R1A 2B3	*Denise Dansante*
Henri En Pointe	Suite 2, 44 Swan Crt., St. Boniface Manitoba R1A 3C4	*Henri Pointe*
Gilles Marie Pieds	1725 Red River Sq., St. Boniface, Manitoba R1A 2B7	*Gilles Pieds*

Note: If any First Director named in paragraph 4 is not an Incorporator, a Form 3 "Consent to Act as a First Director" must be attached. A minimum of three directors is required for incorporation. State the full civic address in paragraphs 2, 4 and 11—a P.O. box number alone is not acceptable. /

Remarque : Si l'un des premiers administrateurs nommés à la rubrique 4 n'est pas un fondateur, joindre la formule 3 intitulée "Consentement à agir en qualité de premier administrateur". Aux fins de la constitution en corporation, il doit y avoir au moins trois administrateurs. Indiquer l'adresse complète dans les rubriques 2, 4 et 11; un numéro de case postale seul n'est pas suffisant.

If there is insufficient space, supplementary pages may be added, but they must be the same size as other pages and have a 1¼" left-hand margin. Each supplementary page should be numbered (for example, if page two has supplementary pages, number them 2A, 2B, etc.). Complete the application in duplicate with original signatures on all documents. Note the following:

Item 1

Enter the name of the corporation (society) in block capital letters on the first line. Be sure it is exactly the same as the name you have had reserved for you.

Item 2

Insert the full address, including postal code. A post office box is not acceptable as the registered address for the corporation.

Item 3

You require at least three first directors who are 18 or more years of age. (For social clubs, there must be at least ten applicants.) A social club is one which is recreational, athletic, community, or fraternal in nature. The names listed here must be repeated in item 6 with no variation in spelling or style. Include all given names (no initials) and full home addresses and postal codes of the required number of applicants.

Item 4

The objects (or purposes) of a corporation without share capital (non-profit society) will be different from those set out by a business. However, a non-profit society may carry out business if the business is incidental to its main objects and does not financially benefit members. These powers are set out in section 23 and section 133(1) of the Corporations Act. You therefore need to enter nothing here related to business except to include in the objects the power to accept donations, gifts, legacies, and bequests.

For wording of objects (purposes) see the sample constitution earlier in this chapter (Sample #11).

Item 5

Suggested special provisions are:

- rotation of directors
- eligibility for membership
- distribution of assets on dissolution
- no remuneration of directors
- executive officers and responsibilities
- terms of offices

Note that any item that can be made the subject of a by-law can be included here.

However, these provisions will be incorporated into the letters patent, and then may be changed only by following a special procedure regarding supplementary letters patent. In general, write into the articles only provisions that should not be readily changed. Write into the by-laws preferred ways of handling the corporation's affairs that may be changed later by amendment.

Item 6

Repeat here the list of first directors with no variations; that is, all given names (no initials), full home addresses, and occupations. Note additional proceedings are set for a club or corporation whose objects are, in whole or in part, of a social nature. They can make application only after having been in existence for at least one year. The minimum number of applicants for a social club is ten people. For other non-profit organizations, the minimum number is three applicants who must also be first directors and must sign the application. Full instructions are given on the Form 2 guidelines.

The document that authorizes the incorporation of your society is called the letters patent — rather like a licence for your corporation. Be aware that your society will operate under the following conditions, required by Revenue Canada, that the Companies Branch will automatically incorporate into the letters patent for your corporation:

(a) The corporation shall be carried on without the purpose of gain for its members and any profits or other accretions to the corporation shall be used in promoting its objects.

(b) The corporation shall be subject to the Charities Accounting Act, the Charitable Gifts Act, and the Mortmain and Charitable Uses Act.

(c) The directors shall serve without remuneration, and no director shall directly or indirectly receive any profit from his or her position, except to be paid reasonable expenses incurred in the performance of his or her duties.

(d) The borrowing power of the corporation pursuant to any by-law passed and confirmed in accordance with section 59 of the Corporations Act shall be limited to borrowing money for current operating expenses, provided that the borrowing power of the corporation shall not be so limited if it borrows on the security of real or personal property.

(e) Upon the dissolution of the corporation and after the payment of all debts and liabilities, its remaining property shall be distributed or disposed of to charitable organizations which carry on their work solely in Ontario (or in Canada).

(f) If it is made to appear to the satisfaction of the minister, upon report to the public trustee, that the corporation has failed to comply with any of the provisions of the Charities Accounting Act, the Charitable Gifts Act, or the Mortmain and Charitable Uses Act, the minister may authorize an inquiry for the purpose of determining whether or not there is sufficient cause for the Lieutenant-Governor to make an order under subsection 317(1) of the Corporations Act to cancel the letters patent of the corporation and declare it to be dissolved.

A constitution is not specifically required for a non-profit society in Ontario; it may operate under its articles of incorporation and the motions and resolutions recorded in the minutes.

These rules of procedure may be changed by a majority vote of the members when required. A constitution and by-laws are recommended, however, to summarize the purposes of the society, including what purposes and requirements are unalterable, to declare the charitable nature of the society, if you plan to register as a charity with Revenue Canada, and to include a wind-up clause as described in section **b. 3.** of this chapter.

This space is for
Ministry Use Only
Espace réservé à
l'usage exclusif
du ministère

Ontario Corporation Number
Numéro de la personne morale en Ontario   1.

Form 2
Corporations
Act

Formule 2
Loi sur les
personnes
morales

APPLICATION FOR INCORPORATION OF A CORPORATION WITHOUT SHARE CAPITAL
REQUÊTE EN CONSTITUTION D'UNE PERSONNE MORALE SANS CAPITAL ACTIONS

1.   The name of the corporation is/Dénomination sociale de la personne morale :

R	E	N	A	I	S	S	A	N	C	E		T	R	A	N	S	I	T	I	O	N		H	O	U	S	E			
C	O	R	P	O	R	A	T	I	O	N																				

2.   The address of the head office of the corporation is/Adresse du siège social:

13579 New Road
(Street & No., or R.R. No., or Lot & Concession No., or Lot & Plan No.,Post Office Box No. not acceptable; if Multi-Office Building give Room No.)
(Rue et numéro, ou R.R. et numéro, ou numéro de lot et de concession, ou numéro de lot et de plan; numéro de boîte postale inacceptable; s'il s'agit d'un édifice à bureaux, numéro du bureau)

Kent, Ontario   N 3 A 0 Y 0
(Name of Municipality)   (Postal Code/Code postal)
(Nom de la municipalité)

3.   The applicants who are to be the first directors of the corporation are:
Requérants appelés à devenir les premiers administrateurs de la personne morale :

Name in full, including all first, middle names Nom et prénoms au complet	Residence address, giving Street & No., or R.R., No. or Lot & Concession No., or Lot & Plan No., and Postal Code (Post Ofice Box No. not acceptable) Adresse personnelle y compris la rue et le numéro ou la R.R. et le numéro, ou le numéro de lot et de concession, ou Le numéro de lot et de plan, ainsi que le code postal (Numéro de boîte postale inacceptable)
Olive Here	19702 Fresh St., Kent, Ontario N3A 1Y8
Chester Short-Stay	Suite 401, Second Ave., Kent, Ontario N3A 3X7
Otto Bea Gowan	5040 Reprieve Rd., Kent, Ontario N3A 0Y1

07109 (04/94)

2.

4. The objects for which the corporation is incorporated are:
   Objets pour lesquels la personne morale est constituée:

   (a) to provide premises and all necessary equipment and
       furniture for former inmates on their return to society;
       and
   (b) to staff those premises with counsellors trained to offer
       transitional services.

07109 (04/94)

68

3.

5. The special provisions are/Dispositions particulières:

The corporation shall be carried on without the purpose of gain for its members, and any profits or other accretions to the corporation shall be used in promoting its objects.

La personne morale doit exercer ses activités sans rechercher de gain pécuniaire pour ses membres, et tout bénéfice ou tout accroissement de l'actif de la personne morale doit être utilisé pour promouvoir ses objets.

(a) For the purpose of the objects of the corporation, to accept gifts, donations, and bequests

(b) The corporation shall be carried on without the purpose of gain for its members, and any profits or other accretions to the corporation shall be used in promoting its objects.

07109 (04/94)

SAMPLE #15 — Continued

6. The names and residence addresses of the applicants:
   Nom et prénoms et adresse personnelle des requérants :

4.

Name in full, including all first, middle names Nom et prénoms au complet	Residence address, giving Street & No., or R.R., No. or Lot & Concession No., or Lot & Plan No., and Postal Code (Post Ofice Box No. not acceptable) Adresse personnelle y compris la rue et le numéro ou la R.R. et le numéro, ou le numéro de lot et de concession, ou Le numéro de lot et de plan, ainsi que le code postal (Numéro de boîte postale inacceptable)
Olive Here	19702 Fresh St., Kent, Ontario N3A 1Y8
Chester R. Short-Stay	Suite 401, Second Ave., Kent, Ontario N3A 3X7
Otto Bea Gowan	3040 Reprieve Rd., Kent, Ontario N3A 0Y1

This application is executed in duplicate.
La présente requête est faite en double exemplaire.

Signatures of applicants/Signature des requérants

Olive Here
Chester Short-Stay
Otto Bea Gowan

70

8
FINAL STEPS TO INCORPORATION
(BY-LAWS AND OTHER DOCUMENTS)

This chapter outlines the final documentation process for incorporating as a society, including drafting your by-laws.

The constitution of a society defines its goals and objectives; the by-laws of a society define the everyday rules of management. They set out in detail such matters as who can be members of the society and under what conditions, how meetings are to be conducted, and the responsibilities of the board of directors and its executive.

Your society might operate for years without the president or anyone else referring to the by-laws. But when a problem arises, all eyes turn to them. They are, in effect, the contract terms or the understanding among members of the society, and, like a good contract, should anticipate potential problems and make simple statements to address those problems. This may be stating the obvious, but most of us know from experience that nothing is too obvious and that the fine print is vitally important.

By-laws are not required by every province, but the Society Act or its equivalent in each province will have certain provisions or rules built in, and these rules will apply unless the by-laws of your society provide differently. Read your provincial act carefully.

Most provinces include a sample constitution or charter and by-laws with the forms you are sent when you request registration as a society. Some (like British Columbia) have sample by-laws written as an appendix (Schedule B) to the Society Act. Others (like Saskatchewan and Manitoba) write the general rules for operating a society into the act, but allow variations as part of the constitution or articles of incorporation.

In any case, or if you are given no samples, ask for a copy of the constitution and by-laws from one or two other provincial societies already registered. Try to find one fairly recently accepted in your province so as to avoid really old-fashioned language and style. Documents from societies that have similar aims to yours would be useful, for example, another day care society. However, by-laws of very different societies can be essentially alike, because they describe the means by which a group's work gets done, not the goals or objectives of the society. A badminton club and an arts association may operate essentially the same way and have essentially the same by-laws.

The general rule is to follow the framework your province provides, but to alter specifics to suit the needs of your new society. You must, however, comply with the requirements of the Society Act or its equivalent in your province.

a. BRITISH COLUMBIA

1. By-laws

In British Columbia, the Society Act includes sample forms as well as sample by-laws.

As a society registering in British Columbia, you will have three choices of format. You may adopt the by-laws as set out in Schedule B of the act (see Sample #16):

The by-laws of the society are those set out in Schedule B to the Society Act.

Or you may make additions and deletions (removing some clauses). For example:

The by-laws of the society are those set out in Schedule B of the Society Act, with the following variations, deletions and additions:
1.
2.
3.

Be sure to list what you have taken out as well as the by-laws you have altered or added.

Your third alternative is to adopt a new format in which the by-laws have been completely rewritten. This will make up five or six pages to insert before the signatures. In this case, the statement on the constitution will read:

Here set forth, in numbered clauses, the by-laws providing for the matters referred to in section 6(1) of the Society Act and any other by-laws.

Most new societies use the sample by-laws but with some changes for clarity. If many changes are planned, it is wise to retype the by-laws.

2. Comments on the by-laws

Item 4

This section states, "A person may apply to the directors for membership in the society and on the acceptance by the directors shall be a member." Such a statement implies unlimited membership. However, it may be more appropriate to define or limit membership in some other way such as:

A member is any person who contributes annually to the society not less than $_____.

or

The membership of the society shall be limited to the members of the Board of Directors.

or

The membership of the society shall be open to parents of children who are playing junior hockey.

You may also wish to address the age of members. For example:

Members less than 18 years of age are subject to the same fees and society rules as adult members.

Item 6

You may prefer a more flexible arrangement for membership dues than is given in section 6. For example, you might state:

The amount of the first annual membership dues, if any, shall be determined by the directors, and, after that the annual membership dues, if any, shall be determined at the annual general meeting of the society.

Item 7(d)

Concerning members' resignation from the society, section 7(d) states: "A person shall cease to be a member of the society on having been a member not in good standing for 12 consecutive months."

An alternative might be to change the last part of this clause to read "on having been a member not in good standing for a period of time prescribed by the directors," or "when the member no longer qualifies for membership in accordance with these by-laws."

Item 8

You may want to set out procedures for expulsion of members. It is, of course, far more common for members who no longer agree with the goals of a society to simply resign or fail to renew membership. But procedures to ensure fairness are a good idea. An alternative to section 8 would be:

A member may be expelled from the organization by a majority vote of the members at any general meeting.

SCHEDULE B

SOCIETY ACT

BYLAWS OF ....
(Name of Society)

Part 1 — Interpretation

1. (1) In these bylaws, unless the context otherwise requires,
    (a) "directors" means the directors of the society for the time being;
    (b) "*Society Act*" means the *Society Act* of the Province of British Columbia from time to time in force and all amendments to it;
    (c) "registered address" of a member means his address as recorded in the register of members.

    (2) The definitions in the *Society Act* on the date these bylaws become effective apply to these bylaws.

2. Words importing the singular include the plural and vice versa; and words importing a male person include a female person and a corporation.

Part 2 — Membership

3. The members of the society are the applicants for incorporation of the society, and those persons who subsequently have become members, in accordance with these bylaws and, in either case, have not ceased to be members.

4. A person may apply to the directors for membership in the society and on acceptance by the directors shall be a member.

5. Every member shall uphold the constitution and comply with these bylaws.

6. The amount of the first annual membership dues shall be determined by the directors and after that the annual membership dues shall be determined at the annual general meeting of the society.

7. A person shall cease to be a member of the society
    (a) by delivering his resignation in writing to the secretary of the society or by mailing or delivering it to the address of the society;
    (b) on his death or in the case of a corporation on dissolution;
    (c) on being expelled; or
    (d) on having been a member not in good standing for 12 consecutive months.

8. (1) A member may be expelled by a special resolution of the members passed at a general meeting.

    (2) The notice of special resolution for expulsion shall be accompanied by a brief statement of the reason or reasons for the proposed expulsion.

    (3) The person who is the subject of the proposed resolution for expulsion shall be given an opportunity to be heard at the general meeting before the special resolution is put to a vote.

9. All members are in good standing except a member who has failed to pay his current annual membership fee or any other subscription or debt due and owing by him to the society and he is not in good standing so long as the debt remains unpaid.

Part 3 — Meetings of Members

10. General meetings of the society shall be held at the time and place, in accordance with the *Society Act*, that the directors decide.

11. Every general meeting, other than an annual general meeting, is an extraordinary general meeting.

12. The directors may, when they think fit, convene an extraordinary general meeting.

13. (1) Notice of a general meeting shall specify the place, day and hour of meeting, and, in case of special business, the general nature of that business.

(2) The accidental omission to give notice of a meeting to, or the non-receipt of a notice by, any of the members entitled to receive notice does not invalidate proceedings at that meeting.

14. The first annual general meeting of the society shall be held not more than 15 months after the date of incorporation and after that an annual general meeting shall be held at least once in every calendar year and not more than 15 months after the holding of the last preceding annual general meeting.

Part 4 — Proceedings at General Meetings

15. Special business is
(a) all business at an extraordinary general meeting except the adoption of rules of order; and
(b) all business transacted at an annual general meeting, except,
    (i) the adoption of rules of order;
    (ii) the consideration of the financial statements;
    (iii) the report of the directors;
    (iv) the report of the auditor, if any;
    (v) the election of directors;
    (vi) the appointment of the auditor, if required; and
    (vii) the other business that, under these bylaws, ought to be transacted at an annual general meeting, or business which is brought under consideration by the report of the directors issued with the notice convening the meeting.

16. (1) No business, other than the election of a chairman and the adjournment or termination of the meeting, shall be conducted at a general meeting at a time when a quorum is not present.

(2) If at any time during a general meeting there ceases to be a quorum present, business then in progress shall be suspended until there is a quorum present or until the meeting is adjourned or terminated.

(3) A quorum is 3 members present or a greater number that the members may determine at a general meeting.

17. If within 30 minutes from the time appointed for a general meeting a quorum is not present, the meeting, if convened on the requisition of members, shall be terminated; but in any other case, it shall stand adjourned to the same day in the next week, at the same time and place, and if, at the adjourned meeting, a quorum is not present within 30 minutes from the time appointed for the meeting, the members present constitute a quorum.

18. Subject to bylaw 19, the president of the society, the vice president or in the absence of both, one of the other directors present, shall preside as chairman of a general meeting.

19. If at a general meeting
(a) there is no president, vice president or other director present within 15 minutes after the time appointed for holding the meeting; or
(b) the president and all the other directors present are unwilling to act as chairman,
the members present shall choose one of their number to be chairman.

20. (1) A general meeting may be adjourned from time to time and from place to place, but no business shall be transacted at an adjourned meeting other than the business left unfinished at the meeting from which the adjournment took place.

(2) When a meeting is adjourned for 10 days or more, notice of the adjourned meeting shall be given as in the case of the original meeting.

(3) Except as provided in this bylaw, it is not necessary to give notice of an adjournment or of the business to be transacted at an adjourned general meeting.

21. (1) No resolution proposed at a meeting need be seconded and the chairman of a meeting may move or propose a resolution.

(2) In case of an equality of votes the chairman shall not have a casting or second vote in addition to the vote to which he may be entitled as a member and the proposed resolution shall not pass.

22. (1) A member in good standing present at a meeting of members is entitled to one vote.

(2) Voting is by show of hands.

(3) Voting by proxy is not permitted.

23. A corporate member may vote by its authorized representative, who is entitled to speak and vote, and in all other respects exercise the rights of a member, and that representative shall be reckoned as a member for all purposes with respect to a meeting of the society.

Part 5 — Directors and Officers

24. (1) The directors may exercise all the powers and do all the acts and things that the society may exercise and do, and which are not by these bylaws or by statute or otherwise lawfully directed or required to be exercised or done by the society in general meeting, but subject, nevertheless, to

    (a) all laws affecting the society;

    (b) these bylaws; and

    (c) rules, not being inconsistent with these bylaws, which are made from time to time by the society in general meeting.

(2) No rule, made by the society in general meeting, invalidates a prior act of the directors that would have been valid if that rule had not been made.

25. (1) The president, vice president, secretary, treasurer and one or more other persons shall be the directors of the society.

(2) The number of directors shall be 5 or a greater number determined from time to time at a general meeting.

26. (1) The directors shall retire from office at each annual general meeting when their successors shall be elected.

(2) Separate elections shall be held for each office to be filled.

(3) An election may be by acclamation, otherwise it shall be by ballot.

(4) If no successor is elected the person previously elected or appointed continues to hold office.

27. (1) The directors may at any time and from time to time appoint a member as a director to fill a vacancy in the directors.

(2) A director so appointed holds office only until the conclusion of the next following annual general meeting of the society, but is eligible for re-election at the meeting.

28. (1) If a director resigns his office or otherwise ceases to hold office, the remaining directors shall appoint a member to take the place of the former director.

(2) No act or proceeding of the directors is invalid only by reason of there being less than the prescribed number of directors in office.

29. The members may by special resolution remove a director before the expiration of his term of office, and may elect a successor to complete the term of office.

30. No director shall be remunerated for being or acting as a director but a director shall be reimbursed for all expenses necessarily and reasonably incurred by him while engaged in the affairs of the society.

Part 6 — Proceedings of Directors

31. (1) The directors may meet together at the places they think fit to dispatch business, adjourn and otherwise regulate their meetings and proceedings, as they see fit.

(2) The directors may from time to time fix the quorum necessary to transact business, and unless so fixed the quorum shall be a majority of the directors then in office.

(3) The president shall be chairman of all meetings of the directors, but if at a meeting the president is not present within 30 minutes after the time appointed for holding the meeting, the vice president shall act as chairman; but if neither is present the directors present may choose one of their number to be chairman at that meeting.

(4) A director may at any time, and the secretary, on the request of a director, shall, convene a meeting of the directors.

32. (1) The directors may delegate any, but not all, of their powers to committees consisting of the director or directors as they think fit.

(2) A committee so formed in the exercise of the powers so delegated shall conform to any rules imposed on it by the directors, and shall report every act or thing done in exercise of those powers to the earliest meeting of the directors to be held next after it has been done.

33. A committee shall elect a chairman of its meetings; but if no chairman is elected, or if at a meeting the chairman is not present within 30 minutes after the time appointed for holding the meeting, the directors present who are members of the committee shall choose one of their number to be chairman of the meeting.

34. The members of a committee may meet and adjourn as they think proper.

35. For a first meeting of directors held immediately following the appointment or election of a director or directors at an annual or other general meeting of members, or for a meeting of the directors at which a director is appointed to fill a vacancy in the directors, it is not necessary to give notice of the meeting to the newly elected or appointed director or directors for the meeting to be constituted, if a quorum of the directors is present.

36. A director who may be absent temporarily from British Columbia may send or deliver to the address of the society a waiver of notice, which may be by letter, telegram, telex or cable, of any meeting of the directors and may at any time withdraw the waiver, and until the waiver is withdrawn,

    (a) no notice of meeting of directors shall be sent to that director; and

    (b) any and all meetings of the directors of the society, notice of which has not been given to that director shall, if a quorum of the directors is present, be valid and effective.

37. (1) Questions arising at a meeting of the directors and committee of directors shall be decided by a majority of votes.

(2) In case of an equality of votes the chairman does not have a second or casting vote.

38. No resolution proposed at a meeting of directors or committee of directors need be seconded and the chairman of a meeting may move or propose a resolution.

39. A resolution in writing, signed by all the directors and placed with the minutes of the directors is as valid and effective as if regularly passed at a meeting of directors.

Part 7 — Duties of Officers

40. (1) The president shall preside at all meetings of the society and of the directors.

(2) The president is the chief executive officer of the society and shall supervise the other officers in the execution of their duties.

41. The vice president shall carry out the duties of the president during his absence.

42. The secretary shall

    (a) conduct the correspondence of the society;

    (b) issue notices of meetings of the society and directors;

    (c) keep minutes of all meetings of the society and directors;

    (d) have custody of all records and documents of the society except those required to be kept by the treasurer;

    (e) have custody of the common seal of the society; and

    (f) maintain the register of members.

43. The treasurer shall

    (a) keep the financial records, including books of account, necessary to comply with the *Society Act;* and

    (b) render financial statements to the directors, members and others when required.

44. (1) The offices of secretary and treasurer may be held by one person who shall be known as the secretary treasurer.

(2) When a secretary treasurer holds office the total number of directors shall not be less than 5 or the greater number that may have been determined pursuant to bylaw 25 (2).

45. In the absence of the secretary from a meeting, the directors shall appoint another person to act as secretary at the meeting.

Part 8 — Seal

46. The directors may provide a common seal for the society and may destroy a seal and substitute a new seal in its place.

47. The common seal shall be affixed only when authorized by a resolution of the directors and then only in the presence of the persons prescribed in the resolution, or if no persons are prescribed, in the presence of the president and secretary or president and secretary treasurer.

Part 9 — Borrowing

48. In order to carry out the purposes of the society the directors may, on behalf of and in the name of the society, raise or secure the payment or repayment of money in the manner they decide, and, in particular but without limiting the foregoing, by the issue of debentures.

49. No debenture shall be issued without the sanction of a special resolution.

50. The members may by special resolution restrict the borrowing powers of the directors, but a restriction imposed expires at the next annual general meeting.

Part 10 — Auditor

51. This Part applies only where the society is required or has resolved to have an auditor.

52. The first auditor shall be appointed by the directors who shall also fill all vacancies occurring in the office of auditor.

53. At each annual general meeting the society shall appoint an auditor to hold office until he is re-elected or his successor is elected at the next annual general meeting.

54. An auditor may be removed by ordinary resolution.

55. An auditor shall be promptly informed in writing of appointment or removal.

56. No director and no employee of the society shall be auditor.

57. The auditor may attend general meetings.

Part 11 — Notices to Members

58. A notice may be given to a member, either personally or by mail to him at his registered address.

59. A notice sent by mail shall be deemed to have been given on the second day following that on which the notice is posted, and in proving that notice has been given it is sufficient to prove the notice was properly addressed and put in a Canadian post office receptacle.

60. (1) Notice of a general meeting shall be given to
    (a) every member shown on the register of members on the day notice is given; and
    (b) the auditor, if Part 10 applies.
(2) No other person is entitled to receive a notice of general meeting.

Part 12 — Bylaws

61. On being admitted to membership, each member is entitled to and the society shall give him, without charge, a copy of the constitution and bylaws of the society.

62. These bylaws shall not be altered or added to except by special resolution.

1977-80-Sch. B.

———

Two additional sections related to membership can be included to define rights and limitations:

> Every member of the society shall be entitled to attend any meeting of the society and to vote at any meeting of the society and to hold any office, but there shall be no proxy voting.

> Membership in the society shall not be transferable.

Note that proxy is the transfer of voting rights from a member to someone else authorized to vote in that member's absence.

These sections do not include any stipulation for different classes of membership.

What about honorary members or associate members? In British Columbia, the act does not prohibit such membership, though the sample by-laws in the act do not include it.

But lawyers who advise on the writing of by-laws recommend against different classes of membership because of the complexity of determining the rights, duties, acceptance, and expulsion procedures, and how these procedures differ from those for regular members.

Item 10

Regarding meetings of members, section 10 may be altered to read:

> General meetings of the society shall be held at such time and place, in accordance with the Society Act, as the directors decide, and shall be held as often as the business of the society requires.

Items 11 and 12

Either or both of these sections may be omitted.

Item 14

This clause stipulates the date of the annual general meeting. Many societies meet within three months of the end of each fiscal year. Some include this date as a regulation in by-laws.

Note that Parts 3 and 4 of Schedule B deal with meetings of members (including the annual general meeting and any special meetings) as distinct from meetings of directors (see Part 6, Proceedings of Directors). Parts 4 and 6 each provide separate and detailed rules of notice for the two types of meetings and have different requirements regarding quorum.

It is possible and perhaps desirable to write rules that apply to all meetings of the society, including a statement such as the following:

> _____ members in good standing shall constitute a quorum at any meeting of the society.

(See the next section for minimum quorum requirements.)

Item 16(3)

Quorum (the minimum number of members who must be present in order to hold a valid meeting) is set out here. It is possible to revise the number upwards from the three members prescribed. Remember, however, to be realistic about attendance; you do not want to obstruct the normal business of the society.

Item 22(2)

The voting procedures in section 22(2) may be changed to read:

> Voting is by show of hands, unless the members otherwise decide.

Item 25(2)

This clause covers the number of directors. The sample by-laws specify five directors; the Society Act requires at least three. Some flexibility is a good idea; for example, you could insert a clause reading "not less than three and not more than fifteen directors."

Most directors hold office for more than one fiscal year so that the organization can benefit from the expertise and experience they gain. A term may be one or more years.

Some by-laws include the number of terms directors may serve, for example, "may be elected for a second or third term, but no more than four terms."

Item 26

Section 26 concerns the election of officers. Note that in these sample by-laws, the president and other officers have been elected to office at the annual general meeting. Another common model is to elect directors at the annual general meeting, but at the next general meeting following, the directors elect from among themselves the various officers, including chairperson, president, or both. For example, the clause in your by-laws could read:

> The officers of the society shall be president, vice-president, treasurer, and secretary. The offices of treasurer and secretary may be combined.

> The directors shall elect one of their number to be president of the society, and shall elect from their number a vice-chair, secretary, and treasurer.

Item 30

This clause is necessary to be eligible for registration as a charity with Revenue Canada. This statement should be written into the constitution, although you may prefer the wording "but a director may be reimbursed."

In general, the by-laws will give as much power as possible to the directors to act on behalf of the society. An addition to Part 5 could be:

> The board shall, subject to the by-laws or directions given it by majority vote at any meeting properly called and constituted, have full control and management of the affairs of the society.

Another useful addition to Part 5 would be:

> A director shall be a member in good standing of the organization.

Item 31(3)

To establish the proceedings of directors, section 31(3) may be simplified to read:

> The president shall be chairperson of all meetings of the directors, unless the directors otherwise decide.

Item 32

You can ensure flexibility in the society's committee work by changing section 32 to read:

> The directors may delegate any, but not all, of their powers to committees consisting of the director or directors as they think fit, or may delegate to committees consisting of other persons as they see fit.

Note that many societies set up committees of board members, but may also set up committees from general members of the society and possibly other non-member individuals by invitation, especially for ad hoc committees or task forces. Generally, a committee is chaired by a board member who reports to the board on committee activities and recommendations. Section 32 (in its altered form as above) allows delegation of powers to committees composed in this way.

Item 33

Further, section 33 may be replaced by:

> Subject to directions of the directors, the committee shall determine its own procedure.

Item 37

The section on voting at committee meetings, while the same as section 21(2) on voting at general meetings, will require discussion. Your group may decide to revert to the more traditional tie-breaking vote for the chair.

Item 40

The president's duties could be revised to read:

> The president shall preside at all meetings of the society and of the directors, unless the

members or directors otherwise decide.

The president is the chief executive officer of the society.

Note that some by-laws include the following clause: "The president shall be ex officio a member of all committees." *Ex officio* means by virtue of office (that is, because he or she is president).

Item 42

The duties of the secretary are defined in section 42. The Society Act requires that an accurate list of current members be kept, therefore an additional by-law could read:

> The secretary shall also keep a record of all the members of the society and their addresses.

Another useful addition to this section would be:

> In the absence of the secretary from a meeting, the directors shall appoint another person to act as secretary at the meeting.

Item 43

The duties of the treasurer given in section 43 should be expanded to read:

> The treasurer shall
>
> (a) keep such financial records, including books of account, as are necessary to comply with the Society Act, and receive all monies paid to the society, and be responsible for the deposit of same into whatever bank the board may order; and
>
> (b) render financial statements to the director, members and others when required, and prepare for submission to the annual meeting a statement of the financial position of the society.

An additional article in this section might read:

> Officers shall perform such duties as the members decide.

Items 46 and 47

The society's seal is described in sections 46 and 47. Note that a society is not required to have a seal. If your society chooses to have a seal from the beginning, or to adopt one later on, the seal must bear the name of the society.

An additional article might read:

> Whenever the seal is used, it shall be authenticated by the signature of the secretary and the president or, in the case of the death or inability of either to act, by the vice-president.

Items 48, 49, and 50

Part 9 defines the terms for borrowing money. Borrowing is a serious matter, only possible under these circumstances:

- if proof of payment or grant acceptance is presented to the bank as a basis to advance funds

- if a loan is guaranteed by the directors or some other persons

- if the society owns assets greater than the value of the loan (which involves the registering of a mortgage on any real property)

- if debentures are issued (a debenture is an official acknowledgment of a loan which is secured by assets of the society)

- if a "line of credit" is extended with or without the personal guarantee of the directors.

The directors should request that a lawyer explain all procedures and obligations which fall to the society and to themselves personally. Under the British Columbia Society Act, the special resolution, if passed, allows the directors to issue debentures "for a period not exceeding one year from the date the resolution is passed." These various limitations on the powers of the directors are to protect the society, lenders, and directors alike.

An alternative article might be:

For the purposes of carrying out its objects, the society may borrow or raise or secure the payment of money in such manner as it thinks fit, and in particular by the issue of debentures, but this power shall be exercised only under the authority of the society, and in no case shall debentures be issued without the sanction of a special resolution of the society.

Items 51 to 57

Part 10 defines the process for appointing an auditor. An audit is an official examination of the society's financial records. A reporting society is a society with a large budget and is required to have an auditor. A non-reporting society (that is, a small non-profit society) may choose to have one, but is not required to do so.

Item 61

Section 61 describes access to by-laws. In the event you change or rewrite the sample by-laws, the items which must be included are defined in the act as follows:

> 6.(1) The by-laws of a society incorporated under this act shall contain provisions in respect of
>
> (a) admission of members, their rights and obligations and when they cease to be in good standing;
>
> (b) conditions under which membership ceases and the manner, if any, in which a member may be expelled;
>
> (c) procedure for calling general meetings;
>
> (d) rights of voting at general meetings, whether proxy voting is allowed, and if so, provisions for it;
>
> (e) appointment and removal of directors and officers and their duties, powers and remuneration, if any:
>
> (f) exercise of borrowing powers; and

(g) preparation and custody of minutes of meetings of the society and directors.

3. Preparing your by-laws

(a) Type out the constitution and by-laws on 8½" x 11" paper.

(b) Each applicant must sign in the presence of a witness. You will require at least one witness who is not a founding member of the society.

(c) After each signature, type in the name (so as to be read easily and spelled correctly), current addresses, and postal codes of witnesses and applicants.

(d) Do not use initials in the signatures or typed names.

(e) Make two photocopies of all pages of the constitution and by-laws.

(f) You now have three sets of documents, and all three must be signed by all applicants and witnesses.

See Sample #17 for a sample first page and signature page for your by-laws.

4. List of first directors

This form repeats in a different format the names listed in the constitution and by-laws (see Sample #18). The form is signed by one "subscriber" to the constitution. You will need two copies with original signatures.

Fill in the last line (relationship to the society) with "founding member." In British Columbia, the director ordinarily must be resident in British Columbia, and a majority ordinarily must be resident in Canada.

5. Notice of address

This form tells the Registrar how to write to the new society (see Sample #19). Two copies are required. Type it on regular paper (8½" x 11"), or use the copy of the form the Registrar sends you.

If your society does not have an office address, the address of an executive officer will do.

(Name of Society)

CONSTITUTION

1. The name of the society is_____

2. The purpose(s) of the society is
(are)_____

(Body of constitution)

BY-LAWS

Here, set forth in numbered clauses, the by-laws providing for matters referred to in section 6(1) of the Society Act and any other by-laws.

(Body of by-laws)

Dated this _____ day of _____, 19__.

Signatures:

WITNESSES	APPLICANTS FOR INCORPORATION
1. _____	1._____
Signature	Signature
_____	_____
Name	Name
_____	_____
Address	Address

SAMPLE #17 — Continued

2. _____
Signature

_____
Name

_____
Address

3. _____
Signature

_____
Name

_____
Address

4. _____
Signature

_____
Name

_____
Address

5. _____
Signature

_____
Name

_____
Address

2. _____
Signature

_____
Name

_____
Address

3. _____
Signature

_____
Name

_____
Address

4. _____
Signature

_____
Name

_____
Address

5. _____
Signature

_____
Name

_____
Address

83

The first time this form is filed (as part of the application for incorporation), cross out the line in brackets that says: "[The day after this is filed with you.]" Then have the first form submitted signed by a "subscriber" to the constitution and thereafter by a director.

Whenever your society moves, another copy of this form should be sent to the Registrar within 15 days. Note that if you are advising of a change of address, type the certificate of incorporation number in the upper right-hand corner to assist the Registrar in locating your file.

If you were issued an administrative number in earlier correspondence, add it to the letter.

6. Submitting your documents

If you make an error on your initial submission, you will be charged a $5 re-examination fee. The likelihood of error increases the more changes you make to the by-law format.

If you decide to submit your own version of the by-laws check the final copy for the following common errors and omissions:

(a) Society's name is not shown consistently throughout the incorporation document

(b) Name chosen by the society is not available

(c) Documents were completed pursuant to former society act. The current act is the Society Act R.S.B.C., 1979.

(d) Full names and residential addresses of all applicants and witnesses are not shown.

(e) One or more of the provisions of section 6 of the Society Act are missing from the by-laws:

- admission of members, their rights and obligations, and when they cease to be in good standing

- conditions under which membership ceases and the manner in which a member may be expelled

- procedure for calling general meetings

- rights regarding voting at general meetings, whether proxy voting is allowed and, if so, its provisions

- appointment and removal of directors and officers and their duties, powers, and remuneration, if any

- exercise of borrowing powers

- preparation and custody of minutes of meetings of the society and directors

After checking this list, write a covering letter to the Registrar (see Sample #20) and include with it the following:

(a) Constitution and by-laws (two copies)

(b) List of First Directors (one copy)

(c) Notice of Address of Society (one copy)

(d) Written information on approved name

(e) Registration fee of $65 made out to Minister of Finance and Corporate Relations

The fee for registration of a society based outside British Columbia is $65. Mail to:

Societies Unit
Ministry of Finance and Corporate
   Relations
940 Blanshard Street
Victoria, BC   V8W 3E6

Providing you have taken the necessary steps early in this procedure to reserve your society's name, you should hear from the Registrar within ten working days. The fee for priority processing is $100 and will bring a response within three working days. The copy of your constitution and by-laws will be returned to you, certified as registered by the Registrar. You will also receive a Certificate of Incorporation with the Certificate of Incorporation number indicated in its upper right-hand corner.

SAMPLE #18
LIST OF FIRST DIRECTORS (BRITISH COLUMBIA)

Form 4
(Section 3)

———

SOCIETIES ACT

———

LIST OF FIRST DIRECTORS OF Vulnerable Valley Environmental Society
(Name of Society)

Full Names	*Resident Addresses*
1. Janet Gabrielle Grey	R.R. 1, Road 7, Anyville, B.C. V0N 1C0
2. Peter Ray White	55 Sawmill Rd., Anyville, B.C. V0N 1C1
3. Susan Ann White	55 Sawmill Rd., Anyville, B.C. V0N 1C1
4. Hugh Green	R.R. 3, Vulnerable Valley, B.C. V0M 1B0
5. Gloria Sue Ochre	10010 River Rd., Anyville, B.C. V0N 1C3

Dated the ___sixth___ day of ___July___, 19_9-_

Vulnerable Valley Environmental Society
(Name of Society)

by _*Gloria Ochre*_
(Signature)

Founding Member
(Relationship to Society)

[Note—One director must be ordinarily resident in British Columbia.]

85

FORM 5

(Sections 3 and 10)

————

Certificate of
Incorporation No.* _____

SOCIETIES ACT

————

NOTICE OF ADDRESS OF SOCIETY

The address of the Society is ____55 Sawmill Rd. V0N 1C1_____
                              (Street address and postal code)

_____Anyville_____, B.C. [the day after this is filed with you]† until the day after
        (City or other place)

the next Notice of Address of the Society is filed by the Society.

Dated the ____sixth____ day of ____July_____, 19 9-.

                              Vulnerable Valley Environmental Society
                              _____
                                      (Name of Society)

                         by ____*Gloria Ochre*_____
                                      (Signature)

                              _____Founding Member_____
                                   (Relationship to Society)

To the Registrar of Companies,
   Victoria, B.C.

————

* To be inserted only in case of change of address.
† Strike out words in brackets when the Notice is filed as part of the application for incorporation.

55 Sawmill Road
Anyville, B.C.
V0N 1C1

October 12, 199-

Ministry of Finance and Corporate Relations
Registries
Ministry Support Services Division
Corporate and Personal Property Branch
Societies Section
940 Blanshard Street
Victoria, British Columbia
V8W 3E6

<u>Vulnerable Valley Environmental Society</u>
(Name of proposed society)

Dear Registrar:

We wish to be incorporated under the Society Act with the name set out above, and for this purpose we enclose:

1. Constitution and by-laws in duplicate

2. A list of our first directors

3. A notice setting out the address of our society, and

4. A certified cheque or money order payable to the Minister of Finance for $60.

Please attend to incorporation, and then send us the certificate of incorporation and a certified copy of the constitution and by-laws to the address set out above.

Yours truly,

Gloria Ochre

(Signature)

On behalf of all applicants for incorporation

b. ALBERTA

1. By-laws

The package of materials sent on request from the Corporate Registry of Consumer and Corporate Affairs in Alberta is designed specifically to assist you to form a non-profit society in Alberta, and includes a set of sample by-laws (see Sample #21).

The sample by-laws may prove useful, but may require some alterations to suit your new society and its goals. If you use these sample by-laws, be sure to fill in the name of your society, fiscal year (item 10), annual meeting date, number of days before meeting that notice was delivered (item 12), and quorum (item 14).

Alternatively, you can write entirely new by-laws provided that certain matters required in the Societies Act are addressed. The act states:

> 5.(4) The by-laws that accompany the application shall contain provisions for all the following matters:
>
> (a) terms of admission of members and their rights and obligations;
>
> (b) the conditions of withdrawal of members and the manner, if any, in which a member may be expelled;
>
> (c) the mode and time of calling general and special meetings of the society and number constituting a quorum at any such meeting and rights of voting;
>
> (d) the appointment and removal of directors and officers and their duties, powers and remuneration;
>
> (e) the exercise of borrowing powers;
>
> (f) the audit of accounts;
>
> (g) the custody and use of the seal of the society;
>
> (h) the manner of making, altering and rescinding by-laws;

> (i) the preparation and custody of minutes of proceedings of meetings of the society and of the directors, and other books and records of the society; and
>
> (j) the time and place, if any, at which the books and records of the society may be inspected by members.

2. Comments on the by-laws

Item 1

Terms of admission of members, their obligations, and their rights must be spelled out. The sample by-laws define membership very broadly — anyone in the province over 18 is eligible, and in fact anyone under 18 as well (if there is a fee, the young person or child pays half). This clearly may not be appropriate for organizations not designed to be so broad-based or inclusive. You may choose to define a member as a person who applies for membership according to the by-laws and who will "uphold the constitution and comply with the by-laws."

Item 2

The conditions of withdrawal of members and the manner, if any, in which a member may be expelled, must be stated.

Items 3 to 9

Your by-laws must define the method of appointment and removal of directors and other officers, as well as their duties, powers, and frequency of meetings. Include whether or not the directors will be paid. Notice of special meeting requires ten days' notice in writing to board members or three days by telegram or telephone unless you alter these notice periods (see also item 12).

Items 10 and 11

By-laws must set out who will audit the society's financial records. You may state that a qualified auditor will be hired for this purpose, or you may state that two officers will perform this function. It is

CORPORATE REGISTRY

THE SOCIETIES ACT
BY-LAWS

The Name of the Society is

Ashford Day Care Society

MEMBERSHIP

1. Membership fee, if any, in the society shall be determined, from time to time, by the members at a general meeting. Any persons residing in Alberta, and being of the full age of 18 years, may become a member by a favourable vote passed by a majority of the members at a regular meeting of the society, and upon payment of the fee. Such voting shall be by ballot, unless the meeting by resolution otherwise decides. Any person under the age of 18 years may in the same manner become a member upon payment of half of the said fee.

2. Any member wishing to withdraw from membership may do so upon a notice in writing to the Board through its Secretary. If any member is in arrears for fees or assessments for any year, such member shall be automatically suspended at the expiration of six months from the end of such year and shall thereafter be entitled to no membership privileges or powers in the society until reinstated. Any member upon a majority vote of all members of the society in good standing may be expelled from membership for any cause which the society may deem reasonable.

PRESIDENT

3. The President shall be ex-officio a member of all Committees. He shall, when present, preside at all meetings of the society and of the Board. In his absence the Vice-President shall preside at any such meetings, and in the absence of both a chairman may be elected by the meeting to preside thereat.

BOARD OF DIRECTORS

4. Board of Directors, Executive Committee or Board, shall mean the Board of Directors of the society.

5. The Board shall, subject to the by-laws or directions given it by majority vote at any meeting properly called and constituted, have full control and management of the affairs of the society, and meetings of the Board shall be held as often as may be required, but at least once every three months, and shall be called by the President. A special meeting may be called on the instructions of any two members thereof provided they request the President in writing to call such meeting, and state the business to be brought before the meeting. Meetings of the Board shall be called by ten days' notice in writing mailed to each member or by three days' notice by telegram or telephone. Any four members shall constitute a quorum, and meetings shall be held without notice if a quorum of the Board is present, provided, however, that any business transactions at such meeting shall be ratified at the next regularly called meeting of the Board; otherwise they shall be null and void.

6. Any director or officer upon a majority vote of all members in good standing may be removed from office for any cause which the society may deem reasonable.

SECRETARY

7. It shall be the duty of the secretary to attend all meetings of the society and of the Board, and to keep accurate minutes of the same. He shall have charge of the Seal of the society which seal whenever used shall be authenticated by the signature of the Secretary and the President, or, in the case of the death or inability of either to act, by the Vice-President. In case of the absence of the Secretary, his duties shall be discharged by such officer as may be appointed by the Board. The Secretary shall have charge of all the correspondence of the society and be under the direction of the President and the Board.

8. The Secretary shall also keep a record of all the members of the society and their addresses, send all notices of the various meetings as required, and shall collect and receive the annual dues or assessments levied by the society, such monies to be promptly turned over to the Treasurer for deposit in a Bank, Trust Company, Credit Union or Treasury Branch as hereinafter required.

TREASURER

9. The Treasurer shall receive all monies paid to the society and shall be responsible for the deposit of same in whatever Bank, Trust Company, Credit Union or Treasury Branch the Board may order. He shall properly account for the funds of the society and keep such books as may be directed. He shall present a full detailed account of receipts and disbursements to the Board whenever requested and shall prepare for submission to the Annual Meeting a statement duly audited as hereinafter set forth of the financial position of the society and submit a copy of same to the Secretary for the records of the society. The office of the Secretary and Treasurer may be filled by one person if any annual meeting for the election of officers shall so decide.

AUDITING

10. The books, accounts and records of the Secretary and Treasurer shall be audited at least once each year by a duly qualified accountant or by two members of the society elected for that purpose at the Annual Meeting. A complete and proper statement of the standing of the books for the previous year shall be submitted by such auditor at the Annual Meeting of the society. The fiscal year of the society in each year shall be _____ .

11. The books and records of the society may be inspected by any member of the society at the annual meeting provided for herein or at anytime upon giving reasonable notice and arranging a time satisfactory to the officer or officers having charge of same. Each member of the Board shall at all times have access to such books and records.

MEETINGS

12. This society shall hold an annual meeting on or before ___March 31___ in each year, of which notice in writing to the last known address of each member shall be delivered in the mail ___30___ days prior to the date of the meeting. At this meeting there shall be elected a President, Vice-President, Secretary, Treasurer, (or Secretary-Treasurer), and three directors. The officers and directors so elected shall form a Board, and shall serve until their successors are elected and installed. Any vacancy occurring during the year shall be filled at the next meeting, provided it is so stated in the notice calling such meeting. Any member in good standing shall be eligible to any office in the society.

13. General meetings of the society may be called at any time by the Secretary upon the instructions of the President or Board by notice in writing to the last known address of each member, delivered in the mail eight days prior to the date of such meeting. A special meeting shall be called by the President or Secretary upon receipt by him of a petition signed by one-third of the members in good standing, setting forth the reasons for calling such meeting, which shall be by letter to the last known address of each member, delivered in the mail eight days prior to the meeting.

14. ___Forty per cent of___ members in good standing shall constitute a quorum at any meeting.

VOTING

15. Any member who has not withdrawn from membership nor has been suspended nor expelled as herein provided shall have the right to vote at any meeting of the society. Such votes must be made in person and not by proxy or otherwise.

REMUNERATION

16. Unless authorized at any meeting and after notice for same shall have been given no officer or member of the association shall receive any remuneration for his services.

BORROWING POWERS

17. For the purpose of carrying out its objects, the society may borrow or raise or secure the payment of money in such manner as it thinks fit, and in particular by the issue of debentures, but this power shall be exercised only under the authority of the society, and in no case shall debentures be issued without the sanction of a special resolution of the society.

BY-LAWS

18. The By-Laws may be rescinded, altered or added to by a "Special Resolution".

DATED this ___fourteenth___ day of ___September___ 19_9-_ .

NAME (SIGNATURE) PLEASE PRINT NAME BELOW SIGNATURE   COMPLETE ADDRESS

Betty Able   49 Elm St., Ashford, AB TOL 1A2
Betty B. Able, Homemaker

Harry Best   18 Oak St., Ashford, AB TOL 2B3
Harry M. Best, Carpenter

Wendy Caring   8 Pine Ave., Ashford, AB TOL 3C4
Wendy R. Caring, Lawyer

WITNESS:
NAME (SIGNATURE)   COMPLETE ADDRESS

Shawn Dependable   52 Oak St., Ashford, AB TOL 2B4
Shawn L. Dependable, Teacher

important to have an auditor because, under the Alberta Societies Act, an audited financial statement must be presented to the society members every year at the annual meeting and attached to the annual return for filing with the Corporate Registry.

Items 12 to 14

The procedure for calling annual meetings and special meetings of the society must be set out. Include how members will be notified and what the quorum will be for each type of meeting.

A useful rule of thumb is to set the date for the annual meeting no more than three months after the end of the fiscal year.

If you are in a rural community, or if your members are scattered beyond regular postal service, you may choose to increase the notice period given in item 12, or you may wish to make item 5 (notice of special meeting to directors) and item 12 consistent.

The quorum set for general meetings of your society will depend on whether the organization is very broad-based (many members) or quite small. Note that a quorum for the board of directors is four members in the sample by-laws.

Item 15

Exactly who has the right to vote and how members vote (by show of hands or by secret ballot) must be set out. Whether or not proxy votes are allowed should be included. (A proxy vote is the transfer of voting rights from a member to another person authorizing him or her to vote in the member's absence.)

Item 16

A statement is required regarding payment of directors and other officers. Remember that the federal government requires a clear statement that members will not profit from the resources or capital of a non-profit charitable organization. Reimbursement of expenses is permitted, but should be carefully monitored and reported.

Item 17

Your by-laws must set out whether or not the society can borrow money. If your society can borrow money, make sure you define how this will be done. If your society is going to raise money by issuing debentures, it must pass a special resolution each time debentures are issued.

Item 18

The manner of adding, altering, and rescinding (cancelling) by-laws must be stated. By-laws can be changed only by special resolution and a statement to this effect must be included.

A change in your by-laws does not come into effect until the special resolution has been registered at the Corporate Registry. Make sure that all special resolutions sent to the Registrar are dated and verified by a person authorized by the society.

The procedure for a special resolution is defined in the Societies Act and in the kit you receive containing other non-profit materials. Read the details carefully and keep a copy of the definition in your board manual along with the constitution and by-laws. Also, keep a copy (including date) of any by-law changes.

3. Arbitration

Unless the by-laws provide otherwise, disputes will be settled by arbitration, and the arbitration will be regulated by the Arbitration Act. A copy of the act is available from the Queen's Printer in Alberta (the address is in the **Reading and Resources** section at the end of chapter 6).

4. Custody and use of the society's seal

In the sample by-laws, the secretary is designated as having care of the seal of the society (item 7). A corporate seal may be purchased from a rubber stamp company, but is not required. However, should your society be dealing with legal documents, the purchase of a seal is advisable. Note that the by-laws must state who shall have custody and use of the seal, whether or not one is ever purchased.

5. Minute books and records

Your by-laws must set out which officers will prepare and keep the minutes of meetings of the society and the minutes of meetings of the directors. They must also set out which officers will keep any other books and records of the society (items 8 and 9).

By-laws must also set out the time and place at which books and records of the society may be inspected by society members (item 11).

6. Preparing your by-laws

If, instead of using the sample by-laws you write your own, then type them in the same format on 8½" x 11" paper.

The same people (at least five) who signed the application form should sign the by-laws, and their signatures must be witnessed. Each applicant must actually sign in the presence of the witness, who must not be one of the persons signing as a director. Do not use initials — sign names in full, use the home addresses of all persons signing, and list their occupations.

Only one copy of the by-laws is required for submission to the Corporate Registry; be sure to keep a photocopy of all documents for your own files.

7. Notice of address

This form is also called Notice of Registered Office (Form 3). It is used for two purposes: on incorporation and for notifications of change of official address. The Corporate Registry must have an up-to-date Alberta address for each registered society, including postal code, so that they are sure to be able to reach you by mail. If your society does not have an office, use the address

of an executive member (an officer of the board, for example, the secretary).

Sample #22 shows a completed Notice of Address. It must be submitted in duplicate. Item 4 applies if society records are kept at a place in Alberta other than the registered office. Remember that under the act, the records of the society must be accessible to the public during business hours. Item 5 is completed only if the registered office is not normally accessible to the public during business hours. This address must be within Alberta and must be a post office box. A director or officer of the board must sign the form and indicate his or her title (for example, president).

This form is also used to advise the Registry of changes of address, so keep a few extra photocopies on hand. You must notify the Registrar of a change of address within 15 days. Write the corporate access number (from the top right-hand corner of the Certificate of Incorporation) in item 2.

8. Submitting your documents

A form is supplied called Request for Corporate Services (see Sample #23). Instructions for completing the form are on the back and are explained again in the Alberta information kit. Be sure to check off item 5 (incorporation) as this is the service you are requesting.

If you are paying by cheque, the cheque number must be filled in. Make the cheque payable to the Provincial Treasurer. The form should be signed by a director or officer of the society.

Keep the last page for your records and mail the other three copies with the following items:

(a) Notice of registration of society's name and original search report

(b) Application to register as a society (two copies). Attach a note requesting one copy be returned stamped "filed and dated" for your records.

SAMPLE #22
NOTICE OF ADDRESS (ALBERTA)

IMPORTANT: PLEASE READ INSTRUCTIONS ON THE BACK OF THIS FORM

Alberta
REGISTRIES
Corporate Registry

BUSINESS CORPORATIONS ACT
(SECTION 19)

FORM 3

NOTICE OF ADDRESS OR
NOTICE OF CHANGE OF ADDRESS

1. NAME OF CORPORATION:	2. CORPORATE ACCESS NUMBER:
Ashford Day Care Society	N/A

3. ADDRESS OF REGISTERED OFFICE (ONLY A STREET ADDRESS, INCLUDING POSTAL CODE, OR LEGAL LAND DESCRIPTION).

1160 School Road
Ashford, AB
T0L 3C5

4. RECORDS ADDRESS (ONLY A STREET ADDRESS, INCLUDING POSTAL CODE, OR LEGAL LAND DESCRIPTION)

49 Elm Street
Ashford, AB
T0L 1A2

5. ADDRESS FOR SERVICE BY MAIL, IF DIFFERENT FROM ITEM 3 (ONLY A POST OFFICE BOX, INCLUDING POSTAL CODE).

N/A

6. DATE	SIGNATURE	TITLE
Sept. 14, 199-	Betty Alo Ce	President
		TELEPHONE NO.
		539-1234
FOR DEPARTMENTAL USE ONLY		FILED

CCA-06.103
(Rev. 07/93) THIS FORM WILL BE REJECTED IF NOT PROPERLY COMPLETED

93

SAMPLE #23
REQUEST FOR CORPORATE SERVICES (ALBERTA)

IMPORTANT: PLEASE READ INSTRUCTIONS ON THE BACK OF THIS FORM

Alberta

REQUEST FOR CORPORATE SERVICES

CCA-06.079
(Rev. 90/11)

CONSUMER AND
CORPORATE AFFAIRS
Corporate Registry

8th Floor John E. Brownlee Bldg.
10365 - 97 Street
Edmonton, Alberta
T5J 3W7
(403) 427-2311

Suite 310 Canada Place
407 - 2nd Street S.W.
Calgary, Alberta
T2P 2Y3
(403) 297-3442

FOR CASH REGISTER USE ONLY

1.

YOUR FILE NUMBER		NAME OF CORPORATION — EXISTING OR PROPOSED (FOR WHICH SERVICES ARE REQUIRED)	AMOUNT		CORPORATE ACCESS NUMBER (if known)
		Ashford Day Care Society			

2. NAME   Ms. Betty Able

ADDRESS   49 Elm Street

Ashford, AB

POSTAL CODE   TOL 1A2

4. PAID BY:
☐ VISA
☐ MASTERCARD

TELEPHONE NO. RES. 123-4567

BUS. 891-1234

FAX 891-1222

DATE Sept. 14, 199-

AUTHORIZATION NUMBER _____

EXPIRY DATE _____

SIGNATURE OF CARDHOLDER _____

3. SERVICE WILL BE:
☐ EDMONTON   ☐ RED DEER   ☐ PICKED UP   ☐ MAILED OUT
☐ CALGARY   ☐ LETHBRIDGE   ☐ PEACE RIVER   ☐ GRANDE PRAIRIE
☐ CAMROSE   ☐ FORT McMURRAY   ☐ MEDICINE HAT

☐ CASH   ☒ CHEQUE NO. 123

5.   PLEASE COMPLETE A SEPARATE REQUEST FOR EACH TRANSACTION REQUESTED ☑

☐ CERTIFICATE OF STATUS   ☐ DISSOLUTION/LIQUID.   ☒ INCORPORATION   ☐ DISCHARGE/RECEIVER

☐ PHOTO COPIES   ☐ DISCONTINUANCE   ☐ NAME CHANGE   ☐ APPOINTMENT OF RECEIVER

☐ DIAZO COPIES   ☐ REVIVAL/RESTORATION   ☐ ENGLISH/FRENCH EQUIV.   ☐ ARTICLES OF REORG.

☐ CERTIFIED COPIES   ☐ AMALGAMATION   ☐ ARTICLES OF AMEND.   ☐ REGISTRATION

☐ ANNUAL RETURN   ☐ CONTINUATION   ☐ RESTATED ARTICLES   ☐ FAX

☐ PHONE SEARCH   ☐ WRITTEN SEARCH

6. SPECIAL INSTRUCTIONS
(Client)
                                                            ☐ OBJECT OR BYLAWS AMENDMENTS   ☐ OTHER

_____

_____

_____

_____

_____

7. REQUESTED BY:

Betty Able

(PLEASE SIGN CLEARLY)

Betty B. Able, President   CORPORATE REGISTRY - AUDIT   o

94

(c) By-laws (two copies)

(d) Notice of address (three copies)

(e) Payment of $50 for incorporation. Make cheques payable to the Provincial Treasurer.
Mail to:
Corporate Registry
Box 1007
Main Post Office
Edmonton, AB
T5J 2M1

Remember, all documents must be submitted within 90 days of reservation of a society's name. You should have a reply in seven to nine working days.

If the documents are approved, a Certificate of Incorporation will be issued to your society indicating a "corporate access number" in the top right-hand corner, proving that your society is incorporated in Alberta under the Societies Act.

c. SASKATCHEWAN

1. By-laws

Societies are not required to draft by-laws for incorporation in Saskatchewan. The Non-Profit Corporations Act is sufficiently complete to allow the society to operate without by-laws.

However, by-laws may still be written in order to alter certain provisions of the act that apply to your society. Therefore, it is important to know the provisions of the act, to understand the operation and management requirements laid down, and to draft any necessary alterations that will apply to your society.

Such by-laws do not become part of the articles of incorporation of the society as this is considered to create problems if you need to change your by-laws. They should not be listed on the articles of incorporation (Form 1, shown in Sample #13), and should not be sent to the Corporations Branch.

Copies must, however, be available for members at the registered office of the society.

2. The Saskatchewan Non-Profit Corporations Act

Sample #24 lists the provisions of the act which constitute by-laws for all non-profit societies, *unless their articles or by-laws provide otherwise*.

Some provisions of the act may be altered by including them in your articles of incorporation, some by including them in your by-laws, and some by either. Where you put them depends on how difficult you want changing them to be.

Note that items listed in Sections A and D in the excerpts from the act may only be altered by making them different in your articles of incorporation. Sections B, C, and E may be altered in *either* the articles or in the by-laws. In general, it is better to make any changes you want in the by-laws rather than the articles, because by-laws are easier to change later on.

Section A

Section A items may be altered by inclusion in your articles *only*. Unless these items are changed in your articles, the sections as contained in the act are in effect.

Item A(2)

Under this section, a director of a corporation is not required to be a member of the corporation. You may choose to change this to:

> A director is required to be a member of the corporation.

Items A(3) and (5)

You may choose to have directors elected for two two-year terms, or some variation.

Section B

These items may be altered in *either* the articles of incorporation or the by-laws, but, unless some alteration is present, the section as contained in the act will apply.

Item B(5)

A quorum at a general meeting is a majority of people eligible to vote. If this isn't appropriate for your society, you may alter

SAMPLE #24
SASKATCHEWAN NON-PROFIT CORPORATIONS ACT

PROVISIONS OR EXCERPTS FROM THE ACT

In Sections A, B, C, D and E, "articles" means the articles of the corporation including articles of amendment, if any, in respect of which the Director has issued a Certificate of Amendment.

Note that reference is made to articles only in Section A and Section D and to articles or by-laws in the other sections.

Section A

Unless the articles otherwise provide:

1. A corporation may by vote of its members at a special meeting remove any director or directors from office but the articles may not require greater than a majority vote.

2. A director of a corporation is not required to be a member of the corporation.

3. Directors may not be elected to hold office for a term exceeding three years following election. A director not elected for an expressly stated term ceases to hold office at the close of the first meeting of members following his election at which an election of directors is required.

4. Directors may fill a vacancy among their number for the unexpired term of the vacant director.

5. Members of a corporation shall at the first meeting of members and at each succeeding meeting at which an election of directors is required, elect directors to hold office for a term not exceeding three years.

6. A director or officer may receive reasonable remuneration for his services to the corporation and indemnification for his expenses incurred on behalf of the corporation as a director or officer and a director or member may receive reasonable remuneration and expenses for his services to the corporation in any other capacity.

Section B

Unless the articles or by-laws otherwise provide:

1. Any resolution of the directors admitting a person as a member or honorary member is not effective until the resolution has been confirmed by the members in general meeting.

2. The directors may meet at a place and upon such notice as the by-laws may require. If the by-laws do not require notice, the directors may determine the notice required.

3. A membership interest of a member in the corporation is not transferable and is terminated when:

   (a) he dies or resigns;

   (b) he is expelled or his membership is otherwise terminated in accordance with the articles or by-laws of the corporation;

   (c) his term of membership expires; or

   (d) the corporation is liquidated and dissolved.

4. The rights and privileges of a member in a corporation, including any rights in the property of the corporation, cease to exist when his membership interest in the corporation is terminated.

5. A quorum of members is present at a meeting of members if a majority of voting persons is present in person.

6. Each member of a corporation is entitled to one vote at a meeting of members.

7. Voting at a meeting of members shall be by show of hands except where a ballot is demanded by a member. A member may demand a ballot either before or after any vote by show of hands.

8. The directors may, by resolution, make, amend or repeal any by-laws that regulate the activities and affairs of the corporation.

9. The articles are deemed to state that the directors of a corporation may, without authorization of the members:

(a) borrow money upon the credit of the corporation;

(b) issue, re-issue, sell or pledge debt obligations of the corporation;

(c) give a guarantee on behalf of the corporation to secure performance of an obligation of any person; [*The act should be examined before any guarantee is given under clause (c) as there are restrictions and limitations with respect to guarantees.*]

(d) mortgage, hypothecate, pledge or otherwise create a security interest in all or any property of the corporation, owned or subsequently acquired, to secure an obligation of the corporation.

10. The directors may, by resolution, delegate the powers mentioned in the preceding item to a director, a committee of directors or an officer. This assumes, of course, that the powers of the directors to do these things have not been restricted by the articles or by-laws.

Section C

Subject to the articles or by-laws:

1. A majority of the number of directors or minimum number of directors required by the articles constitutes a quorum at any meeting of directors and, notwithstanding any vacancy among the directors, a quorum of directors may exercise all the powers of the directors.

2. A director may, if all the directors of the corporation consent, participate in a meeting of directors or of a committee of directors by means of such telephone or other communications facilities as permit all persons participating in the meeting to hear each other, and a director participating in such a meeting by such means is deemed for the purposes of this act to be present at that meeting.

3. The directors may designate the offices of the corporation, appoint as officers persons of full capacity, specify their duties and delegate to them any powers that the directors may lawfully delegate except powers to:

(a) submit to the members any question or matter requiring the approval of members;

(b) fill any vacancy among the directors or in the office of auditor;

(c) issue securities (memberships) except in the manner and on the terms authorized by the directors;

(d) purchase, redeem or otherwise acquire securities issued by the corporation;

(e) approve any financial statements; or

(f) adopt, amend or repeal by-laws.

4. The directors of a corporation may fix the remuneration of the directors, officers and employees of the corporation provided the articles do not prohibit remuneration to any such person [*see item 6 of section A*].

Section D

The articles may provide that:

1. A greater number of votes of directors or members is required than the number required by the act [*the act requires a majority of two-thirds for a special resolution*] to effect any action excepting that not more than a majority of votes shall be required to remove any director or directors.

2. A vacancy in the office of auditor shall only be filled by a vote of the members. [*The act provides that the directors shall immediately fill a vacancy in the office of auditor.*]

3. A vacancy among the directors [*see item 4 of section A*] shall only be filled by a vote of the members. [*Or by a vote of the members of any class of members having an exclusive right to elect one or more directors if the vacancy occurs among the directors elected by that class.*]

Section E

The articles or by-laws may provide that:

1. An officer of the corporation is, by virtue of this office, a director of the corporation.

2. A representative of a specific organization is a director of the corporation. [*But no director mentioned in sections 1 and 2 may be a salaried officer of the corporation and the number of such directors shall not exceed one-third of the total number of directors.*]

3. Members of a corporation may cast a ballot by mail to decide any issue in respect of which the members are entitled to vote and, where the articles or by-laws so provide, the procedures that relate to collecting, counting and reporting the results of any mail ballot shall be set out in the articles or by-laws of the corporation.

4. A membership corporation may in lieu of sending its members financial statements or publishing its financial statements publish a notice stating that the financial statements are available at the registered office of the corporation and any member may, upon request, obtain a copy thereof, free of charge, by prepaid mail to his address, or by calling at the registered office of the corporation during usual business hours of the corporation.

5. A charitable corporation shall publish the financial statement or where the by-laws or articles permit publish a notice that the financial statements are available at the registered office of the corporation to be examined during the usual business hours of the corporation by any person and that person may make extracts therefrom free of charge.

6. Members may vote through a representative of any subdivision of members of the corporation notwithstanding that the members of the subdivision do not constitute a separate class.

7. A resolution of directors admitting a person as a member or honorary member is not effective until it has been confirmed by the members in general meeting.

this section and include it in either the articles or by-laws.

Item B(8)

Note that directors have the power to make, amend, or repeal any by-laws. They are not required to present them to a general membership meeting. An alternative might be:

> Except in the case of first by-laws after incorporation, all by-laws shall be made, amended or repealed by the members in general meeting. First by-laws shall be submitted at the first meeting of members and may by ordinary resolution be confirmed, rejected, or amended.

It would make sense for this particular item to be included in the articles of incorporation and thus harder to alter without full consideration by a majority of general members.

Item B(9)

Note that directors may borrow money without authorization of the membership, and that these powers may be delegated to an individual director or committee of directors providing "the powers of the directors to do these things have not been restricted by the articles or by-laws."

Section C

This section is subject to alteration in either articles or by-laws, but unless some alteration is incorporated into either, this section of the act will apply.

Item C(1)

Unless altered by articles or by-laws, this section provides that a majority of directors constitute a quorum at meetings of directors.

Item C(3)

This item contains a list of duties which the directors may *not* delegate.

Section D

The items in section D may be included in the *articles only*. They provide a list of alternatives that would still fit the requirements of the act.

Item D(1)

If added to the articles of incorporation, this item may provide for a greater number of votes of directors or members than the act requires to effect any action (pass a resolution or motion). The act requires a majority of two-thirds for a special resolution, but not more than a majority of votes shall be required to remove any director.

Section E

This section contains alternatives that fit the requirements of the act, but which may be included in *either* articles or by-laws. For instance:

> An officer of the corporation is, by virtue of this office, a director of the corporation.

Note that your articles might instead say:

> A director is required to be a member of the corporation.

Or you may require that a representative of a specific organization be a director of the corporation. (However, the act stipulates that the number of such directors may not exceed one-third of the total number of directors.)

Remember that references to salaried directors will not apply to you if your organization intends to become a registered charity.

It is also possible to build in the provision that members may vote by mail, or that admission of persons as members is not effective until confirmed by the members at a general meeting.

General

If your society decides to draft by-laws, these will probably address specific details related to the following areas:

- eligibility for membership
- membership fees (if any)
- what records will be kept

- whether or not an audit will be required (the act is flexible on this point)

- duties of officers

- meetings of members (fiscal year, quorum, date of annual meeting)

A set of sample by-laws are included in the incorporation kit from Consumer and Corporate Affairs.

3. Preparing your documents

(a) Be sure to date each document.

(b) Print or type the name of the person signing any document.

(c) Where the phrase "description of office" is used, show the office that person holds (for example, president, secretary, director).

(d) Forms may refer to "incorporators"; these are people who sign documents as the original directors. It is possible for an incorporator to be another corporation. In this case, a person authorized by that corporation signs the articles, and the address of the corporation is given.

(e) Do not attach by-laws as an appendix to the articles of incorporation.

4. Notice of directors

Form 6 must be completed (see Sample #25), though items 2 and 3 are not required for incorporation. Be sure to enter the name of the corporation in exactly the same way as in the articles of incorporation (Form 1).

Note the instructions on the back of Form 6. For each director, set out:

- first given name, initial, and family name

- full home address and postal code

- occupation (for example, farmer, nurse, retired, homemaker)

Complete two copies of this form with original signatures on each form. Make a copy of the completed form for your own records.

Note that the same form is used to notify the Registrar of the registration and election of directors in the future (see chapter 9).

Make sure the proper number of directors is listed (not fewer than or more than the number authorized in Form 1, item 5 of the Articles of Incorporation).

5. Notice of registered office

Complete Form 3, Notice of Registered Office (see Sample #26). Be sure you are consistent in writing out the society's name and the municipality exactly as recorded in the articles of incorporation (Form 1). Note the instructions on the back of Form 3, Items 4, 5, and 7 apply only to change of address (see chapter 9).

Location of the office within the municipality (item 3) is ordinarily a street address or office number and address. If the office is in a rural municipality, give the legal description of the land (NW-10-43-18 W2) or "at the home of Peter Smith, president, in the hamlet of Kipling."

6. Submitting your documents

Be sure to submit all documents within 90 days of having a name reserved for you.

If there is not enough room in the space provided on any form, type in that space: "The annexed Schedule 1 [or 2, etc.] is incorporated in this form." A separate page is required for each schedule attached. Assemble the completed forms for mailing:

(a) Articles of Incorporation (Form 1) (with two copies of any annexed schedule)

(b) Notice of Registered Office (Form 3) (two copies)

(c) Notice of Directors (Form 6) (two copies)

(d) Verification of name search and name reservation on Form 27 if name is not already reserved

SAMPLE #25
NOTICE OF DIRECTORS (SASKATCHEWAN)

Government of Saskatchewan

The Non-profit Corporations Act
Notice of Directors
(Sections 90 and 97)

Form 6

1. Name of corporation: Centretown Society for Exceptional Children Inc.   Corporation No. 1789-01

2. On the **twentieth** day of **October** ,19 **9-** , the following persons ceased to be directors of the corporation:

Full name	Address	Occupation	Citizenship

3. On the **twentieth** day of **October** ,19 **9-** , the following persons became directors of the corporation:

Full name	Address	Occupation	Citizenship

4. The directors of the corporation are:

Full name	Address	Occupation	Citizenship
Ivan P. Petit	49 High St., Centretown, Sask., S1A 4B5	Teacher	Canadian
Joan A. Brown	123 Field St., Centretown, Sask., S1A 2B3	Farmer	Canadian
Alice B. White	456 Garden St., Centretown, Sask., S1A 2Z3	Nurse	Canadian
Juan W. Pequeno	99 Circle Dr., Centretown, Sask., S1A 4X4	Geologist	Canadian
Ellen E. Enfant	678 Main St., Centretown, SK S1A 1Z3	Homemaker	Canadian

Date	Name	Description of office	Signature
October 20, 199-	John A. Brown	President	*John A. Brown*

101

The Non-profit Corporations Act

Notice of Directors

Form 6

Instructions

Format

Documents required to be sent to the Director pursuant to the Act must conform with sections 2 to 6 of the regulations under the Act.

Item 1:

Set out the full legal name of the corporation and, except where a number has not been assigned, state the corporation number.

Items 2, 3 and 4:

With respect to each director:

(a) set out first given name. initial and family name;

(b) state full residential address and postal code; and

(c) specify occupation clearly, e.g. manager, farmer, geologist.

Signature:

A director or authorized officer of the corporation shall sign the notice. Upon incorporation, an incorporator shall sign the notice.

Completed document, in duplicate, is to be sent to:

Director, Corporations Branch
1871 Smith Street
Regina, Saskatchewan
S4P 3V7

Government of Saskatchewan	**The Non-profit Corporations Act** **Notice of Registered Office** (Sections 19 (2) and (4))	**Form 3**

1. Name of corporation: Corporation No.

   Centretown Society for Exceptional Children Inc.   1789-01

2. Name of municipality in which registered office is situated:

   The City of Centretown

3. Location of registered office within the municipality:

   123 Field St.
   Centretown, Saskatchewan
   S1A 2B3

4. Mailing address of registered office including postal code:

   Same as above

5. Effective date:

   November 1, 199-

6. If change of address, give previous address of registered office:

   N/A

7. If change of municipality, give name of previous municipality:

   N/A

Date	Name	Description of office	Signature
October 20, 199-	John A. Brown	President	John A. Brown

The Non-profit Corporations Act

Notice of Registered Office

Form 3

Instructions

Format:
Documents required to be sent to the Director pursuant to the Act must conform to sections 2 to 5 of the regulations under the Act.

Item 1:
Set out the full legal name of the corporation and except where a number has not yet been assigned, state corporation number.

Item 2:
Set out the city, town, village, rural municipality or local improvement district, or The Municipal Corporation of Uranium City and District, or a local community authority established under The Northern Administration Act, or the Northern Saskatchewan Administration District as defined in The Northern Administration Act.

Item 3:
Set out in full the location of the registered office including street address and, if multi-office building, room number.

Item 4:
Mailing address should include postal code and may include post office box number. If mailing address is the same as in item 3 state "same as above."

Items 5 and 6:
These items need to be completed only if there is a change in the location or address of the registered office.

Item 7:
This item needs to be completed only if the location of the registered office is moved to another municipality. Section 156 of the Act sets out the requirements for changing the municipality within which the registered office is to be situated.

Signature:
A director or an authorized officer of the corporation shall sign the notice. Upon incorporation, an incorporator shall sign the notice.

Service of Documents:
Note that documents may, under section 264 of the Act, be sent to or served upon the corporation at its registered office.

Completed document, in duplicate, is to be sent to:

Director, Corporations Branch
1871 Smith Street
Regina, Saskatchewan
S4P 3V7

(e) Incorporation fee of $50

Mail documents to:

Corporations Branch
1871 Smith Street
Regina, SK S4P 3V7

If forms are not completed correctly, they will be returned and a re-examination fee of $20 will be charged when the documents are re-submitted. If you wish documents to be examined within 48 hours of being received, include this in a covering letter at the time of application.

It will take about two weeks for the Registrar to return the duplicate copy of these documents with a notation about their registration and date. The Certificate of Incorporation will be sent to you with the corporate registration number in the upper right-hand corner.

d. MANITOBA

1. By-laws

By-laws describe the way in which the organization will operate. The by-laws are not part of the constitution or articles of incorporation under the Corporations Act, but should be adopted by the organization at the first general meeting. Also at the first meeting, the board of directors will be elected and officers appointed.

You are not required to send your society's by-laws to the Department of Cooperative, Consumer and Corporate Affairs. They are considered to be internal to your society. You are, however, bound by certain provisions of the act. Your by-laws should include:

- details of operation of the society
- conditions under which the society may borrow money
- how the membership list is kept up to date (for example, listed as one of the duties of the secretary)

- the fiscal year of the organization (usually December 31 or March 31); remember that your annual meeting must be held within three months of the end of the fiscal year
- details of notice of annual meeting
- quorum for annual meetings
- quorum for directors' meetings
- details of directors' term of office (usually for more than one fiscal year so the organization can benefit from their experience)
- the following statement:

  The directors of the organization shall serve without remuneration and no director shall directly or indirectly receive any profit from his or her position as such; provided that a director may be paid reasonable expenses incurred by him or her in the performance of his or her duties, and any director who is a bona fide employee of the organization (whether full time or part time) may be paid remuneration with respect to services performed by him or her as an employee.

- details of any insurance to save directors and employees from liability — whenever the society holds meetings or invites the public to attend gatherings, the society is liable (if negligent) or responsible by virtue of occupying the property where meetings are held
- a dissolution or wind-up clause which is required by Revenue Canada for registration of a society as a charity

A set of sample by-laws is contained in Sample #27.

2. Submitting your documents

A Request for Service (Form 19) is provided to accompany documents on filing (see Sample #28). The form is also used when filing other documents later in the life of your society.

Submit to Cooperative, Consumer and Corporate Affairs the following:

(a) Articles of Incorporation (without share capital) (Form 2) (two copies)

(b) Request for Service (two copies)

(c) Approved Corporate Name Request

(d) Original copy of NUANS computer search report

(e) Certified cheque or money order for $70 made payable to the Minister of Finance of Manitoba.

Note that if you send in the name reservation (Form 23) and incorporation form (Form 2) at the same time, you must submit separate cheques for the two fees. The cheque for incorporation accompanying Form 2 must be certified. If only one cheque is submitted, all documents will be returned to you without being processed. Send to:

Corporations and Business
  Names Branch
1010 - 405 Broadway
Winnipeg, MB   R3C 3L6

You will receive one of the originals of Form 2 with the top half stamped with the date of incorporation.

BY-LAW NO. 1

Be it enacted and it is hereby enacted as a by-law of
(hereinafter called the "Organization"), as follows:

1. REGISTERED OFFICE

The Registered Office of the Organization shall be at such places
in the Province of Manitoba as the Directors of the Organization
may decide.

2. SEAL

The Seal, an impression whereof is stamped in the margine hereof,
shall be the seal of the Organization.

3. MEMBERSHIP

(a) any person who is interested in the Organization may
apply for membership.
(b) the Board of Directors shall have discretion to accept
or reject any application for membership, subject to
the review by the members at any general meeting of the
Organization.
(c) a member may withdraw by giving notice in writing to the
Board of Directors.
(d) a member may be expelled from the Organization by a
majority vote of the members at any general meeting.

4. FISCAL YEAR

The fiscal period of the Organization shall terminate on the
_____ day of _____, in each year or on such other date as
the Directors may by resolution determine.

5. MEETINGS

(a) the originating meeting shall be the first annual meeting.
(b) the annual meeting shall be held during the month of
_____ on a day named by the Board of Directors and
21 days notice of such meeting shall be given to every
member of the Organization.
(c) The Board of Directors or 5% of the members of the
Organization may requisition the Directors to call a general
meeting of the Organization for any of the purposes stated
in the requisition. It shall be the responsibility of
the Board of Directors to ensure that 21 days notice of
such meetings shall be given to every member of the Organization.
(d) every notice of the general meeting shall state the
nature and the business of the meeting.
(e) questions arising at any meeting of the Organization shall
be decided by a majority of votes. In case of an equality
of votes, the chairman shall call a second vote. In the
event the second vote results in an equality of votes
the resolution shall be lost.
(f) the quorum for transaction of business at any general meeting
of the Organization shall be a majority of the number of
members.

SAMPLE #27 — Continued

(g) every member shall be entitled to one vote at general
     meetings; no voting by proxy will be permitted.
(h) the rules of procedure at general meetings of the
     Organization shall be determined at the first general
     meeting and may be amended by ordinary resolution.

6. BOARD OF DIRECTORS

(a) the affairs of the Organization shall be managed by a
     Board of Directors, each having one vote, and of whom
     a majority shall constitute a quorum.
(b) the Board of Directors shall be appointed by the majority
     of the membership at the annual meeting of the Organization.
(c) the qualification of the Director shall be that he or she
     be a member in good standing of the Organization.
(d) Directors shall be eligible for re-election at the annual
     meeting of the members.
(e) the office of Directors shall be automatically vacated;
     (i)   if by notice in writing to the Organization he resigns
           his office.
     (ii) if at any special meeting of the Organization a
           majority of the members present so decide that he
           be removed from office; provided that if any
           vacancy shall occur for any reason in this paragraph
           contained prior to an annual meeting, the Directors
           may by resolution fill the vacancy with any person
           who could qualify as a Director at an annual meeting.
           The person so chosen shall hold office (subject to
           the provisions aforesaid), for the balance of the
           unexpired term of the vacating Director.
(f) all Directors of the corporation shall hold office for one
     year or until their successors are elected or appointed
     in their stead.
(g) the Directors of the Organization shall serve without
     remuneration and no Director shall directly or indirectly
     receive any profit from his position as such; provided
     that a Director may be paid reasonable expenses incurred
     by him in the performance of his duties, and any Director
     who is a bona fide employee of the Organization (whether
     full time or part time), may be paid remuneration with
     respect to services performed by him as an employee.

7. DUTIES OF DIRECTORS

(a) The Directors of the Organization shall be responsible for
     co-ordination of the work of the Organization and for
     carrying out the policies and directives of the Organization
     as determined by the Organization's general meeting.
(b) The Board of Directors shall be responsible for ensuring
     that one member chairs meetings of the Organization, for
     ensuring that funds of the Organization are accounted for,
     and for ensuring that minutes of meetings of the Organization
     are maintained.
(c) The Board of Directors cannot authorize non-routine
     expenditures over_____without authority from a
     general meeting of the membership.
(d) The Directors may exercise all such powers of the Organization
     as are not by the Manitoba Corporations Act or by the by-laws

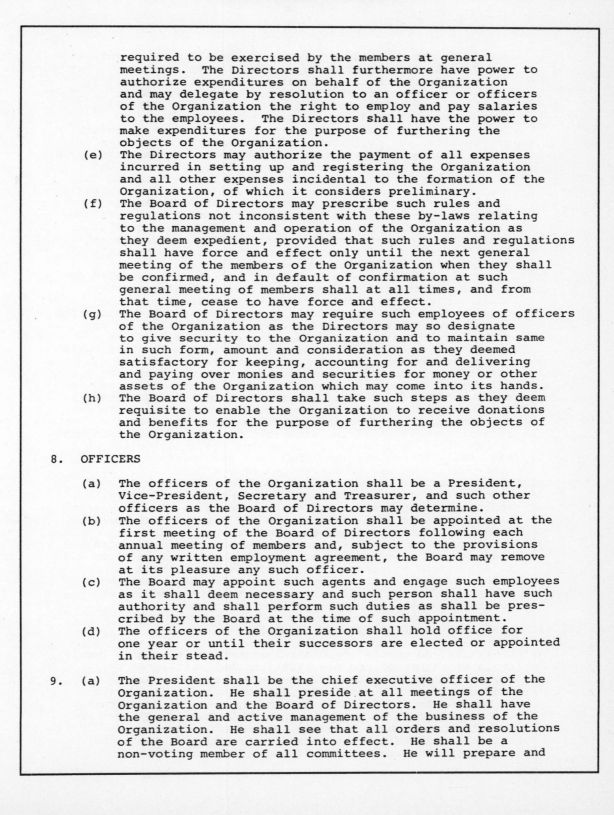

required to be exercised by the members at general meetings. The Directors shall furthermore have power to authorize expenditures on behalf of the Organization and may delegate by resolution to an officer or officers of the Organization the right to employ and pay salaries to the employees. The Directors shall have the power to make expenditures for the purpose of furthering the objects of the Organization.

(e) The Directors may authorize the payment of all expenses incurred in setting up and registering the Organization and all other expenses incidental to the formation of the Organization, of which it considers preliminary.

(f) The Board of Directors may prescribe such rules and regulations not inconsistent with these by-laws relating to the management and operation of the Organization as they deem expedient, provided that such rules and regulations shall have force and effect only until the next general meeting of the members of the Organization when they shall be confirmed, and in default of confirmation at such general meeting of members shall at all times, and from that time, cease to have force and effect.

(g) The Board of Directors may require such employees of officers of the Organization as the Directors may so designate to give security to the Organization and to maintain same in such form, amount and consideration as they deemed satisfactory for keeping, accounting for and delivering and paying over monies and securities for money or other assets of the Organization which may come into its hands.

(h) The Board of Directors shall take such steps as they deem requisite to enable the Organization to receive donations and benefits for the purpose of furthering the objects of the Organization.

8. OFFICERS

(a) The officers of the Organization shall be a President, Vice-President, Secretary and Treasurer, and such other officers as the Board of Directors may determine.

(b) The officers of the Organization shall be appointed at the first meeting of the Board of Directors following each annual meeting of members and, subject to the provisions of any written employment agreement, the Board may remove at its pleasure any such officer.

(c) The Board may appoint such agents and engage such employees as it shall deem necessary and such person shall have such authority and shall perform such duties as shall be prescribed by the Board at the time of such appointment.

(d) The officers of the Organization shall hold office for one year or until their successors are elected or appointed in their stead.

9. (a) The President shall be the chief executive officer of the Organization. He shall preside at all meetings of the Organization and the Board of Directors. He shall have the general and active management of the business of the Organization. He shall see that all orders and resolutions of the Board are carried into effect. He shall be a non-voting member of all committees. He will prepare and

submit to the members at the annual meeting a statement
and report of the preceding year for its approval.

(b)   The Vice-President shall act in the absence or disability
of the President and shall exercise the powers of the
President and shall perform such other duties as shall
from time to time be imposed upon him by the Board.
Should both the President and the Vice-President be absent
or disabled, the performance of their powers and duties
shall be delegated to a chairman appointed by the Board.

(c)   The Secretary shall attend all sessions of the Board and
all meetings of the members and act as clerk thereof
and record all votes and minutes of all proceedings in the
books to be kept for that purpose. He shall give or
cause to be given notice of all meetings of the members
and of the Board of Directors, and shall perform such other
duties as may be prescribed by the Board of Directors or
President under whose supervision he shall be. He shall
be custodian of the seal of the Organization.

(d)   The Treasurer shall have the custody of the corporate funds
and securities and shall keep full and accurate accounts
of receipts and disbursements in books belonging to the
Organization and shall deposit all monies and other valuables
in the name and to the credit of the Organization and at
such depositories as may be designated by the Board of
Directors. The Accounts maintained in such depository shall
be in the name of _____. He shall disburse
the funds of the Organization as may be ordered by the
Board taking proper vouchers for such disbursements, and
shall render to the President and Directors at the regular
meetings of the Board, or whenever they may require it, an
account of all transactions as Treasurer and of the
financial position of the Organization. He shall be designated
as one of the signing officers of the Organization in
any financial transaction. He shall also perform such
other duties as may be determined by the Board.

(e)   In all cases of death, resignation, retirement or removal
from office of an officer, all books, papers, vouchers,
money and other property of whatever kind in his possession
or under his control belonging to the Organization shall
be delivered to the Board of Directors.

(f)   The chairman may with the consent of any meeting adjourn
the same and no notice of such adjournment need be given
to all of the Directors. Any business may be brought
before or dealt with at any meeting which might have been
brought before or dealt with at the original meeting in
accordance with the notice calling for same.

10. SIGNATURE AND CERTIFICATION OF DOCUMENTS

(a)   Contracts, documents, or other instruments in writing requiring a signature of the Organization shall be signed by
any two of the President, Vice-President, Secretary or
Treasurer, and all contracts, documents, and instruments
in writing so signed shall be binding upon the Organization
without any further authorization or formality. The
Directors shall have power to appoint an officer or
officers on behalf of the Organization to sign contracts,
documents, instruments in writing. The seal of the

Organization when required may be affixed to contracts, documents, instruments in writing signed as aforesaid or by any officer or officers appointed by a resolution of the Board of Directors.

The terms "contract, documents, or any instruments in writing": as used herein shall include deeds, mortgages, hypothecs, charges, conveyances, transfers and assignments of property real or personal, immovable or movable, agreements, releases, receipts and discharges for the payment of money or other obligations, conveyances, transfers and assignments of shares, stocks, bonds, debentures, or other securities and all paper writings.

11. RESOLUTIONS AND AMENDMENTS

   (a)   The by-laws of the Organization may be amended at any general meeting of the Organization by an ordinary resolution adopted by a majority vote of the members of the Organization present and voting at any general meeting.

   (b)   Notice to amend any by-laws or introduce a new one shall be given in writing at a meeting of the Organization prior to the meeting or circulated to the members of the organization present at any general meeting.

   (c)   Any resolution other than a special resolution shall be deemed passed if a majority of the members present vote in favour of such resolution.

   (d)   For all purposes of the Organization, "special resolution": shall mean a resolution passed by no less than two-thirds majority of such members entitled to vote as are present in person at a general meeting of which notice specifying the intention to propose a resolution as a special resolution has been duly given.

12. INDEMNITIES TO DIRECTORS AND OTHERS

Every Director or officer of the Organization or other person who has undertaken or is about to undertake any liability on behalf of the Organization and their heirs, executors, administrators and estate, respectively, shall at all times, be indemnified and saved harmless, out of the funds of the Organization from and against:

   (a)   All costs, charges, and expenses whatsoever which such Director, officer or other person sustains or incurs in or about any action, suit or proceedings which is brought or prosecuted against him for, or in respect of any act, deed, matter or thing whatsoever made, done or permitted by him in or about the execution of the duties of his office except such costs, charges or expenses as are occasioned by his own willful neglect.

   (b)   all other costs, charges and expenses, which he sustains or incurs in or about or in relation to the affairs thereof, except such costs, charges or expenses as are occasioned by his own willful neglect.

13. INTERPRETATION

In all by-laws and special resolutions of the Organization the singular shall include the plural, the singular; the word "person": shall include firms and corporations, the masculine shall include

the feminine. Whenever references are made in any by-law or
any special resolution of the Organization or to any statute or
section thereof, such references shall be deemed to extend and
apply to any amendment or re-enactment or such by-law, statute
or section thereof as the case may be.

14. BOOKS AND RECORDS

The books and records of the Organization shall be open to the
inspection by members at all reasonable times, upon reasonable
notice at the office of the Organization.

15. WINDING UP

It is the unalterable provision of this by-law that members
of this Organization shall have no interest in the property and
assets of the Organization; and that upon dissolution or winding up
of the Organization, any funds and assets of the Organization
remaining after satisfaction of its debts and liabilities, shall be
distributed to a recognized Charitable Organization in the area
whose objects most closely accord with those of this Organization
as determined by its members at dissolution.

PER: _____

PER: _____

PER: _____

SAMPLE #27 — Continued

<u>BY-LAW NO. 2:   BORROWING</u>

1. The Directors may borrow money upon the credit of the Organiz-
    ation.

2. The Directors may authorize any Director or Directors, member
    or members, employee or employees of the Organization to make
    arrangements with reference to money to be borrowed as aforesaid.
    Whereas to the terms and conditions of the loan thereof and as
    to the security to be given, therefore with power to vary
    or modify such arrangements, terms and conditions and to give
    such additional securities for any monies borrowed or remaining
    due by the Organization as the Directors of the Organization
    may authorize and generally to manage, transact and settle
    the borrowing of money by the Organization.

3. The Directors may authorize a Director of Directors, officer
    or officers, employee or employees of the Organization or
    other person or persons whether connected with the Organization
    or not, to sign, execute, and give on behalf of the Organization,
    all documents, agreements, and promises necessary or desirable
    for the purpose aforesaid and to draw, make and accept, endorse,
    execute and issue cheques, promissory notes, bills of exchange,
    bills of lading and other negotiable or transferrable instru-
    ments in the name and all renewals thereof, or substitutions
    therefore, if so signed shall be binding upon the Organization.

4. The powers hereby conferred shall be deemed to be in supplement
    of, not substitution for, any power to borrow money for the
    purposes of the Organization, possessed by its Directors or
    officers independently of this by-law.

        DATED this   day of   , 19 .

                PER:_____

                PER:_____

                PER:_____

SAMPLE #28
TRANSMITTAL NOTICE (MANITOBA)

The Corporations Act /
Loi sur les corporations
REQUEST FOR SERVICE
DEMANDE DE SERVICE

Manitoba

A Name and address of sender / Nom et adresse de l'expéditeur

St. Boniface Folk Dancing Society Inc.
1879 Reel Raod
St. Boniface, Manitoba
R1A 2B3

Contact person / Personne ressource

Denise Dansante

Tel(8:30-4:30) / /Tél.(8 h 30-16 h 30) __347-5689__

Fee enclosed / Droit inclus $ 70.00

B Current name of the corporation/ Dénomination de la corporation

As above, new incorporation

Corporation number / Numéro de la corporation

C IF YOU ARE FILING ARTICLES OR AN APPLICATION, PLEASE IDENTIFY THE FORM BEING FILED /
EN CAS DE DÉPÔT DE STATUTS OU D'UNE DEMANDE, INDIQUER LA FORMULE DÉPOSÉE :

- [x] Articles of incorporation / Statuts constitutifs
- [ ] Articles of / Statuts (Clauses) _____
- [ ] Application for registration / Demande d'enregistrement
- [ ] Application for supplementary registration / Demande d'enregistrement supplémentaire
- [ ] Other / Autre _____

D IF YOU WANT CERTIFICATES AND/OR COPIES, PLEASE IDENTIFY THE DESIRED ITEM (S) /
POUR OBTENIR DES CERTIFICATS OU DES PHOTOCOPIES, PRIÈRE D'INDIQUER LES DOCUMENTS DÉSIRÉS

- [x] Certificate of status / Certificat de statut
- [ ] Certificate of search / Certificat de recherche
- [ ] Photocopy of / Photocopie de _____
- [x] Certified copy of / Copie certifiée conforme de __Status__

E OFFICE REPLY / RÉPONSE

- [ ] Forms accepted, your copy enclosed.
  Les formules sont acceptées, votre copie est jointe aux présentes
- [ ] Requested item(s) enclosed / Les documents demandés sont joints aux présentes
- [ ] REMARKS / REMARQUES _____

_____

_____

SIGNATURE FOR RECEIPT / ACCUSÉ DE RÉCEPTION (SIGNATURE)

RETURN FEE AND TWO COPIES OF FORM TO :
CORPORATIONS AND BUSINESS NAMES BRANCH
1010-405 BROADWAY
WINNIPEG, MANITOBA R3C 3L6

(204) 945-2500
MG10235 (REV.SEP/92)

ENVOYER LE DROIT ET DEUX COPIES DE LA FORMULE À
CORPORATIONS ET NOMS COMMERCIAUX
405, BROADWAY, BUREAU 1010
WINNIPEG (MANITOBA) R3C 3L6

(204) 945-2500
FORM 19 /FORMULE 19

e. ONTARIO

1. By-laws

While it is assumed that by-laws for the operation of a new society will be drawn up, they are not required for submission to the Ministry of Consumer and Corporate Relations.

Any by-laws adopted, however, must not contravene the act or contradict the letters patent of the society.

Letters patent is the name of the document returned to you from the Ministry of Consumer and Corporate Affairs that authorizes the incorporation of your society.

A sample set of by-laws is shown in Sample #29. Generally, by-laws include clauses covering the following:

(a) admission of members, their rights and obligations, when they cease to be in good standing, and dues;

(b) conditions under which membership ceases and the manner, if any, in which a member may be expelled;

(c) procedure for calling general meetings and annual general meetings, including notice and quorum;

(d) rights of voting at general meetings, whether proxy voting is allowed, and, if so, provisions for it;

(e) appointment and removal of directors and officers, their duties, powers, and remuneration, if any, and methods of nomination and election;

(f) exercise of borrowing powers;

(g) preparation and custody of minutes of meetings and other documents of the society and directors;

(h) special resolutions or notice of motion by which new or amended by-laws or changes to the constitution are proposed;

(i) appointment of auditors (required in Ontario);

(j) provisions for the adoption of a corporate seal (required in Ontario); and

(k) any other particulars related to the conduct of the corporation's affairs.

Note that during the first year of operation of the society, any by-law or resolution signed by all directors and any resolution signed by all members is as valid and effective as if passed at a meeting.

A director must be at least 18 years of age and a member of a society within ten days of election to the board.

The Corporations Act stipulates (and by-laws must reflect) that directors are to be elected at a yearly general meeting unless letters patent provide otherwise. No director should be elected for a term of more than five years and at least three directors shall retire from office in each year. Where a vacancy occurs on the board, the directors may appoint a member to serve the remainder of the term.

By-laws may provide for persons serving as directors *ex officio* instead of by election. A person serving ex officio is on the board by virtue of an office or position he or she holds and not as an individual person. For example, a president of a society which works closely with yours may be appointed ex officio, whoever the person who is president happens to be. If provided for in the by-laws, this appointment is not subject to an election by the membership.

Directors elect a president from among themselves and appoint a secretary. They may also appoint one or more vice-presidents and other officers.

Note that by-laws may provide that a membership expires on failure to pay annual dues. Thus, inactive members are automatically dropped from the registry.

Membership is not transferable unless otherwise stated in the letters patent.

A society is required to hold an annual general meeting not later than 18 months

A society is required to hold an annual general meeting not later than 18 months after incorporation, and within 15 months thereafter. The written notice of meeting must include an agenda of the general business to be discussed. A general meeting must be held if at least one-tenth of the eligible members request it of directors.

Approved sample by-laws are contained in the *Ontario Corporations Manual*. This is a private publication addressing all aspects of the Corporation Act. Refer to the section on "Corporations Without Share Capital."

Also see the *Ontario Corporate Law Guide*. Both are found at public libraries, and law and court libraries (see the **Reading and Resources** section in chapter 6).

2. Submitting your documents

Prior to submitting documents to the Corporations Branch, you must first submit them to the Charitable Property Division, Office of the Public Trustee for Ontario.

Office of the Public Trustee for Ontario
Charities Division
595 Bay Street
Toronto, ON M5G 2M6
Tel: (416) 314-2800
Fax: (416) 314-2716

This office will check the proposed objectives of the corporation and the forms for completeness and accuracy.

Every page of the documents will be stamped as evidence that the documents met the criteria for charitable corporations as set out by the Charitable Property Division of the Public Trustee. Once the documents have been approved and returned to you, mail them to the Companies Branch. For both submissions, you will need:

(a) Application for Incorporation (without share capital) (Form 2) (two copies)

(b) Original copy of NUANS computer search report (one copy)

(c) Cheque or money order for $155 made payable to the Minister of Finance to cover the fee for incorporation.

(d) Covering letter with name, address, and telephone number of the person to whom Letters Patent or any correspondence about the application should be sent.

Note that when payment is made by cheque, the name of the corporation must be written on the face of the cheque.

Mail approved forms to:

Companies Branch
Ministry of Consumer and
  Commercial Relations
 Suite 200, 393 University Avenue
Toronto, ON M5G 2M2
Tel: (416) 314-8880

You can expect to receive a reply in four to six weeks. Your corporation number will be printed on the copy of Form 2 which is returned to you and also entered on the certificate page. The society comes into existence on the date of the letters patent incorporating it.

Form XV.7—By-laws of corporation without share capital

BY-LAW No.

A by-law relating generally to the transaction of the affairs of

(here insert name of corporation)

BE IT ENACTED as a by-law of *(here insert name of Corporation)* as follows:

HEAD OFFICE

1. The Head Office of the Corporation shall be in the City of _____, in the Province of Ontario, and at such place therein as the directors may from time to time determine.

SEAL

2. The seal, an impression whereof is stamped in the margin hereof, shall be the corporate seal of the Corporation.

BOARD OF DIRECTORS

3. The affairs of the Corporation shall be managed by a board of _____ directors, each of whom at the time of his election or within 10 days thereafter and throughout his term of office shall be a member of the Corporation. Each director shall be elected to hold office until the first annual meeting after he shall have been elected or until his successor shall have been duly elected and qualified. The whole board shall be retired at each annual meeting, but shall be eligible for re-election if otherwise qualified. The election may be by a show of hands unless a ballot be demanded by any member. The members of the Corporation may, by resolution passed by at least two-thirds of the votes cast at a general meeting of which notice specifying the intention to pass such resolution has been given, remove any director before the expiration of his term of office, and may, by a majority of the votes cast at that meeting, elect any person in his stead for the remainder of his term.

VACANCIES, BOARD OF DIRECTORS

4. Vacancies on the board of directors, however caused, may, so long as a quorum of directors remain in office, be filled by the directors from among the qualified members of the Corporation, if they shall see fit to do so, otherwise such vacancy shall be filled at the next annual meeting of the members at which the directors for the ensuing year are elected, but if there is not a quorum of directors, the remaining directors shall forthwith call a meeting of the members to fill the vacancy. If the number of directors is increased between the terms, a vacancy or vacancies, to the number of the authorized increase, shall thereby be deemed to have occurred, which may be filled in the manner above provided.

QUORUM AND MEETINGS, BOARD OF DIRECTORS

5. A majority of the directors shall form a quorum for the transaction of business. Except as otherwise required by law, the board of directors may hold its meetings at such place or places as it may from time to time determine. No formal notice of any such meeting shall be necessary if all the directors are present, or if those absent have signified their consent to

the meeting being held in their absence. Directors' meetings may be formally called by the President or Vice-President or by the Secretary on direction of the President or Vice-President, or by the Secretary on direction in writing of two directors. Notice of such meetings shall be delivered, telephoned or telegraphed to each director not less than *one day* before the meeting is to take place or shall be mailed to each director not less than *two days* before the meeting is to take place. The statutory declaration of the Secretary or President that notice has been given pursuant to this by-law shall be sufficient and conclusive evidence of the giving of such notice. The board may appoint a day or days in any month or months for regular meetings at an hour to be named and of such regular meeting no notice need be sent. A directors' meeting may also be held, without notice, immediately following the annual meeting of the Corporation. The directors may consider or transact any business either special or general at any meeting of the board.

ERRORS IN NOTICE, BOARD OF DIRECTORS

6. No error or omission in giving such notice for a meeting of directors shall invalidate such meeting or invalidate or make void any proceedings taken or had at such meeting and any director may at any time waive notice of any such meeting and may ratify and approve of any or all proceedings taken or had thereat.

VOTING, BOARD OF DIRECTORS

7. Questions arising at any meeting of directors shall be decided by a majority of votes. In case of an equality of votes, the Chairman, in addition to his original vote, shall have a second or casting vote. All votes at such meeting shall be taken by ballot if so demanded by any director present, but if no demand be made, the vote shall be taken in the usual way by assent or dissent. A declaration by the Chairman that a resolution has been carried and an entry to that effect in the minutes shall be admissible in evidence as *prima facie* proof of the fact without proof of the number or proportion of the votes recorded in favour of or against such resolution. In the absence of the President his duties may be performed by the Vice-President or such other director as the board may from time to time appoint for the purpose.

POWERS

8. The directors of the Corporation may administer the affairs of the Corporation in all things and make or cause to be made for the Corporation, in its name, any kind of contract which the Corporation may lawfully enter into and, save as hereinafter provided, generally, may exercise all such other powers and do all such other acts and things as the Corporation is by its charter or otherwise authorized to exercise and do.

Without in any way derogating from the foregoing, the directors are expressly empowered, from time to time, to purchase, lease or otherwise acquire, alienate, sell, exchange or otherwise dispose of shares, stocks, rights, warrants, options and other securities, lands, buildings and other property, movable or immovable, real or personal, or any right or interest therein owned by the Corporation, for such consideration and upon such terms and conditions as they may deem advisable.

REMUNERATION OF DIRECTORS

9. The directors shall receive no remuneration for acting as such.

OFFICERS OF CORPORATION

10. There shall be a President, a Vice-President, a Secretary and a Treasurer or in lieu of a Secretary and Treasurer, a Secretary-Treasurer and such other officers as the board of directors may determine by by-law from time to time. One person may hold more than one office except the offices of President and Vice-President. The President and Vice-President shall be elected by the board of directors from among their number at the first meeting of the board after the annual election of such board of directors, provided that in default of such election the then incumbents, being members of the board, shall hold office until their successors are elected. The other officers of the Corporation need not be members of the board and in the absence of written agreement to the contrary, the employment of all officers shall be settled from time to time by the board.

DUTIES OF PRESIDENT AND VICE-PRESIDENT

11. The President shall, when present, preside at all meetings of the members of the Corporation and of the board of directors. The President shall also be charged with the general management and supervision of the affairs and operations of the Corporation. The President with the Secretary or other officer appointed by the board for the purpose shall sign all by-laws and membership certificates. During the absence or inability of the President, his duties and powers may be exercised by the Vice-President, and if the Vice-President, or such other director as the board may from time to time appoint for the purpose, exercises any such duty or power, the absence or inability of the President shall be presumed with reference thereto.

DUTIES OF SECRETARY

12. The Secretary shall be *ex officio* clerk of the board of directors. He shall attend all meetings of the board of directors and record all facts and minutes of all proceedings in the books kept for that purpose. He shall give all notices required to be given to members and to directors. He shall be the custodian of the seal of the Corporation and of all books, papers, records, correspondence, contracts and other documents belonging to the Corporation which he shall deliver up only when authorized by a resolution of the board of directors to do so and to such person or persons as may be named in the resolution, and he shall perform such other duties as may from time to time be determined by the board of directors.

DUTIES OF TREASURER

13. The Treasurer, or person performing the usual duties of a Treasurer, shall keep full and accurate accounts of all receipts and disbursements of the Corporation in proper books of account and shall deposit all moneys or other valuable effects in the name and to the credit of the Corporation in such bank or banks as may from time to time be designated by the board of directors. He shall disburse the funds of the Corporation under the direction of the board of directors, taking proper vouchers therefor and shall render to the board of directors at the regular meetings thereof or whenever required of him, an account of all his transactions as Treasurer, and of the financial position of the Corporation. He shall also perform such other duties as may from time to time be determined by the board of directors.

DUTIES OF OTHER OFFICERS

14. The duties of all other officers of the Corporation shall be such as the terms of their engagement call for or the board of directors requires of them.

EXECUTION OF DOCUMENTS

15. Deeds, transfers, licences, contracts and engagements on behalf of the Corporation shall be signed by either the President or Vice-President and by the Secretary, and the Secretary shall affix the seal of the Corporation to such instruments as require the same.

Contracts in the ordinary course of the Corporation's operations may be entered into on behalf of the Corporation by the President, Vice-President, Treasurer or by any person authorized by the board.

The President, Vice-President, the directors, Secretary or Treasurer, or any one of them, or any person or persons from time to time designated by the board of directors may transfer any and all shares, bonds or other securities from time to time standing in the name of the Corporation in its individual or any other capacity or as trustee or otherwise and may accept in the name and on behalf of the Corporation transfers of shares, bonds or other securities from time to time transferred to the Corporation, and may affix the corporate seal to any such transfers or acceptances of transfers, and may make, execute and deliver under the corporate seal any and all instruments in writing necessary or proper for such purposes, including the appointment of an attorney or attorneys to make or accept transfers of shares, bonds or other securities on the books of any company or corporation.

Notwithstanding any provisions to the contrary contained in the by-laws of the Corporation, the board of directors may at any time by resolution direct the manner in which, and the person or persons by whom, any particular instrument, contract or obligations of the Corporation may or shall be executed.

BOOKS AND RECORDS

16. The directors shall see that all necessary books and records of the Corporation required by the by-laws of the Corporation or by any applicable statute or law are regularly and properly kept.

MEMBERSHIP

17. The membership shall consist of the applicants for the incorporation of the Corporation and such other individuals and such corporations, partnerships and other legal entities as are admitted as members by the board of directors.

Members may resign by resignation in writing which shall be effective upon acceptance thereof by the board of directors.

In case of resignation, a member shall remain liable for payment of any assessment or other sum levied or which became payable by him to the corporation prior to acceptance of his resignation.

Each member in good standing shall be entitled to one vote on each question arising at any special or general meeting of the members. Corporations, partnerships and other legal entities may vote through a duly authorized proxy.

Each member shall promptly be informed by the Secretary of his admission as a member.

DUES

18. There shall be no dues or fees payable by members except such, if any, as shall from time to time be fixed by unanimous vote of the board of directors, which vote shall become effective only when confirmed by a vote of the members at an annual or other general meeting.

The Secretary shall notify the members of the dues or fees at any time payable by them and, if any are not paid within 30 days of the date of such notice the members in default shall thereupon automatically cease to be members of the Corporation, but any such members may on payment of all unpaid dues or fees be reinstated by unanimous vote of the board of directors.

ANNUAL AND OTHER MEETINGS OF MEMBERS

19. The annual or any other general meeting of the members shall be held at the head office of the Corporation or elsewhere in Ontario as the board of directors may determine and on such day as the said directors shall appoint.

At every annual meeting, in addition to any other business that may be transacted, the report of the directors, the financial statement and the report of the auditors shall be presented and a board of directors elected and auditors appointed for the ensuing year and the remuneration of the auditors shall be fixed. The members may consider and transact any business either special or general without any notice thereof at any meeting of the members. The board of directors or the President or Vice-President shall have power to call at any time a general meeting of the members of the Corporation. No public notice nor advertisement of members' meetings, annual or general, shall be required, but notice of the time and place of every such meeting shall be given to each member by sending the notice by prepaid mail or telegraph, ten days before the time fixed for the holding of such meeting; provided that any meetings of members may be held at any time and place without such notice if all the members of the Corporation are present thereat or represented by proxy duly appointed, and at such meeting any business may be transacted which the Corporation at annual or general meetings may transact.

ERROR OR OMISSION IN NOTICE

20. No error or omission in giving notice of any annual or general meeting or any adjourned meeting, whether annual or general, of the members of the Corporation shall invalidate such meeting or make void any proceedings taken thereat and any member may at any time waive notice of any such meeting and may ratify, approve and confirm any or all proceedings taken or had thereat. For the purpose of sending notice to any member, director or officer for any meeting or otherwise, the address of any member, director or officer shall be his last address recorded on the books of the Corporation.

ADJOURNMENTS

21. Any meetings of the Corporation or of the directors may be adjourned to any time and from time to time and such business may be transacted at such adjourned meeting as might have been transacted at the original meeting from which such adjournment took place. No notice shall be

required of any such adjournment. Such adjournment may be made notwithstanding that no quorum is present.

QUORUM OF MEMBERS

22. A quorum for the transaction of business at any meeting of members shall consist of not less than *three* members present in person or represented by proxy: provided that in no case can any meeting be held unless there are two members present in person.

VOTING OF MEMBERS

23. Subject to the provisions, if any, contained in the Letters Patent of the Corporation, each member of the Corporation shall at all meetings of members be entitled to one vote and he may vote by proxy. Such proxy need not himself be a member but before voting shall produce and deposit with the Secretary sufficient appointment in writing from his constituent or constituents. No member shall be entitled either in person or by proxy to vote at meetings of the Corporation unless he has paid all dues or fees, if any, then payable by him.

At all meetings of members every question shall be decided by a majority of the votes of the members present in person or represented by proxy unless otherwise required by the by-laws of the Corporation, or by law. Every question shall be decided in the first instance by a show of hands unless a poll be demanded by any member. Upon a show of hands, every member having voting rights shall have one vote, and unless a poll be demanded a declaration by the Chairman that a resolution has been carried or not carried and an entry to that effect in the minutes of the Corporation shall be admissible in evidence as *prima facie* proof of the fact without proof of the number or proportion of the votes accorded in favour of or against such resolution. The demand for a poll may be withdrawn, but if a poll be demanded and not withdrawn the question shall be decided by a majority of votes given by the members present in person or by proxy, and such poll shall be taken in such manner as the Chairman shall direct and the result of such poll shall be deemed the decision of the Corporation in general meeting upon the matter in question. In case of an equality of votes at any general meeting, whether upon a show of hands or at a poll, the Chairman shall be entitled to a second or casting vote.

FINANCIAL YEAR

24. Unless otherwise ordered by the board of directors, the fiscal year of the Corporation shall terminate on the _____ day of _____ in each year.

CHEQUES, ETC.

25. All cheques, bills of exchange or other orders for the payment of money, notes or other evidences of indebtedness issued in the name of the Corporation, shall be signed by such officer or officers, agent or agents of the Corporation and in such manner as shall from time to time be determined by resolution of the board of directors and any one of such officers or agents may alone endorse notes and drafts for collection on account of the Corporation through its bankers, and endorse notes and cheques for deposit with the Corporation's bankers for the credit of the Corporation, or the

same may be endorsed *"for collection"* or *"for deposit"* with the bankers of the Corporation by using the Corporation's rubber stamp for the purpose. Any one of such officers or agents so appointed may arrange, settle, balance and certify all books and accounts between the Corporation and the Corporation's bankers and may receive all paid cheques and vouchers and sign all the bank's forms or settlement of balances and release or verification slips.

DEPOSIT OF SECURITIES FOR SAFEKEEPING

26. The securities of the Corporation shall be deposited for safekeeping with one or more bankers, trust companies or other financial institutions to be selected by the board of directors. Any and all securities so deposited may be withdrawn, from time to time, only upon the written order of the Corporation signed by such officer or officers, agent or agents of the Corporation, and in such manner, as shall from time to time be determined by resolution of the board of directors and such authority may be general or confined to specific instances. The institutions which may be so selected as custodians by the board of directors shall be fully protected in acting in accordance with the directions of the board of directors and shall in no event be liable for the due application of the securities so withdrawn from deposit or the proceeds thereof.

NOTICE

27. Any notice (which term includes any communication or document) to be given, sent, delivered or served pursuant to the Act, the letters patent, the by-laws or otherwise to a member, director, officer or auditor shall be sufficiently given if delivered personally to the person to whom it is to be given or if delivered to his recorded address or if mailed to him at his recorded address by prepaid air or ordinary mail, or if sent to him at his recorded address by any means of prepaid transmitted or recorded communication. A notice so delivered shall be deemed to have been given when it is delivered personally or at the recorded address as aforesaid; a notice so mailed shall be deemed to have been given when deposited in a post office or public letter box; and a notice sent by any means of transmitted or recorded communication shall be deemed to have been given when dispatched or delivered to the appropriate communication company or agency or its representative for dispatch. The Secretary may change or cause to be changed the recorded address of any member, director, officer or auditor in accordance with any information believed by him to be reliable.

BORROWING

28. The directors may from time to time
(a) borrow money on the credit of the Corporation; or
(b) issue, sell or pledge securities of the Corporation; or
(c) charge, mortgage, hypothecate or pledge all or any of the real or personal property of the Corporation, including book debts, rights, powers, franchises and undertakings, to secure any securities or any money borrowed, or other debt, or any other obligation or liability of the Corporation.

From time to time the directors may authorize any director, officer or employee of the Corporation or any other person to make arrangements with reference to the moneys borrowed or to be borrowed as aforesaid and as to the terms and conditions of the loan thereof, and as to the securities to be given therefor, with power to vary or modify such arrangements, terms and conditions and to give such additional securities for any moneys borrowed or remaining due by the Corporation as the directors may authorize, and generally to manage, transact and settle the borrowing of money by the Corporation.

INTERPRETATION

29. In these by-laws and in all other by-laws of the Corporation hereafter passed unless the context otherwise requires, words importing the singular number or the masculine gender shall include the plural number or the feminine gender, as the case may be, and *vice versa*, and references to persons shall include firms and corporations.

Passed by the board of directors and sealed with the corporate seal this _____ day of _____, 19_____.

(Corporate Seal)

_____   _____
President   Secretary

9

MAINTAINING YOUR
LEGAL STATUS

Let's suppose that your society has followed all the steps in the last three chapters, and that you now exist as a legal entity in your province. The legal obligations of your society have not ended. There are still certain yearly reporting requirements that all societies must comply with.

Once a year, all non-profit societies are required to account for their financial and administrative affairs to the provincial government. A yearly report is also required by the federal government if your society is registered as a charity (see chapter 11).

You also need to know what steps to take if and when you want to make changes; for example, if your board of directors changes or you want to modify your by-laws.

Because the constitution (also called articles of incorporation) of a non-profit society states its fundamental purpose, changes to the constitution are fundamental in nature, and require a special general meeting or attention at an annual general meeting for which all the membership has been notified in advance.

Your society's constitution may be altered through modifications to existing clauses, additions, or deletions, except for those clauses which are required to be unalterable or are stated in your constitution as unalterable.

Changing the by-laws — the rules and procedures for operating your society — is more common and is also generally done at a special or annual general meeting.

In both cases, notice of the changes must be duly submitted to provincial authorities so that they have on record an accurate description of non-profit societies active in the province.

You must also notify the provincial Registrar of non-profit societies if your registered address changes. The registered address is the office address of the society, or the home address of a responsible person who is a member of that society.

Similarly, the Registrar needs to know the names of the people responsible for speaking and acting on behalf of the non-profit society. Most registrars like to be informed of each change as it happens. At the very least, the yearly report of the society must list the members of the board of directors at the time of the annual general meeting.

Yearly requirements and notifications of changes are given below on a province-by-province basis.

a. BRITISH COLUMBIA

1. Ongoing requirements

(a) Seal

The use of a seal for official documents is optional in British Columbia. If used, it may be reproduced by a rubber stamp or impression seal.

(b) Annual general meeting

An annual general meeting must be held at least once every calendar year, with not more than 15 months between meetings. Proper notice must be given to all members. The

Society Act requires not less than 14 days' written notice. The by-laws of your society may contain additional requirements.

The act requires that the members who attend the annual general meeting receive the following documents:

- a financial statement (showing receipts, disbursements, and assets, and signed by two directors)
- an auditor's report (if any)
- a directors' report to members

(c) Annual report

The annual report of a society must be received by the Registrar within 30 days of the annual meeting, using Form 11 (see Sample #30). With Form 11 submit the following:

- date and place of annual meeting
- full names and home addresses of the society's directors, indicating who are officers of the society
- number of voting (and, if any, non-voting) members of the society
- the financial statement that was presented to the annual general meeting signed by the directors. If you have an auditor, his or her report must be attached to the financial statement.
- filing fee of $15 made out to the Minister of Finance

If the Registrar requires more information or clarification, you will receive a follow-up letter.

If no annual report has been filed for a two-year period, the Registrar may "strike the society from the register," which in effect revokes or cancels the society's registration.

In this event, a Notice of Commencement of Dissolution will be sent by registered mail to the last official address of the society. The society then has one month to reply.

2. Registering changes

(a) Special general meeting

Extraordinary meetings of the full membership may be called (with proper notice) usually for the purpose of amending a by-law or the constitution. The act also describes a procedure by which a special general meeting can be called by the agreement of 10% or more of the society's voting members. This takes the form of a written demand to the directors stating the purpose of the proposed meeting. The directors must then call a meeting within 21 days; after that time, if a meeting is not called, the members themselves may call a valid meeting.

(b) Special resolutions

A special resolution is defined in section 1 of the act as:

> (a) a resolution passed in general meeting by a majority of not less than 75% of the votes of those members of a society who, being entitled to do so, vote in person or, where proxies are allowed, by proxy
>
> > (i) of which the notice that the by-laws provide and not being less than 14 days' notice specifying the intention to propose the resolution as a special resolution has been given; or
> >
> > (ii) if every member entitled to attend and vote at the meeting so agrees, at a meeting of which less than 14 days' notice has been given;
>
> (b) a resolution consented to in writing by every member of a society who would have been entitled to vote on it in person or, where proxies are allowed, by proxy at a general meeting of the society; and a resolution so consented to shall be deemed to be a special resolution passed

SAMPLE #30
ANNUAL REPORT NOTICE (BRITISH COLUMBIA)

<table>
<tr><td>**Province of British Columbia**</td><td>**Ministry of Finance and Corporate Relations**
REGISTRAR OF COMPANIES</td><td>CORPORATE AND PERSONAL
PROPERTY REGISTRIES
940 BLANSHARD STREET
VICTORIA, BRITISH COLUMBIA
V8W 3E6</td></tr>
</table>

Form 11
(Section 68)

Certificate of Incorporation No. __S-19056__

SOCIETY ACT

Annual Report of ___Vulnerable Valley Environmental Society___
(Name of Society)

1. This report contains information as at the close of the annual general meeting which was held on

___May 30, 199-___ at ___Anyville, B.C.___ .
(Date)   *(City)*

2. The directors of the Society and their resident addresses are:
(attach list if space is insufficient):

FULL NAMES	RESIDENT ADDRESSES (P.O. Box is not acceptable. If no civic address available, supply legal description of land)
Gloria Sue Ochre	10010 River Road, Anyville, B.C. VON 1C3
Peter Ray White	55 Sawmill Road, Anyville, B.C. VON 1C1
Janet Gabrielle Grey	R.R.#1, Road 7, Anyville, B.C. VON 1C0
Susan Ann White	55 Sawmill Road, Anyville, B.C. VON 1C1
Hugh John Green	R.R.#3 Vulnerable Valley, B.C. VON 1B0

3. The society has:

___103___ voting members
and
___n/a___ non voting members (fill in the proper numbers).

4. A signed copy (copies) of the financial statement(s) presented to the Annual General Meeting is (are) attached.

Dated the ___15th___ day of ___June___ , 19 __9-__ .

by ___Gloria Ochre___
(Signature)

___President___
(Relationship to Society)

Note: a) An Annual Report must be filed with the Registrar of Companies within 30 days after each Annual General Meeting.
b) If the Society has an auditor his report must be attached to the financial statement. (The financial statement must be signed by two directors.)

(Note that an annual report must be filed with the Registrar of Companies within 30 days after each annual general meeting.)

at a general meeting of the society;

(c) where a society has adopted a system of indirect or delegate voting or voting by mail, a resolution passed at least 75% of the votes cast in respect of the resolution; or

(d) an extraordinary resolution passed before January 5, 1978.

Generally, a special resolution must be put in writing prior to an annual general meeting or a special general meeting if the purpose is to alter the constitution or by-laws. Members should receive a copy of the changes by mail with their notice of meeting.

Note that 14 days' written notice is required informing members of the meeting and the wording of the resolution. If changes to both constitution and by-laws are planned, a separate resolution is required to alter the by-laws and to alter the constitution.

The only parts of the constitution that may be altered are:

- name of the society (with prior approval and reservation of the new name)

- purposes (providing any new purposes are also charitable purposes)

- any other statements in the constitution which are not designated as unalterable. However, once a statement is declared unalterable, it cannot then be deleted or changed.

Special resolutions must be filed with the Registrar, and do not come into effect until the Registrar receives and approves them. Exceptions are special resolutions that change the name of directors or remove a director; these come into effect immediately.

To file a special resolution, type out Form 10 (see Sample #31). Send two copies to the Registrar and keep one for your files.

The form must be signed by a director, the lawyer for the society, or another person authorized by the board or the general meeting.

(c) Change of registered address

The Registrar must know who to write to about the society and who is responsible for its affairs. If your society moves its office or if the secretary or other designated person whose address is registered either moves or resigns, you must notify the Registrar within 15 days of the change. Use Form 5 (see Sample #19 in chapter 8). Be sure to add your society's incorporation number to the upper right-hand corner of the notice.

(d) Notice of change of directors

If directors change (other than at an annual general meeting) use Form 7 (shown in Sample #32) and return it to the Registrar as soon as possible after the change is made.

b. ALBERTA

1. Ongoing requirements

(a) Seal

A corporate seal is optional, but the purchase of a seal from a rubber stamp company is advised. By-laws must state who has the use of a seal whether or not one is purchased.

(b) Books

You are required to keep minutes of meetings of the general membership and of the board of directors. Your by-laws say who is responsible for these records. They should be kept at the registered address of your society and organized in an orderly way — a three-ring binder is a good idea. Society members have a right to know where the books and other records are kept and to have access to them.

SAMPLE #31
SPECIAL RESOLUTION NOTICE (BRITISH COLUMBIA)

Province of British Columbia

Form 10
(Section 66 and 67)

Certificate of Incorporation No. __S-19056__

SOCIETY ACT

COPY OF RESOLUTION

The following is a copy of

☐ a special resolution* passed

☐ an ordinary resolution

☒ a directors' resolution

in accordance with the by-laws of the Society on the __14th__ day of __August__ , 19 _9-_ :

"RESOLVED

That directors may appoint committees and may delegate to such committees any but not all of their powers.

Dated the __21st__ day of __August__ , 19 _9-_ ."

Vulnerable Valley Society
(Name of Society)

by _Gloria Ochee_
(Signature)

President
(Relationship to Society)

* **Strike out words which do not apply.**

[Note— (a) No special resolution has effect until accepted by the Registrar of Companies.
　　　(b) Send, in duplicate, to the Registrar of Companies, 2nd Floor - 940 Blanshard Street, Victoria, B.C., V8W 3E6, together with applicable fee.]

(Note that no special resolution has effect until accepted by the Registrar of Companies.)

SAMPLE #32
NOTICE OF CHANGE OF DIRECTORS (BRITISH COLUMBIA)

Province of British Columbia

Ministry of Finance and Corporate Relations

REGISTRAR OF COMPANIES

CORPORATE AND PERSONAL PROPERTY REGISTRIES
940 BLANSHARD STREET
VICTORIA, BRITISH COLUMBIA
V8W 3E6

FORM 7

(Section 24)

———

SOCIETIES ACT

———

Certificate of Incorporation No. __S-19056__

NOTICE OF CHANGES IN DIRECTORS OTHER THAN AT AN ANNUAL GENERAL MEETING

The person(s) described as follows:

1. Became a director (or became directors) on the date(s) shown:

Full Name	*Resident Address(es)*	*Date*

John Alan Black, 246 Railway Ave., Anyville, B.C. VON 1C3, August 21, 199-

2. Ceased to be a director (or ceased to be directors) on the date(s) shown:

Full Name	*Date*

Janet Gabrielle Grey, RR#1, Rd., 7, Anyville, B.C., VON 1CO, August 21, 199-

Date

3. [List present directors] Are the directors as of__August 21, 199-__

Note — Full names and residential addresses are required for all directors listed in item 3.

Dated the ___21st___ day of ___August___ , 19 9-

__Vulnerable Valley Society__
(Name of Society)

by ___*Gloria Oche*___
(Signature)

__President__
(Relationship to Society)

(c) Annual general meeting

You are required to have at least one annual general meeting a year — usually set before the annual return is due and after the end of the fiscal year.

At the annual general meeting you must present a financial statement setting out income, disbursements, assets and liabilities. It must be audited and signed by the society's auditor.

(d) Annual filing

A Society Annual Return (Sample #33) must be submitted to the Corporate Registry each year. Note that failure to do so will result in the cancellation of your Society's registration. The form requires the full legal name of the society, the current official address, and the corporate access number from the top right hand corner of the certificate of incorporation. The date of incorporation is on the same certificate. Enter the year, month, and day that the information on the form covers. The attachments required are a listing of all officers and directors of the society including their name, mailing address, postal code, and the position in the society held by each person. Use full given names, not initials. The form must be dated and signed by one director with contact telephone numbers included. Enclose the $8 filing fee made out to the Provincial Treasurer. You can hand deliver the return to either of the addresses listed at the end of chapter 6 or mail it to:

Alberta Municipal Affairs
Registries
P.O. Box 1007, Station Main
Edmonton, AB T5J 2M1

(e) Register of members

The register of members is a list of all people who have been and currently are members of the society. Members must have access to this list, which is to be kept at the registered address of the society. A copy must be provided on request at a fee of no more than 25¢ for every 100 words copied.

Include in the register of members the following information:

- name and home address
- date of becoming member
- date of ceasing to be a member
- class of membership (if there are several classes)

2. Registering changes

(a) Changing objects

A special resolution of the general membership is required to change the objects or purposes of a society. A "special resolution" is defined in section 1(d) of the act as:

> (i) a resolution passed
>
>> (a) at a general meeting of which not less than 21 days' notice specifying the intention to propose the resolution has been duly given, and
>>
>> (b) by the vote of not less than 75 percent of those members who, if entitled to do so, vote in person or by proxy,
>
> (ii) a resolution proposed and passed as a special resolution at a general meeting of which not less than 21 days' notice has been given, if all the members entitled to attend and vote at the general meeting so agree, or
>
> (iii) a resolution consented to in writing by all the members who would have been entitled at a general meeting to vote on the resolution in person or, where proxies are permitted, by proxy.

The special resolution must then be registered with the Corporation Registry. Make sure the notice of special resolution is identified with your society name and registration number, and is dated and signed by a director of the society. Submit a request for Corporate Services and include the fee of $50 for Articles of Amendment.

Alberta

MUNICIPAL AFFAIRS
Registries

Societies Act
CCA-06.002

SOCIETY ANNUAL RETURN

IMPORTANT: An annual return and required attachments must be filed each year with the Registrar of Corporations. <u>Failure to do so will result in the cancellation of your Society's registration.</u>

1. SOCIETY NAME

2. ADDRESS OF REGISTERED OFFICE OF THE SOCIETY

N.B. If there has been a change in the address as listed, a Notice of Change of Address (Form 3) must be completed and filed with the Registrar of Corporations within fifteen days of the date of the change

3. CORPORATE ACCESS NUMBER

4. THE SOCIETY'S DATE OF INCORPORATION IS
_____ _____ _____
Year   Month   Day

5. THIS RETURN COVERS THE YEAR ENDING EFFECTIVE AS OF THAT DATE.
_____ _____ _____ , WITH THE INFORMATION PROVIDED
Year   Month   Day

THE FOLLOWING ATTACHMENTS MUST ACCOMPANY THIS RETURN:

a) A listing of all officers and directors with the name (surname, followed by given name), complete mailing address including postal code, and position held by each.

b) $8.00 filing fee

Please ensure that this return is dated and signed by a director or authorized officer of the society.

DATE	SIGNATURE	TELEPHONE NO. Bus. Res.	FILED (For dept. use only)

07/94   This form will be rejected if not properly completed

A notice of the alteration of the society's objectives will be published in the Registrar's Periodical at the expense of the society.

(b) Changing by-laws

By-law changes also require a special resolution at a members' general meeting. Thereafter, the change does not come into effect until the special resolution is registered at the Corporate Registry. When submitting your special resolution, identify it with your society's name and registration number, dated and signed by a director, and include a completed copy of the Request for Corporate Services form (see Sample #23).

(c) Changing registered address

You must notify the Registrar of any change of registered office within 15 days of the change. Send the Notice of Change of Address (see Sample #22), completing items 1, 2, 3, 4 or 5, and 6.

If your registered address is that of an officer or director who resigns, remember that a change of address notification must be submitted.

(d) Change of name, dissolution, and revival

A separate set of forms is available from the Corporate Registry for changing the name of a society (Form 4) or for dissolution of a society (Form 17).

It is also possible to revive a society that has been removed from the active register (Form 15.1).

c. SASKATCHEWAN

1. Ongoing requirements

(a) Annual general meeting

You are required to have a general meeting of all society members at least once a year.

At the annual general meeting, the directors are responsible for presenting a financial statement to the membership and for the appointment of an auditor (if required) by the members. Whether or not the financial statement must be audited depends on the amount of income the society receives. In excess of $100 000 per year, an audited statement must be submitted. Between $25 000 and $100 000 per year, a resolution must be passed with a decision to have an audit or to have a review conducted. Under $25 000, no audit or review is required, but a resolution regarding the decision must still be passed.

The financial statement shows assets, liabilities, revenue, and expenditures calculated to a date not more than three months before the date of the annual meeting.

Remember that you must submit a copy of your financial statement to the Director not less than 21 days before the annual general meeting of members of the society.

(b) Annual return

At the end of the fiscal year you will receive an annual return (Form 26) for completion prior to the date indicated on the form. List all directors' full given names with their current home address (see Sample #34). Return with the filing fee of $10 payable to the Minister of Finance to the address listed at the end of chapter 6.

2. Registering changes

During the course of the fiscal year, you are required to keep the Corporations Branch informed about the following matters:

(a) changes in your list of directors (use Notice of Directors, Form 6; see Sample #25)

(b) change of registered address (use Notice of Registered Office, Form 3; see Sample #26)

(c) any amendments to the articles of incorporation. A fee of $20 will be charged for each change (use Articles of Amendment, Form 4 shown in Sample #35).

Amendments are not effective until a certificate of amendment is returned to your society.

SAMPLE #34
ANNUAL RETURN (SASKATCHEWAN)

Saskatchewan Justice
Corporations Branch
1871 Smith Street
2nd Floor
Regina, Saskatchewan
S4P 3V7

The Non-profit Corporation Act
Annual Return (Saskatchewan Corporation)

Incorporating
Jurisdiction

Return due date   Y Y M M D D 9- 0903

By Due Date $ 10   Fees

After due date $

Payable to:
Minister of Finance

Corporation Name	**01**	Centretown Society for Exceptional Children Inc.

		Street, Hamlet, or Land Description	City, Town, Village, R.M., L.I.D., N.A.D.	Province	Postal Code
Registered Office Location	**02**	123 Field Street	Centretown	SK	S1A 2B3

Main Types of activities	**03**	Funding development of children, teaching, transportation, equipment
Mailing Agent	**04**	n/a

		Street, P.O. Box, or R.R. #	City/Province	Postal Code
Mailing Address	**05**	same as above		

Classes of Membership
If more than 6 classes use an attachment.

Class of membership	VOTE	Number of members	Class of membership	VOTE	Number of members	Class of membership	VOTE	Number of members
1	YES X / NO	38	2	YES / NO		3	YES / NO	
4	YES / NO		5	YES / NO		6	YES / NO	

Authorized No. of Directors   Fixed Number [ ]   or Min. [ ]   and Max. [ ]   Number

Directors:
If more than 10 Directors use an attachment.

		Name (Surname followed by first name and initial)	Office Held	Res-Can.
	06	John A. Brown	President	Yes
		Residential Address	City / Province	Postal Code
	07	123 Red Street	Centretown, SK	S1T 3L5
	08	Ivan M. Petit	Director	Yes
		Residential Address	City / Province	Postal Code
	09	49 High Street	Centretown, SK	S1T 2V3
	10	Joan Little	Vice President	Yes
		Residential Address	City / Province	Postal Code

Directors
(Continued on page 2 . . .)

	11	152 Back Street	Nearbytown, SK	S4T6V7

Form 26   Signature required on Page 2   Page 1 of 2

Annual Return

Corporation Name

Corporation No.

Directors: (continued)		Name (Surname followed by first name and initial)	Office Held	Res.-Can.
	12	Heinz L. Jung	Treasurer	Yes
		Residential Address	City / Province	Postal Code
	13	66 Rail Road	Centretown, SK	S7T 8V9
	14	Name (Surname followed by first name and initial)	Office Held	Res.-Can.
		Alice B. White	Secretary	Yes
		Residential Address	City / Province	Postal Code
	15	87 Falls Street	Centretown, SK	S9T 4R9
	18	Name (Surname followed by first name and initial)	Office Held	Res.-Can.
	19	Residential Address	City / Province	Postal Code
	20	Name (Surname followed by first name and initial)	Office Held	Res.-Can.
	21	Residential Address	City / Province	Postal Code
	22	Name (Surname followed by first name and initial)	Office Held	Res.-Can.
	23	Residential Address	City / Province	Postal Code
	24	Name (Surname followed by first name and initial)	Office Held	Res.-Can.
	25	Residential Address	City / Province	Postal Code
	26	Name (Surname followed by first name and initial)	Office Held	Res.-Can.
	27	Residential Address	City / Province	Postal Code

For use of Corporations Branch only

		Organization			Jurisdiction		Incorp. Date			Register Date			Fiscal Year End		
		Type	Group	Code	Name	X - P File No.	C C Y Y	M M	D D	C C Y Y	M M	D D	Y Y	M M	D D
28															

		Annual Return				Status				Continuance	Directors		Share	Sub
		Y Y	M M	D D	Fee	Code	Y Y	M M	D D	New Numbers	Filed	Min.	Max.	Holders	File
29															

I ____Alice B. White____ being ____Secretary____ of the corporation
Name of office (President, Director, Solicitor)

Do hereby certify that the foregoing information respecting the corporation is correct as of ___August 12___ 19_9-_.

Date ___August 15, 199-___ Signature _Alice white_

Government of Saskatchewan	**The Non-profit Corporations Act** **Articles of Amendment** (Section 159)	**Form 4**

1. **Name of corporation:** Centretown Society for Exceptional Children Inc.   **Corporation No.**   1789-01

2. **The articles of the corporation are amended as follows:**

   In Section B, article 5,

   > 5. A quorum of members is present at a meeting of members if a majority of voting persons is present in person.

   is changed to read:

   > 5. A quorum of members is present at a meeting of members if forty per cent of voting persons is present in person.

   See Schedule 1 attached (copy of authorized special resolution required under sections 156 and 158 of the Saskatchewan Non-Profit Corporations Act).

3. **The amendment has been duly authorized by the members pursuant to sections 156 and 158 of the Act on the** thirtieth **day of** June **, 19 9-.**

   OR

4. **The amendment has been duly authorized by the directors pursuant to section 87 of the Act on the** **day of** 19.

Date	Name	Description of office	Signature
30 June 198-	John A. Brown	President	*John A. Brown*

SAMPLE #35
(Back)

The Non-profit Corporations Act

Articles of Amendment

Form 4

Instructions

Format:

Documents required to be sent to the Director pursuant to the Act must conform to sections 2 to 5 of the regulations under the Act.

General:

(a)   Any change in the Articles of the corporation must be made in accordance with section 159 of the Act. If an amendment is to change a corporate name, the new name must comply with sections 10 to 12 of the Act and with sections 7 to 9 of the regulations. Where a new name has not been reserved a copy of Request for Name Search and Name Reservation (Form 27) should be attached.

(b)   Each amendment must correspond to the appropriate provisions of the Articles being amended, e.g. sections, subsections, clauses, etc.

(c)   A director or authorized officer shall sign the Articles.

(d)   Articles of Amendment shall be accompanied by a copy of the authorizing special resolution required under sections 156 and 158 of the Act. The resolution may be attached as a schedule in accordance with section 5 of the regulations.

Other Notices:

The Articles must be accompanied by Notice of Registered Office (Form 3) or Notice of Directors (Form 6) if there has been a change in registered office or a change of directors.

Completed documents, in duplicate, and the prescribed fee payable to the Minister of Fiance are to be sent to:

Director, Corporations Branch

1871 Smith St.

Regina, Saskatchewan

S4P 3V7

d. MANITOBA

1. Ongoing requirements

(a) Seal

If you choose to purchase a corporate seal, have a rubber stamp company prepare one, but make sure it states the name of the society correctly, including the legal definition, such as "Incorporated" or "Inc." Put a sample stamp in the margin of By-law (1), Article (2) (see Sample #27). Then use it to stamp by-laws and resolutions, minutes and contracts. These documents, however, are valid whether or not the seal is used.

(b) Books

You are required to keep a minute book for the society. This is generally a three-ring binder, and it includes your incorporation certificate, by-laws, and any resolutions of the society. Be sure to add not only the resolution but also the date it was passed. Also keep the first set of minutes of the society, all subsequent minutes, and the register of directors of the society (see chapter 4).

(c) Annual general meeting

You are required to have at least one annual general meeting of the full membership of your society giving all members at least 21 days' notice of the meeting. Afterwards, keep the minutes of this yearly meeting in the minute book.

If you decide not to appoint auditors for your annual financial statement, you must record a resolution of the general membership to this effect at the annual general meeting.

(d) Annual returns

You must file an income tax return within three months of the end of your society's fiscal year. You must also file an annual return to the Corporations Branch between March 31 and June 1 of each year (see Annual Return of Information, Sample #36). Your society legally exists only as long as this return is filed on time.

2. Registering changes

(a) Changing by-laws

If you amend by-laws, the resolution must be passed by an ordinary resolution of a majority vote of the general membership of the society — usually at the annual general meeting unless a special general meeting is called. Record the amendments on the Corporations Act Articles of Amendment (Form 10, shown in Sample #37) and submit to the Corporations Branch. Be sure to enter your corporation number, specify the relevant subsection that sets out how amendments will be authorized, and sign and date the document in the areas indicated. Type two copies of Form 10 and two copies of Request for Service (Form 19, shown in Sample #28).

(b) Changing directors

You must notify the Corporations Branch any time there is a change in directors. File any Notice of Change of Directors (Form 21, shown in Sample #38) within 15 days of the change.

Remember that there must be at least three directors at all times. If one resigns, a new director must be appointed on the same date.

(c) Changing registered address

File any Notice of Change of Registered Office (Form 20, shown in Sample #39). This address may change annually if the registered address is the home of an officer of the board (usually the secretary) and if the term of that officer is only one year.

Note that the registered office must be a street address and not a post office box number.

SAMPLE #36
ANNUAL RETURN OF INFORMATION (MANITOBA)

Manitoba

19

The Corporations Act
Loi sur les corporations

ANNUAL RETURN OF INFORMATION
RAPPORT ANNUEL DE RENSEIGNEMENTS

INSTRUCTIONS ON REVERSE / INSTRUCTIONS AU VERSO

RETURN TO:
Corporations Branch
1010 - 405 Broadway
Winnipeg, MB R3C 3L6
WITH THE FEE OF
$ 15

RETOURNER LA FORMULE À
Direction des corporations
405, Broadway - Bureau 1010
Winnipeg, (MB) R3C 3L6
ACCOMPAGNÉE D'UN DROIT DE:
$

Payable to Minister of Finance of Manitoba by :
Payable au ministre des Finances du Manitoba par:

A

1. CORPORATION NUMBER / NUMÉRO DE LA CORPORATION	2. JURISDICTION / RESSORT	3. DATE OF INCORPORATION OR AMALGAMATION / DATE DE CONSTITUTION EN CORPORATION OU DE FUSION	4. LAST ANNUAL RETURN / DERNIER RAPPORT ANNUEL
MA 400 200	St. Boniface	January 15, 199-	January 30, 199-

5. CORPORATION NAME & MAILING ADDRESS / DÉNOMINATION SOCIALE ET ADRESSE POSTALE

St. Boniface Folk Dance Society Ltd.

THE FOLLOWING INFORMATION IS ACCURATE FOR THE CORPORATION AS OF:
LES RENSEIGNEMENTS CI-DESSOUS REFLÈTENT FIDÈLEMENT LA SITUATION DE LA CORPORATION EN DATE DU:

B

1. MAIN TYPE OF BUSINESS (MAKE CHANGES IF NECESSARY) / ACTIVITÉ PRINCIPALE (PRIÈRE DE MODIFIER, SI NÉCESSAIRE)

To promote ethnic dance

2. REGISTERED OFFICE ADDRESS (IF CHANGED, INDICATE THE DATE OF CHANGE (DAY, MONTH, YEAR) AND THE NEW ADDRESS) /
ADRESSE DE BUREAU ENREGISTRÉ (EN CAS DE CHANGEMENT, PRIÈRE D'INDIQUER LA DATE DU CHANGEMENT (JOUR, MOIS, ANNÉE) ET LA NOUVELLE ADRESSE)

1160 Promenade Street, St. Boniface, Manitoba R1A 1X1

3. DIRECTORS (IF CHANGED, DATES MUST BE SHOWN (E.G. APPOINTED FEB. 1, 1990 OR CEASED DECEMBER 4, 1990) /
ADMINISTRATEURS (LA DATE DES CHANGEMENTS SURVENUS EN COURS D'ANNÉE DOIT ÊTRE INDIQUÉE (P.EX. FONCTION DÉBUT 1er FÉVR. 1990 OU FIN 4 DÉC. 1990)

FULL NAME / NOM AU COMPLET	RESIDENCE ADDRESS / ADRESSE RÉSIDENTIELLE	DATE OF CHANGE / DATE DES CHANGEMENTS
Denise Dansante	1879 Reel Road St. Boniface, MA R1A 2B3	No change
Henri En Pointe	Suite #2, 44 Swan Crt. St. Boniface, MA R1A 3C4	No change
Gilles Marie Pieds	1725 Red River Sq. St. Boniface, MA R1A 2B7	Ceased June 30, 199-
Virginia Reel	1160 Promenade St. St. Boniface, MA R1A 1X1	Appointed June 30, 199-
Suzette Crepe	42 Bistro Street St. Boniface, MA R1A 3G8	Appointed June 30, 199-

4. OFFICERS / DIRIGEANTS

FULL NAME / NOM AU COMPLET	RESIDENCE ADDRESS / ADRESSE RÉSIDENTIELLE	OFFICE HELD / POSTE
Denise Elle Dansante	1879 Reel Road St. Boniface, MA R1A 2B3	President
Virginia Reel	1160 Promenade St. St. Boniface, MA R1A 1X1	Secretary
Henri En Pointe	Suite #2, 44 Swan St. St. Boniface	Treasurer

C ONLY SHARE CORPORATIONS COMPLETE SECTION C / SEULES LES SOCIÉTÉS PAR ACTION REMPLISSENT LA SECTION C

1. ☐ SHARES ARE DISTRIBUTED TO THE PUBLIC / LES ACTIONS FONT L'OBJET D'UN PLACEMENT AUPRÈS DU PUBLIC

☐ SHARES ARE NOT DISTRIBUTED TO THE PUBLIC / LES ACTIONS NE FONT PAS L'OBJET D'UN PLACEMENT AUPRÈS DU PUBLIC

2. THE FOLLOWING HOLD 10% OR MORE OF ISSUED VOTING SHARES / ACTIONNAIRES DÉTENANT 10% OU PLUS DES ACTIONS EN CIRCULATION ASSORTIES DU DROIT DE VOTE

FULL NAME - NOM AU COMPLET	NO. & CLASS OF SHARES / CATÉGORIE ET NOMBRE D'ACTIONS	FULL NAME / NOM AU COMPLET	NO. & CLASS OF SHARES / CATÉGORIE ET NOMBRE D'ACTIONS
n/a			

D ATTORNEY FOR SERVICE / PROCURATION
FULL NAME AND ADDRESS OF INDIVIDUAL APPOINTED IN MANITOBA / NOM ET ADRESSE AU COMPLET DE LA PERSONNE NOMMÉE AU MANITOBA

n/a

E THE ABOVE INFORMATION IS CORRECT / LES RENSEIGNEMENTS FIGURANT CI-DESSUS SONTS EXACTS

CONTACT PERSON & PHONE NO. (8:30 4:30)
PERSONNE RESSOURCE ET N° DE TÉLÉPHONE (8 h 30 - 16 h 3

DATE January 30, 199-   SIGNATURE *Denise Dansante*   OFFICE HELD / POSTE President

MG 14269 (REV 12/92)

THIS FORM WILL BE REJECTED IF ALL APPLICABLE QUESTIONS ARE NOT ANSWERED
LE DEFAUT DE FOURNIR DES RÉPONSES COMPLÈTES À TOUTES LES QUESTIONS
APPLICABLE ENTRAINERA LE REJET DE CETTE FORMULE

SAMPLE #36
(Back)

WARNING
FAILURE TO FILE RETURNS FOR TWO YEARS RESULTS IN:
DISSOLUTION OF MANITOBA CORPORATIONS
OR
CANCELLATION OF REGISTRATION OF EXTRA-PROVINCIAL
AND FEDERAL CORPORATIONS.

INSTRUCTIONS
An Annual Return of Information must be filed every year.
It must state information as of the last day of the anniversary month of incorporation or amalgamation.(for example, a corporation incorporated January 5th, 1987, files a return as of January 31st every year.)
If the corporation has stopped doing business in Manitoba, call or write this office for information on the three ways to dissolve / cancel.

SECTION A (basic corporate information)
Section A states information on file in Manitoba. If anything has changed, contact this office for information on what forms and fees must be filed.

SECTION B (main type, registered office, directors, officers)
1 MAIN TYPE OF BUSINESS
—The type of business must be noted.
The Standard Industrial Code (SIC) can be noted, if it is known.
2. REGISTERED OFFICE
—Must be answered completely, including postal code.
—If the registered office has changed, the new registered office and the date of change MUST be noted.
—Manitoba corporations must keep their Registered Office in Manitoba.
—Manitoba corporations must have the Registered Office address identical to the mailing address.
3. DIRECTORS
—Full names and residence addresses (including postal codes) must be noted.
—If any directors have been appointed or ceased, the details of the change must be noted. (example : John Smith, 41 Sykes Blvd, Winnipeg, MB R0A OAO, appointed Jan 01/1991)
—Nonshare (nonprofit) corporations must have at least three directors. Share corporations must have at least one director.
—Attach a list if all the names can't fit on the return.
4. OFFICERS
—Full names and residence addresses (including postal codes) must be noted.
—If no officers have been appointed, write "none appointed".

SECTION C (share information)
(only share corporations complete this section)
1. Asks: does the corporation offer shares or securities to the public? To answer , check off the applicable box.
2. List the full name of the shareholders who hold 10 % or more of issued voting shares, and the number and class of shares they hold. Please indicate if none issued or if no shareholders qualify.
—Attach a list if all the names can't fit on the return.

SECTION D (attorney for service)
A Manitoba corporation with officers or directors living in the province does not have to appoint an attorney for service.
Write N/A.
Otherwise, an attorney for service is needed for :
—any Manitoba corporation without a resident director or officer
—any federal corporation which does not have both a resident director (officer) and a registered office in Manitoba.
—all other non-Manitoba corporations
An Attorney for Service must be appointed and Form #8 filed with this office. Please contact this office for more information.

SECTION E (signature)
Must be signed, in ink, by an officer or director (or agent given authority by the corporation). The office held by the signer must be shown.
Note : An agent must use the word AGENT to describe his/her office.

ANY QUESTIONS ?? CALL (204) 945-2955
HOURS : 8:30 - 4:30 , MONDAY TO FRIDAY

RETURN FEE AND WHITE COPY OF FORM TO :
1010-405 BROADWAY WINNIPEG MANITOBA R3C3L6

AVIS
LE DÉFAUT DE PRODUIRE DES RAPPORTS PENDANT DEUX ANNÉES
CONSÉCUTIVES ENTRAÎNE
LA DISSOLUTION DES CORPORATIONS MANITOBAINES
OU L'ANNULATION DE L'ENREGISTREMENT DES CORPORATIONS
EXTRA-PROVINCIALES OU FÉDÉRALES

INSTRUCTIONS
Un rapport annuel de renseignements doit être produit chaque année. Le rapport doit contenir des renseignements qui sont à jour à la fin du mois anniversaire de la constitution en corporation ou de la fusion (par exemple, une corporation constituée le 5 janvier 1987 doit produire un rapport fournissant des renseignements le 31 janvier de chaque année). Si la corporation a cessé de faire affaires au Manitoba, veuillez communiquer par téléphone ou par écrit avec la Direction des corporations pour obtenir des renseignements concernant les trois manières de dissoudre une corporation ou d'annuler son enregistrement.
SECTION A (renseignements de base concernant la corporation)
La section A énonce les renseignements contenus dans les dossiers de la Direction des corporations. En cas de changements, veuillez communiquer avec la Direction en vue d'obtenir des renseignements sur les formules qui doivent être produites et les droits qui doivent être payés.
SECTION B (activité principale, bureau enregistré, administrateurs, dirigeants)
1. ACTIVITÉ PRINCIPALE
—L'activité principale doit être indiquée.
Le code typé des industries (CTI) peut être indiqué, s'il est connu.
2. BUREAU ENREGISTRÉ
—L'adresse complète doit être indiquée, y compris le code postal.
—Si le bureau enregistré a changé d'adresse, la nouvelle adresse du bureau enregistré et la date du changement DOIVENT être indiquées.
—Le bureau enregistré des corporations manitobaines doit être situé au Manitoba.
- Dans le cas des corporations manitobaines, l'adresse postale et l'adresse du bureau enregistré doivent être identiques.
3. ADMINISTRATEURS
—Les noms et les adresses de domicile au complet (y compris les codes postaux) doivent être indiqués.
Si quelqu'un a commencé ou terminé ses fonctions, l'on doit fournir des détails à cet égard (par exemple : Jean Lapointe, 41, rue Aulneau, Winnipeg (MB) R0A OAO, fonctions commencées le 1er janv. 1991).
—Le conseil d'administration des corporations sans capital-actions (sans but lucratif) doit être constitué d'au moins trois administrateurs, celui des sociétés par actions, d'au moins un administrateur.
—Veuillez annexer une liste si vous ne pouvez faire figurer tous les noms sur le rapport.
4. DIRIGEANTS
—Les noms et les adresses de domicile au complet (y compris les codes postaux) doivent être indiqués.
—Si aucun dirigeant n'a été nommé, inscrivez <<aucune nomination>>

SECTON C (Renseignements concernant les actions)
(SEULES LES SOCIÉTÉS PAR ACTIONS REMPLISSENT LA PRÉSENTE SECTION.)
1) Est-ce que la société effectue un placement de valeurs mobilières auprès du public? Prière de cocher la case appropriée.
2) Indiquez le nom complet des actionnaires qui détiennent 10 % ou plus des actions en circulation assorties du droit de vote ainsi que le nombre et la catégorie des actions en cause. Veuillez indiquer s'il n'y a pas d'action en circulation ou s'il n'y a pas d'actionnaire dans cette situation.
—Veuillez annexer une liste si vous ne pouvez faire figurer tous les noms sur le rapport.

SECTION D (procuration)
Les corporations manitobaines dont certains administrateurs ou dirigeants habitent dans la province NE SONT PAS tenues de nommer un procureur aux fins de signification. Prière d'indiquer <<sans objet>>.
La nomination d'un procureur aux fins de signification est nécessaire dans les cas suivants :
—les corporations manitobaines dont aucun administrateur ou dirigeant n'habite dans la province;
—les corporations fédérales qui ne répondent pas simultanément aux deux conditions suivantes : i) un administrateur ou dirigeant qui habite au Manitoba et ii) un bureau enregistré situé au Manitoba;
—toutes les autres corporations non manitobaines.
Dans tous les cas où la nomination est obligatoire, la formule no 8 doit être déposée auprès de la Direction. Veuillez communiquer avec la Direction pour obtenir de plus amples renseignements.

SECTION E (signature)
Le rapport doit être signé à l'encre par un dirigeant ou un administrateur (ou un mandataire autorisé par la corporation). Le poste qu'occupe le signataire doit être indiqué.
Note : Le mandataire doit indiquer le mot <<mandataire>> pour décrire son poste.

POUR DE PLUS AMPLES RENSEIGNEMENTS, VEUILLEZ
COMMUNIQUER AVEC LA DIRECTION AU NUMÉRO (204) 945-2955,
DE 8 h 30 À 16 h 30, DU LUNDI AU VENDREDI.

ENVOYEZ LES DROITS EXIGIBLES ET L'EXEMPLAIRE BLANC AU :
405 BROADWAY, BUREAU 1010, WINNIPEG (MB) R3C 3L6

SAMPLE #37
ARTICLES OF AMENDMENT (MANITOBA)

MANITOBA

The Corporations Act/
Loi sur les corporations
**ARTICLES OF AMENDMENT/
CLAUSES MODIFICATRICES**

Corporation No.
N° de la corporation

1—Name of Corporation / Dénomination sociale	2—Corporation Number / N° de la corporation
St. Boniface Folk Dancing Society Inc.	MA 400 200

3— a) The amendment to the articles has been authorized by: / La modification apportée aux statuts a été autorisée par résolution:

directors	[X]	administrateurs
shareholders	[ ]	actionnaires
members	[ ]	membres

b) pursuant to Section   6(f)
    conformément à l'article

c) and the articles are amended as follows: / et les statuts de la corporation sont modifiés de la façon suivante:

All Directors of the corporation shall hold office for two years or
until their successors are elected or appointed in their stead.

Date: / Date:	Signature: / Signature:	Description of Office: / Description du poste:
June 10, 199-	*Denise DanGante*	President

Instructions: Specify the relevant subsection pursuant to which the amendment is authorized, and the changes which are being made. Specify whether amendment authorized by directors, shareholders or members. The resolution authorizing the amendment is not required to be attached hereto.

Directives :   Énoncer chacune des modifications apportées aux statuts, en mentionnant la disposition de la loi qui l'autorise. Indiquer également s'il s'agit d'une modification adoptée par résolution des administrateurs ou par résolution des actionnaires ou membres. Il n'est pas nécessaire de fournir une copie de cette résolution.

MG 1646 (Rev. 03/91)   FORM 10 / FORMULE 10

SAMPLE #38
NOTICE OF CHANGE OF DIRECTORS (MANITOBA)

The Corporations Act/
Loi sur les corporations
**NOTICE OF CHANGE OF DIRECTORS/
AVIS DE CHANGEMENT DES ADMINISTRATEURS**

Manitoba

St. Boniface Folk Dancing Society Inc.

NAME OF CORPORATION/DÉNOMINATION DE LA CORPORATION

1879 Reel Road

St. Boniface, Manitoba   R1A 2B3

Address. Please include Postal Code.
Adresse. Inclure le code postal.

Notice is hereby given that on

Avis est par les présentes donné que le

June 30, 199-
(Date)

the following persons ceased to be directors of the above corporation:
les personnes suivantes ont cessé d'être administratrices de la corporation mentionnée ci-dessus :

FULL NAME/NOM COMPLET	ADDRESS/ADRESSE	OCCUPATION/PROFESSION
Gilles Marie Pieds	1725 Red River Square St. Boniface, Manitoba R1A 2B7	Dance Instructor

Notice is also given that on

Avis est également donné que le

June 30, 199-
(Date)

the following persons became directors of the corporation:
les personnes suivantes sont devenues administratrices de la corporation mentionnée ci-dessus :

FULL NAME/NOM COMPLET	ADDRESS/ADRESSE	OCCUPATION/PROFESSION
Virginia Reel	1160 Promenade St. St. Boniface, Manitoba R1A 1X1	Historian

Dated/
Fait le   June 30, 199-

Denise Ansara
(Signature of Officer of the Corporation/
Signature du dirigeant de la corporation)

Corporation Number /
Numéro de la corporation   MA 400 200

MG 1664 (Rev. 02/90)

FORM 21 / FORMULE 21

142

SAMPLE #39
NOTICE OF CHANGE OF REGISTERED OFFICE (MANITOBA)

Manitoba

The Corporations Act/
Loi sur les corporations
**NOTICE OF CHANGE OF REGISTERED OFFICE/
AVIS DE CHANGEMENT DU LIEU DU BUREAU ENREGISTRÉ**

St. Boniface Folk Dancing Society Inc.

NAME OF CORPORATION/DÉNOMINATION DE LA CORPORATIC

1160 Promendae St.

Address. Please include Postal Code.
Adresse. Inclure le code postal.

St. Boniface, Manitoba R1A 1X1

Notice is hereby given that on

Avis est par les présentes donné que depuis   July 1, 199-
                                                    (Date)

the location/address of the registered office of the above corporation was changed to:
le nouveau lieu/la nouvelle adresse du bureau enregistré de la corporation mentionnée ci-dessus est :

1160 Promenade St., St. Boniface, Manitoba R1A 1X1
(Full Address Giving Street Number, and if Multi-Office Building, Give Room Number, and Postal Code)
(Adresse complète : donner le n° de rue, et le n° du local dans le cas d'un immeuble à bureaux, ainsi que le code postal)

Dated/   July 1, 199-
Fait le

(Signature of Officer of the Corporation/
Signature du dirigeant de la corporation)

Corporation Number/   MA400200
Numéro de la corporation

MG 1663 (Rev. 02/90)

FORM 20 / FORMULE 20

143

e. ONTARIO

1. Ongoing requirements

(a) Seal

A corporate seal is required in Ontario. Have an inexpensive rubber stamp produced or use an impression seal.

(b) Initial notice of directors and officers

Generally, the applicants for incorporation are the first directors of a corporation. They elect a president and any other officers from among themselves. Once the executive officers are in place, complete Initial Notice/Notice of Change Form 1 Schedule A (see Sample #40) within 60 days of the date of incorporation. Note that this means your first general meeting must be held within this period.

When completing Form 1 and Schedule A, write in block capitals or type. Complete all sections; if not applicable, state so. Do not leave items blank.

If there are changes in directors, again complete Form 1 and Schedule A and return within 15 days of the change taking place. Use as many Schedule A forms as required to list all directors.

(c) Records and financial statements

A society is required to keep minutes of proceedings at all general meetings and meetings of the board of directors and executive committee. They must also keep available a copy of letters patent and supplementary letters patent, all by-laws and special resolutions, register of members, and register of directors. Books of accounts are also required and an auditor must be appointed at each annual meeting.

(d) Annual general meeting

The act requires that an annual general meeting of members be held within 18 months after incorporation. Subsequent meetings must be held at least every 15 months. At each annual general meeting, directors will be elected.

2. Registering changes

(a) Supplementary letters patent

Changes may be made to the founding documents of a society via supplementary letters patent for the following purposes:

(a) extending, limiting, or otherwise varying the society's objects or purposes

(b) changing the name of the society once a new name has been searched and approved

(c) varying any provision in the letters patent on subsequent supplementary letters patent

(d) providing any new matter which may be included under the letters patent

(e) converting to a company

(f) converting to a corporation with or without share capital

Varying objects or adding new items to the letters patent must be authorized by a special resolution. Converting to a company or to a corporation requires a resolution of the board of directors, supported in writing by 100% of the members, or at least 95% of members subject to requirements in the act, section 131(3) and (4).

An application (Form 3, shown in Sample #41) must be made within six months of confirmation for any of the above changes.

If application is made to change the name of a society, a statement must be made that the society is not insolvent. In other words, a society cannot escape a major deficit by simply changing its name.

The fee for supplementary letters patent is $155. Make cheques or money orders payable to the Minister of Finance. Be sure to remember that the name of the society must be entered on the face of every cheque.

(b) Changing directors

Use Form 1, and Schedule A, (see Sample #40) to notify the Companies Branch of changes in the directors and officers after each annual general meeting. The completed form should be received by the Companies Branch within 15 days after the change takes place. There is no fee for filing this form.

(c) Changing number of directors

A special resolution is required to change the number of directors and must be filed with the ministry within 15 days of the meeting confirming the resolution (use Form 1, shown in Sample #40). Attach a separate page (plain white paper about 8½" x 11" with a left margin of 1¼") that acts as a certified copy of the resolution. The resolution might read:

**NOTICE OF SPECIAL RESOLUTION
CHANGING THE NUMBER
OF DIRECTORS**

Re: [*Name of corporation*]
Ontario corporation no. _____

Notice is hereby given that the number of directors of [*name of corporation*] was [*increased*][*decreased*] from _____ to _____ by a special resolution which was confirmed by the members of the corporation on the _____ day of _____ 19___.

Dated this _____ day of _____ 19___.

Secretary:_____
[*signature*]

This notice of special resolution must be signed by an officer or director of the corporation. The resolution must be filed with the Companies Branch and mailed for publication direct to:

Ontario Gazette
Queen's Printer
880 Bay Street
5th Floor
Toronto, ON M7A 1N8

(d) Requesting permission to remove records from head office

Complete two copies of Form 5 (see Sample #42) if a general meeting of the corporation decides to keep its records somewhere other than the address indicated in the Application for Incorporation filed earlier (see Sample #15).

A change in president or, particularly, treasurer may make such a notice necessary if records are kept at a private home.

The fee for an order permitting change in location of records is $130. However, once Form 5 is submitted, you may also keep the records "at such other address within the same locale as may be determined by the board of directors," providing a notice is filed with the Companies Branch within ten days of the change in location.

Form 5 requires that you give a reason for the application and that you state the exact date of the general meeting at which the decision was made.

The point is that both members and the Companies Branch must know exactly where the corporation's records are kept at any given time.

(e) Changing head office address

If a change is to a new location within the same municipality, submit Form 1 (see Sample #40).

If the change is to another municipality, submit Form 1 along with a certified (which means signed) notice of special resolution approving the change. The fee for filing this form is $130. The resolution should be typed on plain white paper approximately 8½" x 11" with a 1¼" left margin. It should be signed by an officer or director of the corporation.

The special resolution must be filed and published in the *Ontario Gazette* within 15 days of the special resolution being confirmed by the corporation membership.

Such a special resolution might read:

NOTICE OF SPECIAL RESOLUTION CHANGING THE LOCATION OF THE HEAD OFFICE

RE: [*Name of corporation*]
Ontario corporation no.:_____

Notice is hereby given that the location of the head office of [*name of corporation*] was changed from [*name of municipality*] to [*name of municipality*] by special resolution which was confirmed by the members of the corporation on the _____ day of _____, 19____.

Dated this _____ day of _____ 19___.

Secretary:_____
          [*signature*]

(f) Other changes

Forms are also available to apply for:

(a) an order rescinding the order permitting removal of records from head office (Form 8)

(b) the surrender of charter and termination of corporate existence (Form 9)

(c) the revival of a corporation within two years of the date of dissolution (Form 10)

(d) Letters Patent of Amalgamation (Form 11)

(g) Annual Return

You will be mailed a form called "Special Notice" on about the anniversary date of incorporation. This is a yearly update in addition to the other notices of change you have submitted. Send the return to the Companies Branch with a $25 filing fee made out to the Minister of Finance.

SAMPLE #40
INITIAL NOTICE/NOTICE OF CHANGE (ONTARIO)

Ministry of Consumer and Commercial Relations / Ministère de la Consommation et du Commerce
Ontario

Companies Branch
393 University Ave Suite 200
Toronto ON M5G 2M2

Direction des compagnies
393 ave University Bureau 200
Toronto ON M5G 2M2

For Ministry Use Only / À l'usage du ministère seulement
Page/Page 1 of/de _____

Form 1 - Ontario Corporation/
Formule 1 - Personnes morales en Ontario

Initial Notice/Notice of Change/
Avis Initial/Avis de modification
Corporations Information Act/Loi sur les
renseignements exigés des personnes morales

All information must be typewritten in block capital letters using black ink in 10 or 12 pitch.
Tous les renseignements doivent être dactylographiés en caractères d'imprimerie à l'encre noire, en 10 ou 12 points.

1. Business Corporations/Société par actions — Initial Notice/Avis initial / Notice of Change/Avis de modification
   Not-For-Profit Corporation/Personne morale sans but lucratif

For Ministry Use Only À l'usage du ministère seulement	2. Ontario Corporation Number Numéro matricule de la personne morale en Ontario	3. Offering/ Appel à l'épargne Yes/Oui No/Non	4. Date of Incorporation or Amalgamation/ Date de constitution ou fusion
I	8-8884	n/a	Year/Année 199- Month/Mois 03 Day/Jour 31

For Ministry Use Only / À l'usage du ministère seulement

5. Corporation Name Including Punctuation/Raison sociale de la personne morale, y compris la ponctuation

Renaissance Transition House Corporation

6. Address of Registered or Head Office/Adresse du siège social

c/o / attn

Street Number/Numéro civique: 13579 Street Name/Nom de la rue: New Road Suite/Bureau:

Street Name (cont'd)/Nom de la rue (suite)

City/Town/Ville: Kent   ONTARIO, CANADA

Postal Code/Code postal: N3A 0Y0

For Ministry Use Only/ À l'usage du ministère seulement

7. Principal Place of Business in Ontario/Adresse du bureau d'affaire principal en Ontario

[X] Same as Registered or Head Office/ Même que celle du siège social

[ ] Not Applicable/ Ne s'applique pas

Street Number/Numéro civique

Street Name/Nom de la rue

Street Name (cont'd)/Nom de la rue (suite)   Suite/Bureau

City/Town/Ville   ONTARIO, CANADA

Postal Code/Code postal

8. Activity Classification Code/Code de classification des activités

A B C D E F G H I J K L M O P Q R

9. Language of Preference/Langue préférée

English - Anglais [X]   French - Français [ ]   None of the Above Aucun de ces choix [X] [X]

10. Information on Directors/Officers must be completed on Schedule A. If additional space is required, photocopy Schedule A./Renseignements relatifs aux administrateurs/dirigeants doivent être inscrits à l'annexe A. Si vous avez besoin de plus d'espace, photocopiez l'annexe A.

Number of Schedule A(s) submitted/Nombre d'annexes A présentées _____ (At least one Schedule A must be submitted/Au moins une annexe A doit être présentée)

11. I, Je soussigné (Type name in full/Inscrire les noms et prénoms en caractère d'imprimerie)

Olive M. Here

certify that the information set out herein, is true and correct.
Atteste que les renseignements précités sont véridiques et exacts.

Signature: Olive M. Here

Check appropriate box
Cocher la case pertinente

D) [X] Director/Administrateur

O) [ ] Officer /Dirigeant

P) [ ] Other individual having knowledge of the affairs of the Corporation/Autre personne ayant connaissance des activités de la personne morale

NOTE/REMARQUE: Sections 13 & 14 of the Corporations Information Act provide penalties for making false or misleading statements or omissions. Les articles 13 & 14 de la Loi sur les renseignements exigés des personnes morales prévoient des peines en cas de déclaration fausse ou trompeuse, ou d'omission.

FOR MINISTRY USE ONLY À L'USAGE DU MINISTÈRE SEULEMENT [ ] See Deficiency Letter enclosed Voir l'avis d'irrégularité ci-joint

SAMPLE #40
(Back)

Form 1 - Ontario Corporation/Formule 1 - Personnes morales en Ontario
Schedule A/Annexe A

All information must be typewritten in block capital letters using black ink in 10 or 12 pitch.
Tous les renseignements doivent être dactylographiés en caractères d'imprimerie à l'encre noire, en 10 ou 12 points.

For Ministry Use Only
À l'usage du ministère seulement
Page/Page _____ of/de _____

For Ministry Use Only À l'usage du ministère seulement	Ontario Corporation Number Numéro matricule de la personne morale en Ontario	Date of Incorporation or Amalgamation Date de constitution ou fusion
I	8-8884	Year/Année 199- Month/Mois 03 Day/Jour 31

For Ministry Use Only
À l'usage du ministère seulement

DIRECTOR / OFFICER INFORMATION - RENSEIGNEMENTS RELATIFS AUX ADMINISTRATEURS/DIRIGEANTS

Full Name and Residential Address/Nom et adresse personnelle au complet

Last Name/Nom de famille	First Name/Prénom	Middle Names/Autres prénoms
Again	Troy	L.

Street Number/Numéro civique: 49

Street Name/Nom de la rue: Rehab Avenue

Street Name (cont'd)/Nom de la rue (suite): ____ Suite/Bureau: ____

City/Town/Ville: Kent

Province, State/Province, État	Country/Pays	Postal Code/Code postal
Ontario	Canada	N3A 0Y0

Director Information/Renseignements relatifs aux administrateurs

Resident Canadian/ Résident canadien: Yes YES/OUI [ ] NO/NON
(Resident Canadian applies to directors of business corporations only.)/
(Résident canadien ne s'applique qu'aux administrateurs de personnes morales à but lucratif)

Date Elected/ Date d'élection: Year/Année 199- Month/Mois 06 Day/Jour 30
Date Ceased/ Date de cessation: Year/Année 199- Month/Mois 11 Day/Jour 01

Officer Information/Renseignements relatifs aux dirigeants

	PRESIDENT/PRÉSIDENT Year/Année Month/Mois Day/Jour	SECRETARY/SECRÉTAIRE Year/Année Month/Mois Day/Jour	TREASURER/TRÉSORIER Year/Année Month/Mois Day/Jour	GENERAL MANAGER/ DIRECTEUR GÉNÉRAL Year/Année Month/Mois Day/Jour	OTHER/AUTRE Year/Année Month/Mois Day/Jour
Date Appointed/ Date de nomination	19	19	199- 06 03	19	19
Date Ceased/ Date de cessation	19	19	199- 11 01	19	19

DIRECTOR / OFFICER INFORMATION - RENSEIGNEMENTS RELATIFS AUX ADMINISTRATEURS/DIRIGEANTS

Full Name and Residential Address/Nom et adresse personnelle au complet

Last Name/Nom de famille	First Name/Prénom	Middle Names/Autres prénoms
Hopeful	Gloria	R.

Street Number/Numéro civique: 261

Street Name/Nom de la rue: Sunshine Street

Street Name (cont'd)/Nom de la rue (suite): ____ Suite/Bureau: ____

City/Town/Ville: Kent

Province, State/Province, État	Country/Pays	Postal Code/Code postal
Ontario	Canada	N3A 1H3

Director Information/Renseignements relatifs aux administrateurs

Resident Canadian/ Résident canadien: Yes YES/OUI [ ] NO/NON
(Resident Canadian applies to directors of business corporations only.)/
(Résident canadien ne s'applique qu'aux administrateurs de personnes morales à but lucratif)

Date Elected/ Date d'élection: Year/Année 199- Month/mois 11 Day/Jour 01
Date Ceased/ Date de cessation: Year/Année 19

Officer Information/Renseignements relatifs aux dirigeants

	PRESIDENT/PRÉSIDENT Year/Année Month/Mois Day/Jour	SECRETARY/SECRÉTAIRE Year/Année Month/Mois Day/Jour	TREASURER/TRÉSORIER Year/Année Month/Mois Day/Jour	GENERAL MANAGER/ DIRECTEUR GÉNÉRAL Year/Année Month/Mois Day/Jour	OTHER/AUTRE Year/Année Month/Mois Day/Jour
Date Appointed/ Date de nomination	19	19	199- 11 01	19	19
Date Ceased/ Date de cessation	19	19	19	19	19

For Ministry Use Only
À l'usage du ministère seulement

Initials/Paraphes
LI ____ QA ____
DE ____ VER ____

148

SAMPLE #41
APPLICATION FOR SUPPLEMENTARY LETTERS PATENT (ONTARIO)

This space is for
Ministry Use Only
Espace réservé à l'usage
exclusif du ministère

Insert Ontario Corporation Number
Inserer le numéro de la personne morale
en Ontario

1.

Form 3
Corporations
Act

Formule 3
Loi sur les
personnes
morales

APPLICATION FOR SUPPLEMENTARY LETTERS PATENT
REQUETE EN VUE D'OBTENIR DES LETTRES PATENTES SUPPLÉMENTAIRES

1. Name of the applicant corporation / Dénomination sociale de la personne morale requérante :

R	E	N	A	I	S	S	A	N	C	E		T	R	A	N	S	I	T	I	O	N		H	O	U	S	E					
C	O	R	P	O	R	A	T	I	O	N																						

2. The name of the corporation is changed to (if applicable):   La dénomination sociale de la personne morale devient (le cas échéant) :

N	/	A																														

3. Date of incorporation/amalgamation:
    Date de constitution ou de fusion: <u>31</u>   <u>March</u>   <u>199-</u>
    　　　　　　　　　　　　　　　　　　　　(day/jour)　　month/mois　　　year/année)

4. The resolution authorizing this application was confirmed by the shareholders/members of the corporation on
    La résolution autorisant la présente requête a été ratifiée par les actionnaires ou membres de la personne morale
    le :

    　　　<u>30</u>　　　　<u>June</u>　　　<u>199-</u>
    　　(day/jour)　　month/mois　　year/année)

    under section 34 0r 131 of the Corporations Act.
    aux termes de l'article 34 ou 131 de la Loi sur les personnes morales.

5. The corporation applies for the issue of supplementary letters patent to provide as follows:
    La personne morale demande la délivrance de lettres patentes supplémentaires qui prévoient ce qui suit:

07108(04/94)

149

SAMPLE #41 — Continued

2.

5. (cont.)(suite)

In section 3,
    The affairs of the corporation shall be managed by a board of three
    directors.

is changed to read,
    The affairs of the corporation shall be managed by a board of
    five directors.

This application is executed in duplicate.
La présente requête est faite en double exemplaire.

Renaissance Transition House Corporation
(Name of corporation/Dénomination sociale de la personne morale)

By:/Par: _____ President
       (Signature)   (Description of Office)
       (Signature)   (Fonction)

_____ Secretary
(Signature)   (Description of Office)
(Signature)   (Fonction)

(corporate seal)
(sceau de la
personne morale)

07108(04/94)

150

SAMPLE #42
APPLICATION FOR CHANGE IN LOCATION OF RECORDS (ONTARIO)

Insert Ontario Corporation Number
in space below
Inserer le numéro de la personne morale
en Ontario   1.

Form 5
Corporations
Act

Formule 5
Loi sur les
personnes
morales

**APPLICATION FOR AN ORDER PERMITTING REMOVAL OF RECORDS FROM HEAD OFFICE
DEMANDE EN VUE D'OBTENIR UN ARRÊTÉ AUTORISANT LE RETRAIT
DE DOCUMENTS DU SIEGE SOCIAL**

1. Name of the applicant corporation/Dénomination sociale de la personne morale qui fait la demande :

| R | E | N | A | I | S | S | A | N | C | E | | T | R | A | N | S | I | T | I | O | N | | H | O | U | S | E | | | |
| C | O | R | P | O | R | A | T | I | O | N | | | | | | | | | | | | | | | | | | | | |

2. Date of incorporation/amalgamation:
   Date de la constitution ou de la fusion:

   31   March   199-
   (day/jour)   month/mois   year/année)

3. The corporation is not in default in filing notices required under the **Corporations Information Act** and returns.

   La personne morale n'a pas omis de déposer les avis et déclaration exigés par la **Loi sur les renseignements exigés des personnes morales.**

4. It is requested that an order under subsection 304(3) of the **Corporations Act** be made permitting the corporation to remove the records mentioned in subsection 304(1) of the Act from its head office and to keep them at the following address.

   Est demandée la prise d'un arrêté en vertu du paragraphe 304(3) de la **Loi sur les personnes morales** autorisant la personne morale à retirer de son siège social les documents visés au paragraphe 304(1) de cette loi et à les conserver à l'adresse suivante :

   19702 Fresh Street
   Kent, Ontario
   N3A 1Y8

   or at such other address within the same local as may be determined by the board of directors of the corporation by resolution, a notice of which shall be filed, within 10 days after it has been passed, with the Minister.
   ou à toute autre adresse dans la même localité que peut fixer le conseil d'administration de la personne morale par résolution, avis de laquelle est déposé auprès du ministre dans les dix jours de son adoption.

5. The necessity therefor is as follows / La présente demande se fonde sur les motifs suivants :

   Records moved from address of secretarty to address of president.

07087(03/94)

151

SAMPLE #42 — Continued

2.

6. This application has been duly authorized/La présente demande a été dûment autorisée :
   (a) By a resolution approved by a majority of the votes cast at a general meeting of the shareholders/members of the corporation duly called for that purpose and held on

   Par une résolution approuvée par la majorité des voix exprimé à une assemblée générale des actionnaires ou membres de la personne morale dûment convoquée à cette fin et tenue le

   <u>30   June   199-</u>
   (day/jour)   (month/mois)   (year/année)

   or/ou
   (b) By the consent in writing of all the shareholders/members of the corporation entitled to vote at such meeting.
   Par le consentement écrit de tous les actionnaires ou membres de la personne morale ayant droit de vote à pareille assemblée.

7. The corporation hereby acknowledges that it will be a condition of the order that:
   La personne morale reconnaît que l'arrêté sera assujetti aux conditions suivantes :
   (a) If requested by the Minister, the corporation will return forthwith to its head officer or some other place in Ontario designated by the Minister, such of the records as may be removed.
   À la demande du ministre, rapportera sans délai à son siège social ou à tel autre endroit en Ontario désigné par le ministre, les documents qui ont pu en être retirés.
   (b) Such records will be open for examination at the head office of the corporation or some other place in Ontario designated by the Minister, by any person who is entitled to examine them and who has applied to the Minister for such examination.
   Ces documents pourront être consultés au siège social de la personne morale, ou à tel autre endroit en Ontario désigné par le ministre, par toute personne qui a le droit de les consulter et qui en a fait la demande au ministre.

This application is executed in duplicate.
La présente demande est faite en double exemplaire.

Renaissance Transition House Corporation
(Name of corporation/Dénomination sociale de la personne morale)

By/Par: _Oave M. Hill_   President
(Signature)   (Description of Office)
(Signature)   (Fonction)

Chestly Short-Stay   Secretary
(Signature)   (Description of Office)
(Signature)   (Fonction)

(corporate seal)
(sceau de la personne morale)

07087(03/94)

152

10
FEDERAL INCORPORATION

There are some circumstances under which you may choose to register your organization under federal legislation. If you plan to expand from a local or provincial base of membership and activity to a national base, or if you are establishing a national group to begin with, you will incorporate under the federal Canada Corporations Act, Part II.

You will then be able to set up the registered office of your new society anywhere in Canada. Generally, federal incorporation fees are higher than those for provincial societies or corporations.

a. OBTAINING INFORMATION

A client information kit on federal incorporation is available from the Department of Industry. It contains a sample application, model by-laws, a policy summary, copies of documents, and so on. The kit also contains a detailed three-page checklist to use prior to filing.

You may obtain the kit at regional or district offices of the Department of Industry, by mail, telephone, or fax, or from the head office:

Corporations Directorate
Department of Industry
9th Floor
Journal Tower South
365 Laurier Avenue West
Ottawa, ON
K1A 0C8
Tel: (613) 941-9042
Fax: (613) 941-0601

This office is open from 8:30 a.m. to 4:30 p.m. weekdays, eastern standard time. If you need advice or have questions about the kit, they will be able to help you. They can also give you the address and telephone number of the regional or district office nearest you.

To check on the status of an application or to call regarding a rejected application, call (613) 941-4550.

You can obtain a copy of the Canada Corporations Act, Part II (incorporation of a corporation without share capital) by calling (613) 941-9537 or by fax (613) 941-9047.

b. NAME SEARCH AND NAME RESERVATION

Applications for incorporation must be accompanied by a Canada-based NUANS (New Upgraded Automated Name Search) system search report not more than 90 days old.

This report, prepared for a fee (at least $70 paid in advance) by a private search house, will state that the name chosen for your society (corporation) is not already in use anywhere in Canada and will not be confused with the name of any other society or corporation. Name search takes one to three days. Alternatively, send a filing fee of $15 for each name searched and the Corporations Directorate will conduct the NUANS search on your behalf. A bilingual name normally requires two searches. Name search by the Directorate takes one to three days, but faster service is available by fax.

If approved by the Director of Companies, the proposed name of your organization will be reserved for 90 days. Within this time, you should complete and submit the other required documents listed below.

c. APPLICATION AND BY-LAWS

The application form (Sample #43) and sample by-laws (Sample #44) are contained in the kit. The by-laws include the minimum requirements under the act. Other provisions or by-laws may be added if desired. Note the disclaimer that accompanies the model by-laws. It makes clear that the model bylaws contain provisions not specifically dealt with in the Canada Corporations Act. While the model by-laws are acceptable as written for filing with the Corporations Directorate, they may be subject to a validity ruling if they were reviewed by a court.

Note that the final page of the application is an affirmation of the truth and completeness of the application. It must be witnessed (signed) by a commissioner of oaths or notary public.

Your submission to the Corporations Directorate must include the following:

(a) completed application (two originals; see Sample #43).

(b) an affidavit or statutory declaration of one of the applicants, sworn before a commissioner for taking oaths, stating that the details of the application are true, (see Sample #43).

(c) filing fee of $200 payable to the Receiver General for Canada.

(d) Canada-based NUANS name search report not more than 90 days old of the proposed name (two NUANS reports for a bilingual name).

(e) one copy of the proposed by-laws of the new corporation (see Sample #44). These will not be returned to you but are kept on file at the Directorate.

(f) covering letter in the prescribed format specifying the street address of the head office of the new corporation (see Sample #46).

You may file these documents at a regional or district office, but expect an additional ten days for their transferal to the head office. If the application is in order, letters patent (your official document of incorporation) will be returned within two weeks along with one of the original applications, stamped with the date of receipt at the Directorate. For the format of the Letters Patent, see Sample #47.

Applications received by mail will be processed in ten days; applications received by courier will be processed in three days. If your documents are not approved for incorporation, you will receive a form letter and the original pages to be corrected. Your date of application remains the same.

d. STAYING INCORPORATED

You are required under the act to keep minute books and financial records. The Director of Companies should be notified in writing of any change of address of your registered office as soon as possible. Any change in directors will be indicated in the annual summary (Form 3) that your society is required to submit yearly (see Sample #45).

The annual summary will be mailed to you on the anniversary date of incorporation and must be returned within 60 days of that date accompanied by a fee of $50.

Any change in the number of directors or in the by-laws must be filed with the Director of Companies by means of supplementary letters patent. A guide describing how to make application for changes in letters patent is available free (see section **a.** at the beginning of this chapter for the address and phone number).

Supplementary letters patent cost $50. Immediate receipt of forms by fax is available at Telephone Flashfax: (613) 941-0200. The forms related to the Canada Corporations Act Part II are available on the Flashfax menu, code 105. Record your own fax number including the area code. Once you have received the menu, you can order the forms you require. The supplementary letters patent is code 412; the notice of change of directors is code 506.

SAMPLE #43
APPLICATION FOR FEDERAL INCORPORATION

APPLICATION FOR INCORPORATION OF A CORPORATION WITHOUT SHARE CAPITAL UNDER PART II OF THE CANADA CORPORATIONS ACT

To the Minister of Consumer and Corporate Affairs of Canada.

I

The undersigned hereby apply to the Minister of Consumer and Corporate Affairs for the grant of a charter by letters patent under the provisions of Part II of the Canada Corporations Act constituting the undersigned, and such others as may become members of the Corporation thereby created, a body corporate and politic under the name of

XYZ CORPORATION - LA CORPORATION XYZ

The undersigned have satisfied themselves and are assured that the proposed name under which incorporation is sought is not the same or similar to the name under which any other company, society, association or firm, in existence is carrying on business in Canada or is incorporated under the laws of Canada or any province thereof or so nearly resembles the same as to be calculated to deceive (* and, where required by the circumstances: *except that of _____ which has signified its consent to the use of the said name*) and that it is not a name which is otherwise on public grounds objectionable.

II

The applicants are individuals of the full age of eighteen years with power under law to contract. The name, the address and the occupation of each of the applicants are as follows:

JOHN DOE,
100 Dominic Street, Bytown, Ontario K1A 0C9 - Barrister

JAMES SMITH,
200 Dominic Street, Bytown, Ontario K1A 0C9 - Office Manager

ANN JONES,
300 Dominic Street, Bytown, Ontario K1A OC9 - Secretary

The said **JOHN DOE, JAMES SMITH** and **ANN JONES** will be the first directors of the Corporation.

III

The objects of the Corporation are:

(The objects should be set forth in the infinitive form, in general terms and be as brief as possible; they should also be compatible with the type of business implied by any descriptive word which may form part of the corporate name).

(If the corporation is to be a charity registered with Revenue Canada, it is suggested that you have Revenue Canada approve the objects).

*   When drafting, please insert only applicable wording where choices are provided for in this form.

IV

The operations of the Corporation may be carried on throughout Canada and elsewhere.

V

The place within Canada where the head office of the corporation is to be situated is: (Please specify only municipality/city and province here. The complete mailing address should be indicated in the covering letter).

VI

(The following clause should be inserted if the corporation is to be registered as a Canadian charitable organization with Revenue Canada - Taxation):

It is specially provided that in the event of dissolution or winding-up of the corporation all its remaining assets after payment of its liabilities shall be distributed to one or more qualified donees as defined under the provisions of the Income Tax Act (or, "registered charitable organizations in Canada").

(If the corporation is charitable in nature but not intending to be registered as a Canadian charitable organization, the following wording is required):

It is specially provided that in the event of dissolution or winding-up of the corporation, all its remaining assets after payment of its liabilities shall be distributed to one or more organizations in Canada carrying on similar activities.

(If the corporation is not to be charitable in nature but only a membership corporation, you may specify one of the following):

It is specially provided that in the event of dissolution or winding-up of the corporation, all its remaining assets after payment of its liabilities shall be distributed rateably amongst the members.

It is specially provided that in the event of dissolution or winding-up of the corporation, all its remaining assets after payment of its liabilities shall be distributed to _____.

VII
(Optional)

In accordance with Section 65 of the Canada Corporations Act, it is provided that, when authorized by by-law, duly passed by the directors and sanctioned by at least two-thirds of the votes cast at a special general meeting of the members duly called for considering the by-law, the directors of the corporation may from time to time

a) borrow money upon the credit of the corporation;

b) limit or increase the amount to be borrowed;

c) issue debentures or other securities of the corporation;

d) pledge or sell such debentures or other securities for such sums and at such prices as may be deemed expedient; and,

e) secure any such debentures, or other securities, or any other present or future borrowing or liability of the corporation, by mortgage, hypothec, charge or pledge of all or any currently owned or subsequently acquired real and personal, movable and immovable, property of the Corporation, and the undertaking and rights of the corporation.

Any such by-law may provide for the delegation of such powers by the directors to such officers or directors of the corporation to such extent and in such manner as may be set out in the by-law.

Nothing herein limits or restricts the borrowing of money by the corporation on bills of exchange or promissory notes made, drawn, accepted or endorsed by or on behalf of the corporation.

VIII

The by-laws of the corporation shall be those filed with the application for letters patent until repealed, amended, altered or added to.

IX

The corporation is to carry on its operations without pecuniary gain to its members and any profits or other accretions to the corporation are to be used in promoting its objects.

DATED at the City of _____ in the Province of _____, this _____ day of _____, 19__.

_____

_____

_____
Signature of Applicants

SAMPLE #43 — Continued

ANNEX 5

CANADA
PROVINCE OF _____
REGIONAL MUNICIPALITY
OF _____

IN THE MATTER OF the Canada Corporations Act.
RE: Application for incorporation under Part II in
the name of _____
(corporate name)

AFFIDAVIT

I, _____ of the City of _____ in the Province of _____, make oath
and say as follows:

1. I am one of the applicants herein.

2. I have knowledge of the matter, and that the statements in the annexed application contained are, to the
    best of my knowledge and belief, true in substance and in fact.

3. I am informed and believe that each applicant signing the said application is of the full age of eighteen
    years and has power under law to contract and that his or her name and description have been
    accurately set out in the preamble thereto.

4. The proposed corporate name of the company is not on any public grounds objectionable and that it
    is not that of any known company, incorporated or unincorporated, or of any partnership or individual,
    or any name under which any known business is being carried on, or so nearly resembling the same as
    to deceive.

5. I have satisfied myself and am assured that no public or private interest will be prejudicially affected by
    the incorporation of the company aforesaid.

SWORN before me at _____,
in the Regional Municipality of
_____ this _____ day
of _____, 19____.

_____(signature)_____
applicant

_____
A Commissioner, etc.

158

SAMPLE BY-LAWS FOR A FEDERAL CORPORATION

CORPORATIONS DIRECTORATE
MODEL BY-LAW

CORPORATE SEAL

1. The seal, an impression whereof is stamped in the margin hereof, shall be the seal of the corporation.*

CONDITIONS OF MEMBERSHIP

2. Membership in the corporation shall be limited to persons interested in furthering the objects of the corporation and shall consist of anyone whose application for admission as a member has received the approval of the board of directors of the corporation.**

3. There shall be no membership fees or dues unless otherwise directed by the board of directors.

4. Any member may withdraw from the corporation by delivering to the corporation a written resignation and lodging a copy of the same with the secretary of the corporation.

5. Any member may be required to resign by a vote of three-quarters (3/4) of the members at an annual meeting.

HEAD OFFICE

6. Until changed in accordance with the Act, the Head Office of the corporation shall be in the (City - Municipality) of _____, _____.***
    (province)

BOARD OF DIRECTORS

7. The property and business of the corporation shall be managed by a board of * * * * directors of whom * * * * * shall constitute a quorum. Directors must be individuals, 18 years of age, with power under law to contract. Directors need not be members.

8. The applicants for incorporation shall become the first directors of the corporation whose term of office on the board of directors shall continue until their successors are elected.

    At the * * * * * * meeting of members, the board of directors then elected shall replace the provisional directors named in the Letters Patent of the corporation.

9. Directors shall be elected for a term of _____ year(s) by the members at an annual meeting of members.

10. The office of director shall be automatically vacated:

    a) if a director has resigned his office by delivering a written resignation to the secretary of the corporation;

    b) if he is found by a court to be of unsound mind;

    c) if he becomes bankrupt or suspends payment or compounds with his creditors;

    d) if at a special general meeting of members, a resolution is passed by _____ of the members present at the meeting that he be removed from office;

    e) on death;

---

*   seal need not be imprinted until after incorporation
**   if more than 1 class of members, specify which classes are voting
***   please do not include a postal address here
****   a fixed number or a range e.g. 3-10, minimum to be no less than 3
*****   no less than two directors
****** first, second, etc.

provided that if any vacancy shall occur for any reason in this paragraph contained, the board of directors by majority vote, may, by appointment, fill the vacancy with a member of the corporation.

11. Meetings of the board of directors may be held at any time and place to be determined by the directors provided that 48 hours written notice of such meeting shall be given, other than by mail, to each director. Notice by mail shall be sent at least 14 days prior to the meeting. There shall be at least one (1) meeting per year of the board of directors. No error or omission in giving notice of any meeting of the board of directors or any adjourned meeting of the board of directors of the corporation shall invalidate such meeting or make void any proceedings taken thereat and any director may at any time waive notice of any such meeting and may ratify, approve and confirm any or all proceedings taken or had thereat. Each director is authorized to exercise one (1) vote.

If all the directors of the corporation consent thereto generally or in respect of a particular meeting, a director may participate in a meeting of the board or of a committee of the board by means of such conference telephone or other communications facilities as permit all persons participating in the meeting to hear each other, and a director participating in such a meeting by such means is deemed to be present at the meeting.

A resolution in writing, signed by all the directors entitled to vote on that resolution at a meeting of directors or committee of directors, is as valid as if it had been passed at a meeting of directors or committee of directors.

12. The directors shall serve as such without remuneration and no director shall directly or indirectly receive any profit from his position as such; provided that a director may be paid reasonable expenses incurred by him in the performance of his duties. Nothing herein contained shall be construed to preclude any director from serving the corporation as an officer or in any other capacity and receiving compensation therefor.

13. A retiring director shall remain in office until the dissolution or adjournment of the meeting at which his retirement is accepted and his successor is elected.

14. The board of directors may appoint such agents and engage such employees as it shall deem necessary from time to time and such persons shall have such authority and shall perform such duties as shall be prescribed by the board of directors at the time of such appointment.

15. A reasonable remuneration for all officers, agents and employees and committee members shall be fixed by the board of directors by resolution. Such resolution shall have force and effect only until the next meeting of members when such resolution shall be confirmed by resolution of the members, or in the absence of such confirmation by the members, then the remuneration to such officers, agents or employees and committee members shall cease to be payable from the date of such meeting of members.

INDEMNITIES TO DIRECTORS AND OTHERS

16. Every director or officer of the corporation or other person who has undertaken or is about to undertake any liability on behalf of the corporation or any company controlled by it and their heirs, executors and administrators, and estate and effects, respectively, shall from time to time and at all times, be indemnified and saved harmless out of the funds of the corporation, from and against;

a) all costs, charges and expenses which such director, officer or other person sustains or incurs in or about any action, suit or proceedings which is brought, commenced or prosecuted against him, or in respect of any act, deed, matter of thing whatsoever, made, done or permitted by him, in or about the execution of the duties of his office or in respect of any such liability;

b) all other costs, charges and expenses which he sustains or incurs in or about or in relation to the affairs thereof, except such costs, charges or expenses as are occasioned by his own wilful neglect or default.

EXECUTIVE COMMITTEE (OPTIONAL)

17. There shall be an executive committee composed of ___ directors who shall be appointed by the board of directors. The executive committee shall exercise such powers as are authorized by the board of directors. Any executive committee member may be removed by a majority vote of the board of directors. Executive committee members shall receive no remuneration for serving as such, but are entitled to reasonable expenses incurred in the exercise of their duty.

18. Meetings of the executive committee shall be held at any time and place to be determined by the members of such committee provided that forty-eight (48) hours written notice of such meeting shall be given, other than by mail, to each member of the committee. Notice by mail shall be sent at least 14 days prior to the meeting. ___ members of such committee shall constitute a quorum. No error or omission in giving notice of any meeting of the executive committee or any adjourned meeting of the executive committee of the corporation shall invalidate such meeting or make void any proceedings taken thereat and any member of such committee may at any time waive notice of any such meeting and may ratify, approve and confirm any or all proceedings taken or had thereat.

POWERS OF DIRECTORS

19. The directors of the corporation may administer the affairs of the corporation in all things and make or cause to be made for the corporation, in its name, any kind of contract which the corporation may lawfully enter into and, save as hereinafter provided, generally, may exercise all such other powers and do all such other acts and things as the corporation is by its charter or otherwise authorized to exercise and do.

20. The directors shall have power to authorize expenditures on behalf of the corporation from time to time and may delegate by resolution to an officer or officers of the corporation the right to employ and pay salaries to employees. The directors shall have the power to enter into a trust arrangement with a trust company for the purpose of creating a trust fund in which the capital and interest may be made available for the benefit of promoting the interest of the corporation in accordance with such terms as the board of directors may prescribe.

21. The board of directors shall take such steps as they may deem requisite to enable the corporation to acquire, accept, solicit or receive legacies, gifts, grants, settlements, bequests, endowments and donations of any kind whatsoever for the purpose of furthering the objects of the corporation.

OFFICERS

22. The officers of the corporation shall be a president, vice-president, secretary and treasurer and any such other officers as the board of directors may by by-law determine. Any two offices may be held by the same person. Officers need not be directors, nor members.

23. The president shall be elected at an annual meeting of members. Officers other than president of the corporation shall be appointed by resolution of the board of directors at the first meeting of the board of directors following an annual meeting of members.

24. The officers of the corporation shall hold office for ___ year(s) from the date of appointment or election or until their successors are elected or appointed in their stead. Officers shall be subject to removal by resolution of the board of directors at any time.

DUTIES OF OFFICERS

25. The president shall be the chief executive officer of the corporation. He shall preside at all meetings of the corporation and of the board of directors. He shall have the general and active management of the affairs of the corporation. He shall see that all orders and resolutions of the board of directors are carried into effect.

26. The vice-president shall, in the absence or disability of the president, perform the duties and exercise the powers of the president and shall perform such other duties as shall from time to time be imposed upon him by the board of directors.

27. The treasurer shall have the custody of the funds and securities of the corporation and shall keep full and accurate accounts of all assets, liabilities, receipts and disbursements of the corporation in the books belonging to the corporation and shall deposit all monies, securities and other valuable effects in the name and to the credit of the corporation in such chartered bank of trust company, or, in the case of securities, in such registered dealer in securities as may be designated by the board of directors from time to time. He shall disburse the funds of the corporation as may be directed by proper authority taking proper vouchers for such disbursements, and shall render to the president and directors at the regular meeting of the board of directors, or whenever they may require it, an accounting of all the transactions and a statement of the financial position, of the corporation. He shall also perform such other duties as may from time to time be directed by the board of directors.

28. The secretary may be empowered by the board of directors, upon resolution of the board of directors, to carry out his affairs of the corporation generally under the supervision of the officers thereof and shall attend all meetings and act as clerk thereof and record all votes and minutes of all proceedings in the books to be kept for that purpose. He shall give or cause to be given notice of all meetings of the members and of the board of directors, and shall perform such other duties as may be prescribed by the board of directors or president, under whose supervision he shall be. He shall be custodian of the seal of the corporation, which he shall deliver only when authorized by a resolution of the board of directors to do so and to such person or persons as may be named in the resolution.

29. The duties of all other officers of the corporation shall be such as the terms of their engagement call for or the board of directors requires of them.

EXECUTION OF DOCUMENTS

30. Contracts, documents or any instruments in writing requiring the signature of the corporation, shall be signed by any two officers and all contracts, documents and instruments in writing so signed shall be binding upon the corporation without any further authorization or formality. The directors shall have power from time to time by resolution to appoint an officer or officers on behalf of the corporation to sign specific contracts, documents and instruments in writing. The directors may give the corporation's power of attorney to any registered dealer in securities for the purposes of the transferring of and dealing with any stocks, bonds, and other securities of the corporation. The seal of the corporation when required may be affixed to contracts, documents and instruments in writing signed as aforesaid or by any officer or officers appointed by resolution of the board of directors.

MEETINGS

31. The annual or any other general meeting of the members shall be held at the head office of the corporation or at any place in Canada as the board of directors may determine and on such day as the said directors shall appoint. The members may resolve that a particular meeting of members be held outside Canada.

32. At every annual meeting, in addition to any other business that may be transacted, the report of the directors, the financial statement and the report of the auditors shall be presented and auditors appointed for the ensuing year. The members may consider and transact any business either special or general at any meeting of the members. The board of directors or the president or vice-president shall have power to call, at any time, a general meeting of the members of the corporation. The board of directors shall call a special general meeting of members on written requisition of members carrying not less than 5% of the voting rights. ___ members present in person at a meeting will constitute a quorum.

33. Fourteen (14) days' written notice shall be given to each voting member of any annual or special general meeting of members. Notice of any meeting where special business will be transacted shall contain sufficient information to permit the member to form a reasoned judgement on the decision to be taken. Notice of each meeting of members must remind the member that he has the right to vote by proxy.

Each voting member present at a meeting shall have the right to exercise one vote. A member may, by means of a written proxy, appoint a proxyholder to attend and act at a specific meeting of members, in the manner and to the extent authorized by the proxy. A proxyholder must be a member of the corporation.

A resolution in writing, signed by all the members entitled to vote on that resolution at a meeting of members, is as valid as if it had been passed at a meeting of members.

34. No error or omission in giving notice of any annual or general meeting or any adjourned meeting, whether annual or general, of the members of the corporation shall invalidate such meeting or make void any proceedings taken thereat and any member may at any time waive notice of any such meeting and may ratify, approve and confirm any or all proceedings taken or had thereat. For purpose of sending notice to any member, director or officer for any meeting or otherwise, the address of the member, director or officer shall be his last address recorded on the books of the corporation.

MINUTES OF BOARD OF DIRECTORS (AND EXECUTIVE COMMITTEE)

35. The minutes of the board of directors (or the minutes of the executive committee) shall not be available to the general membership of the corporation but shall be available to the board of directors, each of whom shall receive a copy of such minutes.

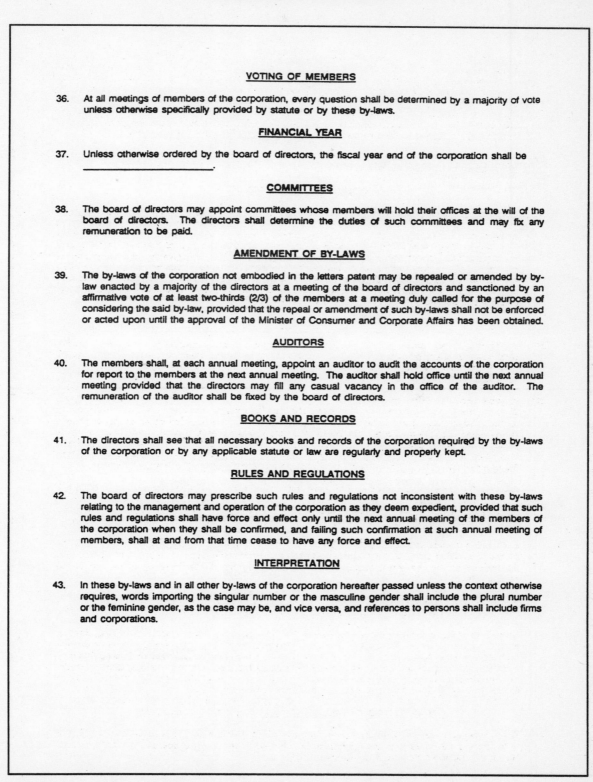

SAMPLE #44 — Continued

VOTING OF MEMBERS

36. At all meetings of members of the corporation, every question shall be determined by a majority of vote unless otherwise specifically provided by statute or by these by-laws.

FINANCIAL YEAR

37. Unless otherwise ordered by the board of directors, the fiscal year end of the corporation shall be _____.

COMMITTEES

38. The board of directors may appoint committees whose members will hold their offices at the will of the board of directors. The directors shall determine the duties of such committees and may fix any remuneration to be paid.

AMENDMENT OF BY-LAWS

39. The by-laws of the corporation not embodied in the letters patent may be repealed or amended by by-law enacted by a majority of the directors at a meeting of the board of directors and sanctioned by an affirmative vote of at least two-thirds (2/3) of the members at a meeting duly called for the purpose of considering the said by-law, provided that the repeal or amendment of such by-laws shall not be enforced or acted upon until the approval of the Minister of Consumer and Corporate Affairs has been obtained.

AUDITORS

40. The members shall, at each annual meeting, appoint an auditor to audit the accounts of the corporation for report to the members at the next annual meeting. The auditor shall hold office until the next annual meeting provided that the directors may fill any casual vacancy in the office of the auditor. The remuneration of the auditor shall be fixed by the board of directors.

BOOKS AND RECORDS

41. The directors shall see that all necessary books and records of the corporation required by the by-laws of the corporation or by any applicable statute or law are regularly and properly kept.

RULES AND REGULATIONS

42. The board of directors may prescribe such rules and regulations not inconsistent with these by-laws relating to the management and operation of the corporation as they deem expedient, provided that such rules and regulations shall have force and effect only until the next annual meeting of the members of the corporation when they shall be confirmed, and failing such confirmation at such annual meeting of members, shall at and from that time cease to have any force and effect.

INTERPRETATION

43. In these by-laws and in all other by-laws of the corporation hereafter passed unless the context otherwise requires, words importing the singular number or the masculine gender shall include the plural number or the feminine gender, as the case may be, and vice versa, and references to persons shall include firms and corporations.

SAMPLE #45
ANNUAL REPORT (FEDERAL CORPORATION)

FORM 3 ANNUAL SUMMARY (Under Section 133 of the Canada Corporations Act) As of 31st March 19 _9-_	FORMULE 3 SOMMAIRE ANNUEL (Article 133 de la Loi sur les corporations canadiennes) Au 31 mars 19 _____

A - Name and Mailing Address of Company Nom et adresse postale de la compagnie	B - Postal Address of Head Office if Different from A Adresse postale du siege social si differente de A
National Council on the Environment 1234 Beaver Square Ottawa, Ontario K1V 1T1	

C - Incorporated by - Incorporée par	D - Date of Incorporation Date de l'incorporation	E - Last annual meeting of shareholders or members held prior to April 1st- Defnière assemblée annuelle des actionnaires ou membres tenue avant le 1er avril.	
[X] Letters Patent Lettres-patentes [ ] Special Act Loi speciale	February 4, 199-	**Date** Mar. 31/9-	**Place - Lieu** Ottawa

F - Names and addresses of the persons who at the date of the return are the Directors of the company. Variations from the authorized number of Directors should be explained. - Noms et adresses des personnes qui à la date du rapport, sont administrateurs de la compagnie. Un changement dans le nombre d'administrateurs devrait être expliqué.

NAMES AND COMPLETE POSTAL ADDRESSES — NOMS ET ADRESSES POSTALES COMPLÈTES

1	Joe A. Pine 98 Ringwood Road Vancouver, B.C. V6N 1X1	9	
2	Sheila Sitka #204-1160 Conifer Place Fredricton, N.B. N8N 1Q1	10	
3	Sylvie L'Arbol 3434 Rue Jeunesse Quebec, P.Q. Q2Q 5L7	11	
4	Michael Maple P.O. Box 333 Terrapin, N.W.T. N6T 7W9	12	
5	Jennifer Juniper 12345 Ardrose Cres. Victoria, B.C. V6V 9Z4	G - Name and complete postal address of the auditor of the Company - Nom et adresse postale complète du vérificateur de la compagnie. Suzanne Spruce #3-949 Bilberry St. Ottawa, Ontario K1X 5Y1	
6			
7		Signature and Title (Officer or Director) Signature et titre (Fonctionnaire ou administrateur) _Joe Pine_ Director	
8		Telephone No. de téléphone (604) 999-1222	Date March 31, 199-
		Received - Reçu	Date

DEPARTMENTAL USE ONLY À L'USAGE DU MINISTÈRE SEULEMENT		
Date received - Date de réception	Validation	
Key Code clé	Cheque - Chèque	Amount - Montant

CCA 1439 (6-77)

SAMPLE #46
SAMPLE LETTER

Sample Letter to Corporations Directorate for Incorporation

Date: Reference:

To: Corporations Directorate
      Department of Industry
      9th Floor
      Journal Tower South
      365 Laurier Avenue West
      Ottawa, ON K1A 0C8

Enclosed herewith are:

1.   Application for Incorporation (2 copies) in the name _____

2.   Affidavit of Bona Fides (or Statutory Declaration) of one applicant sworn (declared) before a commissioner for taking oaths.

3.   By-laws (1 copy):

     i)   CUSTOMIZED (NOT PREVIOUSLY REVIEWED), with checklist duly completed _____.

     or

     ii)   CUSTOMIZED (NOT PREVIOUSLY REVIEWED), without the checklist _____.

     or

     iii) CORPORATIONS DIRECTORATE MODEL BY-LAWS _____.

     or

     iv)   PREVIOUSLY REVIEWED STANDARD BY-LAW BEARING IDENTIFIER NO. ___:_____.

4.   NUANS name search report not more than 90 days old or a cheque payable to the Receiver General for Canada in the amount of $15.00 being the filing fee for searching one proposed name. Bilingual names normally require 2 searches.

5.   Cheque for $200 payable to the Receiver General for Canada.

The street address of the Head Office is:

Instructions for returning Letters Patent to the undersigned when issued:

     __ Call for Pick-up when ready

     __ Regular mail

Reasons for urgency, if any

SIGNED: _____

NAME: _____

ADDRESS: _____

_____

TELEPHONE NUMBER: _____

SAMPLE #47
LETTERS PATENT

ANNEX A

THE ISSUANCE OF THESE LETTERS PATENT DOES NOT CONSTITUTE AUTHORITY TO PRACTICE OR TO REGULATE THE PRACTICE OF THE PROFESSION REFERRED TO HEREIN

C A N A D A

LETTERS PATENT

WHEREAS an application has been filed to incorporate a corporation under the name

THEREFORE the Minister of Consumer and Corporate Affairs by virtue of the powers vested in him by the Canada Corporations Act, constitutes the applicants and such persons as may hereafter become members in the corporation hereby created, a body corporate and politic in accordance with the provisions of the said Act. A copy of the said application is attached hereto and forms part hereof.

DATE of Letters Patent - _____(3)

GIVEN under the seal of office of the Minister of Consumer and Corporate Affairs.

for the Minister of Consumer
and Corporate Affairs

RECORDED

Film   Document

Deputy Registrar General of Canada

ANNEX B

NOTICE

Please note that an incorporation in the proposed name may be in violation of provincial regulatory laws dealing with professions. It is your responsibility to refer to the statutory body, if any, of the province or provinces in which you intend to operate for confirmation of name acceptability.

Evidence of such confirmation is not required for federal incorporation.

11

REGISTERING AS A CHARITY

Once your non-profit society has become a society (or corporation) registered with the provincial or federal government, you may consider applying to the federal government to register as a charity. Just as it is not required that you incorporate, that is, become a registered society, it is not required that you register as a charity either. On the other hand, it is also possible to become a charitable organization without becoming incorporated or registered. However, there are some good reasons why non-profit groups consider registration as a charity to be an essential step:

(a) Becoming a registered charity means your society will be given a charitable tax number. This means that you can write official donation receipts for people who give you money, which they can use as charitable donation credits on their income tax returns. Of course, this is an incentive for donors to give, and in particular to give to your society.

(b) As a registered charitable organization, your society will be exempt from taxation under Part I of the Income Tax Act.

(c) Registered charities are eligible for rebates of the GST on goods and services used in non-taxable activities. This and other benefits are described in chapter 13.

(d) Registered charities may be eligible for exemption from other taxes, such as federal sales tax, provincial sales tax, excise tax, and municipal property tax.

(e) Most foundations require an organization to be a registered charity before grants will be awarded.

(f) Charity status may be a requirement in your province in order for your organization to qualify for exemption from provincial and municipal taxes.

There are also reasons why you might decide not to register as a charity:

(a) Receiving and retaining status as a registered charity requires fitting within certain limits as far as society activity is concerned. You must operate exclusively for charitable purposes. This means that service clubs and fraternal lodges are not eligible for registration because they devote only part of their resources to charitable activities. In some provinces, however, they may qualify as a membership organization for purposes of incorporation and may be exempt from income tax as non-profit organizations.

(b) You must be a non-profit society. Any profits, capital or other holdings must belong to the society and be used for promoting its purposes.

(c) At the wind-up of a non-profit society, all remaining funds and assets must be transferred to a charitable institution with similar purposes. This non-profit commitment must be reflected in your constitution or articles of incorporation.

(d) Until 1985, you would have been excluded from registration by advocacy or political action. This ruling was the subject of controversy in the past several years, and the interpretation of "advocacy" and "political" was challenged by major national organizations. Now, charitable institutions won't lose tax-exempt status for carrying out lobbying activities on public issues providing they are not actively partisan in a direct political way, and that these activities are "ancillary and incidental to their charitable purposes." They may therefore advertise and try to influence public opinion on matters relevant to their organization.

Activities by which a society attempts to influence public policy, seek to inform public opinion, and urge government to take action are now permitted without threat of loss of status. In practical terms, this now allows writing to a newspaper, presenting briefs to MPs or parliamentary committees, demonstrating or speaking publicly, and generally entering into public debate. Note, however, that Revenue Canada still reserves the right to decide the "reasonable limits" of efforts to influence and mobilize public opinion.

You will still not be able to support or oppose any political party, candidate, or public office directly or indirectly. There will be an expenditure limit on the proportion of your society's resources that can be spent on indirectly influencing public opinion by advertising, mailing, or renting meeting facilities. Note that "substantially all" or about 90% of the resources of the society must be devoted to charitable activities in the course of a year.

If you plan such expenditures, keep a record of costs. Adopt a method of bookkeeping that works for your society and that adequately shows expenditures, then apply it consistently. You will be expected to report costs of permitted political activities yearly in the annual return.

a. DEFINITION OF CHARITABLE ORGANIZATION

The definition of a charitable organization for purposes of registration is an organization that has one or more of the following goals:

(a) the relief of poverty (for example, food banks, low-cost rental housing, clothing or furniture, and so on)

(b) the advancement of religion (with benefit of religious instruction for the public good)

(c) the advancement of education (for example, schools, colleges, scholarships, bursaries, research, museums, galleries, and so on)

(d) other purposes beneficial to the community as a whole in a way which the law regards as charitable (for example, disaster relief, sickness and disability funds, social welfare, animal welfare, national heritage, recreation, and so on)

The objectives of your society should fit one or more of these categories. Furthermore, benefits provided by the society must be available to all without discrimination. Specific requirements that will affect your constitution (and statement of goals), articles of incorporation, and letters patent are listed in chapter 7.

Note that local bodies of large organizations that receive donations on their own behalf must register separately as charitable organizations.

Service clubs and fraternal lodges are not eligible for registration as charities because they are not established exclusively for charitable purposes; only part of their resources are devoted to charitable activities. However, such clubs or lodges may still be considered non-profit organizations which can qualify for exemption from income tax.

b. STEPS TO REGISTRATION

1. Applying for registration

Ask for an Application for Registration (Form T2050E) and the most current Information Circular on registered charities (revised in 1993). Also ask for the booklet "Registering Your Charity for Income Tax Purposes" in the Income Tax Charity series. Write to:

Charities Division
Revenue Canada, Customs, Excise
  and Taxation
400 Cumberland Street
Ottawa, ON K1A 0L8

or contact your local district office of Revenue Canada.

2. Completing the application form

Sample #48 shows a completed application form. In Part I, enter the name of your organization exactly the way it is given in the constitution or articles of incorporation and certificate of incorporation you received from the provincial government. This name will also appear on all receipts later issued by the organization once it is registered as a charity.

Note there is a separate line for the address at which books are kept. As well, be sure to complete the postal code and enter when fiscal year ends (for example, March 31).

Part II acts as a checklist of the various documents you will need to send with the application form.

Check the appropriate box in item 15 regarding real property. Note that, as a small non-profit society, your designation as to type of charity will be "charitable organization." In Part III, your answer to item 16 will be "no" unless you will act as a foundation for the purpose of funding other charities.

3. Collecting the necessary documents

(a) Most organizations requesting registration as a charity will have already incorporated either provincially or federally. The governing documents requested in item 10 will be a photocopy of the provincial or federal acknowledgement of approval of registration; that is, your certificate of incorporation or letters patent.

A copy of your constitution, articles of incorporation, or letters patent must accompany the application.

If your organization is affiliated with and abides by the governing documents of a larger organization that is a registered charity, the following documents may be provided instead:

(i) a certificate or certified statement of affiliation, issued by the larger organization, confirming the affiliation of the organization (stating the officially recognized names of both organizations in full and indicating the effective date of affiliation), and

(ii) a certified copy of the resolution confirming that the members of the applying organization have agreed to abide by the governing document of that larger organization (known as the "principal body").

Certification in both (i) and (ii) requires the signatures of at least two executive officers of the relevant organizations.

(b) Include a written statement of your activities as a society. The application asks for "the full details of the activities and/or programs to be carried on by the applicant" in furthering the objectives stated in your constitution or other governing documents. Include all programs; a review of your various committees will give a good idea of what you are now doing or plan to do. Address

SAMPLE #48
APPLICATION FOR INCOME TAX REGISTRATION

Revenue Canada
Customs, Excise and Taxation

Revenu Canada
Accise, Douanes et Impôt

APPLICATION FOR INCOME TAX REGISTRATION FOR CANADIAN AMATEUR ATHLETIC ASSOCIATIONS AND CANADIAN CHARITIES

For Departmental use only
Registration number
Date

PLEASE READ THE INSTRUCTIONS ON THE PERFORATED FLAPS. You will need the information to properly complete this form. The numbered paragraphs in the instructions match the numbers on this form.

All organizations, corporations, trusts, etc. who want to become registered charities or registered Canadian amateur athletic associations must complete this form.

PART I – IDENTIFICATION

1. Name of applicant

Vulnerable Valley Environmental Society

2. Mailing address (Street and no., P.O. Box or R.R. No.)

55 Sawmill Road

3. City or town	4. Province	5. Postal code
Anyville	B.C.	VON 1C1

6. Address at which books and records will be kept

Same as above

7. City or town	8. Province	9. Fiscal year-end	Day	Month
			31	March

PART II – SUPPORTING INFORMATION

Attached

10. Please attach an **official** copy of each of the **governing documents** under which the applicant was established. ..... [X]

Does your organization have by-laws? [X] Yes   [ ] No

If yes, please attach an official copy. .... [X]

11. Please attach a **statement of activities** setting out fully the activities and programs to be carried on by the applicant to further each of the objectives or purposes set out in its governing documents. .... [X]

12. Please attach **financial statements** for the last completed year or fiscal year of operation. If the applicant is not yet in operation, you should attach a copy of a proposed budget or estimate of income and expenditures, as well as anticipated assets and liabilities for the first year of operation. .... [X]

13. Please attach a **list of officers** showing the full name, address and occupation of all the executive or directing officers of the applicant, including, in the case of a parish or congregation, the name of the priest, pastor, minister, or religious leader in charge. .... [X]

14. Is the applicant seeking registration as: [X] a charity?

or

[ ] a Canadian amateur athletic association?

15. Does the applicant own (or intend to own) real property, i.e., land or buildings? [ ] Yes   [X] No

If Yes, please state below the name in which title to the real property will be registered.

Name

PART III – FOR CHARITIES ONLY

Only those applying for registration as charities need to answer questions 16, 17 and 18

	Yes	No
16. Has the applicant been formed for the purpose of giving more than 50% of its income to other registered charities or other "qualified donees?"	☐	☒
17. Are 50% or more of the directing officers named in number 13 (front page) **related** to any other person named in the list? If any of the executive or directing officers are **related** by blood, marriage, adoption, common-law relationship or close business or corporate ties (e.g., business partners, employers and employees), please indicate this relationship on the list provided in response to question number 13 on the front of this form.	☐	☒
18. To the best of your knowledge, will the applicant receive more than 50% of its funds from one person, or from a group of persons who are **related** to each other?	☐	☒

If yes, please explain the funding arrangement:

PART IV – CERTIFICATION

19. **We hereby certify** that the information given in this application and in all documents attached is true and correct.

Officers Name (please print)	Signature	Date
Gloria Sue Ochre	*Gloria Sue Ochre*	May 9, 199-

Position or office within organizational structure of the applicant: **President**
Address: 10010 River Road, Anyville, B.C. VON 1C3
Business Telephone Number: (604) 539-1234
Home Telephone Number: (604) 539-5678

Officers Name (please print)	Signature	Date
Hugh Green	*Hugh Green*	May 9, 199-

Position or office within organizational structure of the applicant: **Vice President**
Address: R.R. #3 Vulnerable Valley B.C. VON 1B0
Business Telephone Number: (604) 539-9012
Home Telephone Number: (604) 539-3456

It is a serious offence to make false or deceptive statements.

20. **Name, address and telephone number of authorized representative, if different from 19 above:**

Name: n/a
Home Telephone Number: ( )
Business Telephone Number: ( )
Address:

each goal specifically in terms of activities and enclose any brochures or other explanatory material. For a small society, a brief factual statement would be less than one page long.

(c) If you have been in operation as a society for over a year, attach a copy of your statement of income and expenses and balance sheet (assets and liabilities) for the last completed year or fiscal year prior to the date of application (see Samples #6 and #7 in chapter 4). If you are new, attach a copy of any budget or an estimate of expenditures for your first year of operation (see Sample #4 in chapter 4).

(d) Attach a list of the executive of the board, showing their full names, home addresses, and occupations. Indicate what office they hold in the society.

In Part IV, print or type the names and addresses of two officers of the board who will both sign the form. Do not use initials.

Make a copy of all documents for your own files, then send one copy of the original application form and the documents listed above to:

Charities Division
Revenue Canada, Taxation
Ottawa, ON K1A 0L8

If you have questions about the forms, use the toll-free number to contact the Charitable and Non-Profit Organization section of Revenue Canada at 1-800-267-2384. Call between 8:00 a.m. and 4:30 p.m., Monday to Friday, eastern standard time.

When your application has been approved as a registered charity, you will receive a Notification of Registration (Form T2051). It will include the date of registration and registration number. Expect a reply in six to eight weeks.

If your organization has existed for some time but has not previously registered as a charity, you will generally be granted registration effective the first day of the society's taxation (fiscal) year during which the application was filed.

c. ISSUING OFFICIAL RECEIPTS

Once you have registered charity status, you can issue official tax-deductible receipts to those who make donations to your society. This is a real incentive to donors and makes donating to your society more attractive. Official receipts issued for donations by your society must bear the following information:

(a) the current name of the society (as recorded with Revenue Canada)

(b) the place or location where the receipt was issued

(c) the registration number Revenue Canada assigned to the organization

(d) the signature of an officer of the society or person the society designates as authorized to acknowledge donations

(e) the serial number of the receipt

(f) full information on amount donated in cash

(g) name and address of donor

(h) a statement to the effect that "this is an official receipt for income tax purposes"

If your receipts are not properly made out, you may have your registration as a charity withdrawn. Official receipts that have missing information or are illegible will be regarded as invalid.

Not all donations are eligible for tax deductible receipts. For non-eligible donations, use receipts that do not include your registration number. Non-eligible donations are:

(a) payments for membership that include some "material advantage" such as use of pools or equipment. Other membership dues are deductible (receipt of the annual report or other routine information is not considered to be a material advantage or personal gain)

(b) tuition fees or other payments for which the donor received some benefit

(c) amounts received in loose collection, that is, no particular donor can be identified as having made donations of a particular amount

(d) donations of merchandise

(e) amounts paid for admission to concerts, dinners, or other fundraising function (unless it is clear that, for example, $20 of a $35 ticket covers costs and $15 is a donation)

It is allowable to give a tax deductible receipt for value of property or services rendered providing money flows in both directions and is recorded on the books of both the society and the donor. For instance, if a painter decorates your office and charges $400, he may choose to then donate the money to the society. But he must be actually paid for the work; the cheque should clear his account. A receipt may then be written by the society receiving his cheque for donation.

In addition to requirements already listed, the receipt should state the day on which the donation of property or service was received, a brief description of it, and the name and address of the appraiser of the property if an appraisal was done. If the donation is a gift of property or service, then list the fair market value at the time the gift was made.

Careful records must be kept of receipts issued to donors for tax deductible purposes. They must be available for audit if required by Revenue Canada. An official receipt issued to replace an official receipt previously issued must show clearly that it replaces the original receipt. In addition to its own serial number, it must show the serial number of the receipt originally issued. A spoiled official receipt form and its duplicate must be marked "cancelled" and retained by the registered society as part of its records.

d. FILING AN ANNUAL RETURN

A non-profit society is required to file a yearly return with Revenue Canada — the Registered Charity Information Return and Public Information Return — together with the appropriate schedules from Schedules 1 to 4 and financial statements for the fiscal year being reported. Financial statements must include a statement of receipts (income), disbursements (expenses) and a statement of assets and liabilities for the financial year the statement covers. The treasurer should sign all such statements; they do not have to be audited. Failing to file a return can mean your society or corporation loses its registration as a charity, making re-application necessary.

1. The Registered Charity Information Return and Public Information Return (Form T3010)

This form (see Sample #49) is similar in format to a personal income tax return. You are responsible for obtaining and submitting a copy whether or not one has reached you from Ottawa. They are available on request from your local taxation office or from Revenue Canada in Ottawa. Revenue Canada must receive this form within six months of the end of the fiscal year set by your society.

Like a personal income tax return, the form has two copies — one that you use as a working copy and one that you file. Fill in every blank space. If the item does not apply, write in N/A (not applicable). A booklet entitled *Your Guide to Charity Information Return* accompanies these forms as well as a mailing envelope. Read the booklet before completing the forms, noting the detailed section called *Glossary of Terms* at the end of the guide.

Calculation of Receipts and Disbursements for the Fiscal Period (p.1)

This is a listing of all income (for example, gifts, donations) and revenue from other

SAMPLE #49
REGISTERED CHARITY INFORMATION RETURN
AND PUBLIC INFORMATION RETURN

Revenue Canada / **Revenu Canada**
Taxation / Impôt

**Registered Charity Information Return And
Public Information Return**

Please complete and mail
this copy together with
confidential schedules
and financial statements

T3010 Rev. 90

Mailing Copy

A IDENTIFICATION

Registration Number

☐☐☐☐☐☐☐☐ – ☐☐

Return for Fiscal Period Ended [Day | Month | Year]

Is this the first return your charity has filed? ☐ Yes ☐ No

If "NO", has the fiscal period changed from that shown on the last return? ☐ Yes ☐ No

Does your charity meet ALL the exemption criteria set out in the Guide? ☐ Yes ☐ No

Is this the final return to be filed by this charity? If so. please attach an explanation ☐ Yes ☐ No

DESIGNATION OF CHARITY:

Is your charity

a Public Foundation   A ☐

a Private Foundation   B ☐

or a Charitable Organization?   C ☐

If the address shown above is incorrect or you can provide a more permanent address, please print the necessary corrections below. If organization's name is incorrect, please see the Guide.

C/O Name or Position

Postal Address

City

Province   Postal Code

B CALCULATION OF RECEIPTS AND DISBURSEMENTS FOR THE FISCAL PERIOD

Receipts from Gifts

Total gifts received for which your charity has issued "official receipts" for income tax purposes .... **100** _____

Please give details about the amounts on line 100 as follows:

- Gifts from foreign sources .... **900** _____
- Gifts of capital received by way of bequest or inheritance .... **901** _____
- Gifts received subject to a trust or direction by the donor that they be held not less than 10 years ..... **902** _____

Total gifts received from other registered charities .... **101** _____

- Gifts from line 101 which have been designated as "specified gifts" .... **903** _____

Total gifts received for which "official receipts" have not been and will not be issued (gifts from other charities on line 101 and grants on line 103 are not to be included) .... **102** _____

- Gifts from line 102 which are from foreign sources .... **904** _____

Receipts from Other Sources

Federal, provincial or municipal grants and payments received .... **103** _____

Investment and property income .... **104** _____

Net realized capital gains (losses) .... **105** _____

Income (loss) from any "related business" .... Gross **905** _____   Net **106** _____

Memberships, subscriptions, fees received .... **107** _____

Other Income (please specify) .... **108** _____

Total Receipts (add lines 100 to 108 inclusive) .... **109** _____ ⇨ _____

Please do not use this area	701	702	703	704

174

SAMPLE #49 — Continued

PAGE 2

Disbursements

Total fund-raising costs . . . . **110** _____

- Total fees from line 110 paid to fund-raising agents . . . . **906** _____

Management and general administration costs . . . . **111** _____

Total amount spent on political activities . . . . **112** _____

Total amount of gifts to "qualified donees" (complete "Summary of Gifts to Qualified Donees" on page 4) . . . . **113** _____

Please give details about the amount on line 113 as follows:

- Gifts designated as "specified gifts" . . . . **907** _____
- Gifts to "associated charities" . . . . **908** _____

Total amount spent on charitable programs carried on by your charity . . . . **114** _____

    Note: Do not include amounts representing disbursements made during the fiscal period for the purpose of property accumulated — see relevant schedule and line 115 below

Please give details about the amount on line 114 as follows:

- In Canada . . . . **909** _____
- Outside Canada . . . . **910** _____

Amount accumulated with the permission of the Minister of National Revenue during the fiscal period . . . . **115** _____

Other disbursements (please specify) . . . . **116** _____

Total Disbursements (add lines 110 to 116 inclusive) . . . . **117** _____ ⇨ _____

C STATEMENT OF ASSETS AND LIABILITIES

Assets

Cash on hand and in bank . . . . **118** _____

Amounts receivable from founders, officers, directors, members, or organizations related to them . . . . **119** _____

Amounts receivable from others (not included on line 119) . . . . **120** _____

Investments other than rental property . . . . **121** _____

Rental Property . . . . **122** _____

Other fixed assets (e.g. land and buildings, etc.) . . . . **123** _____

Inventory . . . . **124** _____

Other assets (please specify) . . . . **125** _____

Total Assets (add lines 118 to 125 inclusive) . . . . **126** _____ ⇨ _____

Liabilities

Contributions, gifts and grants payable . . . . **127** _____

Amounts payable to founders, officers, directors, members, or organizations related to such persons . . . . **128** _____

Amounts payable to others (not included on lines 127, 128 and 130) . . . . **129** _____

Mortgages, notes payable . . . . **130** _____

Total Liabilities (add lines 127 to 130 inclusive) . . . . **131** _____ ⇨ _____

D REMUNERATION

Total remuneration paid to employees carrying out charitable activities . . . . **132** _____

Total remuneration paid to employees carrying out any other activities . . . . **133** _____

Total remuneration paid to all employees (add lines 132 and 133) . . . . **134** _____ ⇨ _____

Total remuneration (including benefits of any kind) paid to employees who were executive officers, directors or trustees of the charity . . . . **135** _____

Number of individuals whose remuneration appears on line 135 . . . . **136** _____

E VOLUNTARY INFORMATION (Your co-operation in completing lines 137 to 143 would be appreciated)

Voluntary Work

Approximate total number of hours contributed by all volunteers on all activities . . . . **137** _____

Percentage of volunteer hours devoted to:

Fundraising activities . . . . **138** _____ %

Charitable activities . . . . **139** _____ %

"Related business" activities . . . . **140** _____ %

Donations

Approximate percentage of donations received from:

Individuals . . . . **141** _____ %

Corporations . . . . **142** _____ %

Other Sources . . . . **143** _____ %

175

SAMPLE #49 — Continued

Staple all required schedules, statements and any other necessary documentation to the top of this page   **PAGE 3**

F   INFORMATION DESCRIBING CHARITY'S PURPOSE(S) AND ACTIVITIES

To be completed by all registered charities.   Note: If you do not have enough space. please attach a separate sheet and label it "Attachment to form T3010"

— Purpose(s) —————————————————————————————————

Give a brief statement of the primary purpose(s) of your charity.

_____

_____

_____

— Activities in Canada ————————————————————————————

Briefly describe the charitable programs which your charity carried on in Canada during the fiscal period. Please specify the location for each activity.

_____

_____

_____

_____

— Activities Outside Canada ————————————————————————

Briefly describe the charitable programs which your charity carried on outside Canada during the fiscal period. Please specify the location for each activity.

_____

_____

_____

_____

Were the activities outside Canada carried on

(a) by the employees of your charity itself?   ☐ Yes ☐ No

If "Yes", print the total amount of salaries (including benefits of any kind) paid to them.   1. _____

Print any other amounts provided to them for the purpose of carrying out these activities (e.g. for equipment, supplies, etc.)   2. _____

(b) through an appointed agent(s) or authorized representative(s) of your charity?   ☐ Yes ☐ No

If "Yes", print the total amount of the fees paid for their services including, in the case of an individual, amounts provided for personal living expenses.   3. _____

any other amounts provided to them for the purpose of carrying out these activities   4. _____

(c) in joint venture with a foreign charity or charities?   ☐ Yes ☐ No

If "Yes", print the total amount your charity spent on projects of this nature.   5. _____

(d) by other means (please specify)   6. _____

Total amount spent on charitable programs outside Canada (add lines 1 to 6 inclusive)
Note: This amount should be equal to the amount printed on line 910 on page 2.   7. _____

Briefly describe the extent to which your charity directs, supervises and controls the application of its funds by agents, representatives or foreign charities acting in joint ventures.

_____

_____

_____

_____

PAGE 4

G SUMMARY OF GIFTS TO "QUALIFIED DONEES"

To be completed by all registered charities that have reported gifts to "qualified donees" on line 113

Note: If you do not have enough space to list all the donees, please attach a separate sheet, using the headings below, and label it "Attachment to form T3010".

Name of Donee	Registration Number of Donee if a Charity	Location	Amount (Omit Cents)	Specified Gift (√)	Associated Charity (√)

H IDENTIFICATION OF EXECUTIVE OFFICERS

To be completed by all registered charities

Please list below the name, address, telephone number and occupation of each current directing officer of the charity including, in the case of a parish or congregation, the name of the priest, minister or religious leader in charge.

Note: If you do not have enough space to list all the officers, please attach a separate sheet, using the headings below and label it "Attachment to form T3010"

Name	Position with Charity	Address	Telephone Number	Occupation

I RETURN COMPLETION

Please provide the name, address, telephone number and occupation of the individual who completed this return.

Name: _____   Occupation: _____

Address: _____   _____

_____   _____

Telephone Number: _____   _____

J CERTIFICATION

To be signed only by a current executive officer of the charity.

I _____ of _____
  Name of officer whose signature appears below (please print)   Address

HEREBY CERTIFY that the information given in this return and in all schedules and statements attached is true, correct and complete in every respect.

Signature of Authorized Officer	Position or Office within the organizational structure of the charity

Charity's Telephone Number	Date
1 __ — __ __ __ — __ __ __ — __ __	Day / Month / Year

Form authorized and prescribed by order of the Minister of National Revenue.

sources, such as memberships or fees. This information is in addition to your society's financial statement for the year covered by the return.

Disbursements may include fundraising costs such as salaries, overhead, promotional material, or postage costs for direct mail campaigns. Total your management and administration costs, including salaries, office space rental, office supplies, equipment, and bookkeeping fees.

The return includes a request for the total amount of money spent on political activities of a non-partisan nature. The guide interprets "political" to mean efforts at influencing and mobilizing public opinion for the purpose of pressuring elected officials to take a certain course of action. However, the guide goes on to say that advocating your society's position on an issue *related to the charitable purpose for which it is registered* falls within general charitable activities and need not be separately designated as "political." The statement also addresses method: "bringing an issue to the attention of government so as to allow full and reasoned consideration." The guide is very clear that engaging in partisan political activities is not permitted. "Partisan" means supporting or opposing political parties or candidates.

Line 114 asks for the total spent on programs as distinct from administration costs (line 111).

Statement of Assets and Liabilities (p. 2)

List all the society's assets (for example, cash on hand, money receivable, fixed assets) and liabilities (for example, accounts payable not already reported).

Remuneration (p. 2)

Include money paid to employees who carry out functions directly related to your charity's objectives. Money paid to employees for management and support are included on a separate line.

Voluntary Information (p. 2)

This information is not required, but is requested from you to aid the Department of Secretary of State to collect statistics on volunteer hours and therefore on the value of volunteer labour in Canada, which will then be made available to the voluntary sector. Remember that "carrying out charitable activities" will include the work of your board of directors.

Also requested is a breakdown by percentage of donations in three categories: corporation, individual, and other sources.

Identification of Executive Officers (p. 2)

Note it is the officers' *home* addresses that are requested here.

Information Describing Charity's Purpose(s) and Activities (p. 3)

The statement of purpose may be repeated as written in the constitution. It should be brief but long enough to convey the purposes for which the society was established. For example:

> To protect Vulnerable Valley and its watershed from damage to its ecological balance or visual beauty.

Activities in Canada (p. 3)

Write a brief description of the charitable programs carried on by the society for the fiscal year covered by the return.

For example, the Ashford Day Care Society might state that they have in the past 12 months:

- provided day care services in Ashford to between 17 and 24 children aged two to six years

- established an advisory committee of parents to assess the need for after-school care in Ashford

- begun a series of staff and parent education meetings on topics such as child sexual abuse and learning disabilities

- joined the Ashford Interagency Council and the Alberta Day Care Association

Summary of Gifts to "Qualified Donees" (p. 4)

This is a list of donations to other registered charities as tax deductible gifts. Not many small and new non-profit societies need complete this section. If you do not, write N/A in the space provided.

Identification of Executive Officer (p. 4)

Note that it is the officer's *home* address that is required here.

Certification (p. 4)

A member of the current board executive should sign the form. Fill in that person's home address and position on the board of the society. The return is not valid unless it is signed.

If you need to add separate sheets, any attachments should be typed on society letterhead, identified with your registration number and the date, and labelled "Attachments to Form T3010."

2. Schedules

There are five schedules in the charity information return. A small non-profit society without property will complete Schedules 1 and 2 only.

These schedules are confidential as are any financial statements submitted. Schedule 1 is general information required for all registered charities.

Question 1 in Schedule 1 (see Sample #50) refers to changes in the constitution or by-laws of the society. Such changes are recorded and acknowledged in writing by the provincial Registrar.

Regarding question 13, note that it is not good practice to give receipts for loose collections. If people require or request a receipt, give it at the time they make the donation unless you have a policy of only writing receipts for amounts over, for example, $3.

Regarding question 14, remember that receipted gifts are not returnable to the donor. They may, however, be given by the society to some other registered charity.

The answer to question 15 should be no; a charity should not receive money designated for the personal use or benefit of any individual.

Question 23 concerns the replacement procedure for lost or spoiled receipts. A common procedure is to issue replacement receipts only if the original receipt is returned to your society.

Schedule 2, Disbursements Quota Calculation for a Charitable Organization (see Sample #51) is a detailed calculation to prove that your society has spent at least 80% of the money received in donations in a given fiscal year.

A charitable organization has met its disbursement quota if the total reported expenditures are equal or greater than 80% of the amount for which official receipts were issued. (Charitable status may be revoked if this is not the case.)

Failure to file annual returns is cause for revocation of a charity's registration. If this happens, reinstatement can be requested with the filing of another Application for Registration (Form T2050E) (see Sample #48).

Mail completed forms and the financial statements to:

Charities Division
Department of National Revenue, Taxation
Ottawa, ON   K1A 0L8

e. KEEPING BOOKS AND RECORDS

Society or corporation records must be kept at the address indicated on your application and annual return.

Revenue Canada audits a number of charities each year to check that they meet the requirements of the Income Tax Act.

Charities are chosen for audit by random selection, and by statistical sampling. They will also audit books and records of charities if irregularities are noted in their annual return or in response to complaints from the public.

Your charity's records must include a record (duplicate copies) of official donation receipts and all bills paid in the running of your organization. (See Information Circular 78-10R, *Books and Records Retention/Destruction*.)

f. CHANGE OF NAME

If your society changes its name after registering as a charity, the original Notification of Registration *must* be returned to Revenue Canada. Enclose documentation to show that the name change has been properly recorded with the provincial Registrar or Companies Branch (the supplementary letters patent of a corporation or a *certified* copy of the resolution by the officers of a society).

A new Notification of Registration will be issued with the new name and, usually, the original registration number.

g. CHANGE OF ADDRESS

Revenue Canada should be advised in writing of changes in the official registered address. Change of address, and therefore not receiving annual report forms, is not an excuse for failing to submit the proper forms.

h. CEASING TO OPERATE AS A CHARITY

If you cease to operate as a charity you must advise Revenue Canada, return the original Notification of Registration, and send in a final Return of Information, financial statements, and a Public Information Return showing the distribution of assets.

READING AND RESOURCES

Revenue Canada Toll-free Service: For non-profit groups wanting information on how to become officially registered as a charity or on other departmental policy. Call the Charities Division between 8:00 a.m. and 4:30 p.m. (eastern standard time), Monday to Friday, at 1-800-267-2384. If you live in Ottawa call 954-0410. There are also toll free services for the visually impaired (1-800-267-1267) and the hearing impaired (1-800-665-0354).

Your Guide to the Charity Information Return (1990). Revenue Canada. Available in French and English.

Registering Your Charity for Income Tax Purposes. Revised 1993. Revenue Canada. Available in French and English.

SAMPLE #50
SCHEDULE 1

Mailing Copy

Name of Charity: _____

Registration Number ⬚⬚⬚⬚⬚⬚⬚ — ⬚⬚   Fiscal Year Ended ⬚⬚⬚⬚

Day Month Year

Schedule 1 General Information Required from All Registered Charities

Note: If you need more space, please attach a separate sheet.

1. Has your charity made any changes to its governing documents that it has not previously reported? If "Yes," please attach a certified copy of the changes to this return. ☐ Yes ☐ No

2. Did your charity spend more than 50% of its income for the fiscal period on gifts to qualified donees other than approved associated charities? ☐ Yes ☐ No

3. Do more than half your charity's directors or like officers deal with each other and with each of the other directors or like officers at arm's length, that is, they are not related by blood, marriage or adoption? If "No," please see the Guide. ☐ Yes ☐ No

4. To the best of your knowledge, has one person or group of people who do not deal with each other at arm's length contributed more than 50% of your charity's capital to date? If "Yes," please see the Guide. ☐ Yes ☐ No

5. Did your charity acquire property from or dispose of property to a related person, other than as a gift to a person who qualifies as an object of charity? ☐ Yes ☐ No

6. At its year-end, was your charity related to another registered charity? ☐ Yes ☐ No

7. Are the receipts your charity uses to acknowledge payments that are not gifts, for example, tuition, hall rentals, etc., distinct from the official receipts that your charity uses to acknowledge donations and which bear your charity's registration number? If "No," please explain below. ☐ Yes ☐ No

8. Did your charity operate a school providing religious or religious and academic instruction? ☐ Yes ☐ No

9. If you answered "Yes" to question 8 above, please report the total amount (in dollars) of contributions or fees your charity received for tuition. 601 $ _____ ☐ Not Applicable

How much (in dollars) of the total at line 601 did your charity treat as charitable donations (gifts) as outlined in Information Circular 75-23? 602 $ _____ ☐ Not Applicable

10. What was the total amount of contributions, if any, your charity received as admission to fund-raising dinners, balls, concerts, shows or similar events? 603 $ _____ ☐ Not Applicable

How much (in dollars) of the total at line 603 did your charity treat as charitable donations (gifts) as outlined in Interpretation Bulletin IT-110R2? 604 $ _____ ☐ Not Applicable

11. Did your charity include any donations postmarked or otherwise submitted after the end of the calendar year in official receipts issued to the donor for that calendar year? ☐ Yes ☐ No

12. Has your charity issued receipts bearing its registration number to acknowledge donations other than cash or cheques, for example, goods, services rendered, etc.? If "Yes," please explain below. ☐ Yes ☐ No

13. Has your charity issued official receipts that include an amount for loose collections, that is, a particular donor cannot be identified with a particular donation? If "Yes," please explain below. ☐ Yes ☐ No

Please do not use this area 800 ⬚⬚⬚⬚

(Please complete reverse side of this schedule)

181

SAMPLE #50 — Continued

14. Has your charity returned any donation to the donor? If "Yes," please explain below.   ☐ Yes   ☐ No

15. Did your charity receive any amount that the donor designated for the personal use or benefit of any individual or for any organization other than a qualified donee? If "Yes," please explain below.   ☐ Yes   ☐ No

16. Has your charity carried on any business activity. If "Yes," please describe below.   ☐ Yes   ☐ No

17. Has your charity earned rental income from real property? If "Yes," please describe below.   ☐ Yes   ☐ No

18. If you reported amounts on lines 132 and/or 133 on page 2 of the return, did your charity issue T4 slips for any salaries included in those amounts?   ☐ Yes   ☐ No

19. If your charity awarded one or more scholarships or bursaries, did it file a T4-T4A Summary and a T4 Supplementary for each scholarship?   ☐ Yes   ☐ No   ☐ Not Applicable

20. Does your charity keep completed books and records at a location in Canada?   ☐ Yes   ☐ No

21. a) Has your charity's registration been revoked?   ☐ Yes   ☐ No

    b) If "Yes," have you applied for its re-registration as a charity?   ☐ Yes   ☐ No   ☐ Not Applicable

22. Your charity's books and records are in the care of:
    (Please print)
    Name
    Mr., Mrs., Miss, Ms.

    Usual first name and initial   Surname, family or last name

    Present Address

    Number, street and apt. no., or R.R. no.

    City   Province or Territory

    Postal Code   Telephone number (home)   Telephone number (office)

23. Please explain the procedure your charity uses to replace lost or spoiled receipts.

24. Please list the people authorized to issue official receipts for your charity.

Name	Position with Charity

182

SAMPLE #51
SCHEDULES 2 AND 3

Name of Charity: _____

Registration Number [ ][ ][ ][ ][ ][ ] — [ ][ ]   Fiscal Year Ended [| | |]

Day   Month   Year

Schedule 2 Disbursement Quota Calculation for a Charitable organization (See Schedule 2 in the Guide)

I. Calculation of Disbursement Quota

Note: You will need your charity's return for the **previous year** to complete this section. Please transfer the appropriate amounts from that return to lines 1, 2, 3 and 4 below.

Total amount for which your charity issued official receipts in the immediately preceding

fiscal period _   1. _____

Minus the following amounts for which your charity **issued official receipts:**

a) Gifts of capital received by way of bequest or inheritance _ _ _ _ _ _ _ _ _ _   2. _____

b) Gifts received subject to a trust or direction by the donor

that they be held not less than 10 years _ _ _ _ _ _ _ _ _ _ _   3. _____

c) Gifts received from other registered charities _ _ _ _ _ _ _ _ _ _ _ _ _   4. _____

Total exclusions (add lines 2 through 4) _ _ _ _ _ _ _ _ _ _ _ _ _ ▶ 5. _____

Subtract line 5 from line 1 _   6. _____

Disbursement Quota (80% of line 6) _ _ _ _ _ _ _ _ _ _ _ _ _ _ _ _ _   7. _____

II. Calculation of whether a charitable organization has met its disbursement quota

Note: Please transfer the appropriate amounts from **this year's** return to lines 8, 9 and 10 below.

Expenditures your organization **actually** made during the fiscal period just ended on its charitable

activities _   8. _____

Gifts to qualified donees _   9. _____

Minus specified gifts _   10. _____

Amount your organization is **considered** to have spent on

charitable activities (subtract line 10 from line 9) _ _ _ _ _ _ _ _ _ _ _ _ ▶ 11. _____

Property accumulated in the fiscal period (from line 2 of Schedule 3) _ _ _ _ _ _ _ _   12. _____

Disbursement excess from previous years _ _ _ _ _ _ _ _ _ _ _ _ _ _ _ _ _ _   13. _____

Deemed charitable expenditure approved by the Minister of National Revenue _ _ _ _ _ _   14. _____

Total expenditures (add lines 8, 11, 12, 13 and 14) _ _ _ _ _ _ _ _ _ _ _ _ _   15. _____

Disbursement excess (subtract line 7 from line 15 — if line 7 is greater than line 15, record

the difference on line 17) _   16. _____

Disbursement shortfall _   17. _____

Portion of the amount on line 16 applied against a disbursement shortfall in your charity's

immediately preceding fiscal period _ _ _ _ _ _ _ _ _ _ _ _ _ _ _ _ _ _   18. _____

Net disbursement excess (subtract line 18 from line 16) _ _ _ _ _ _ _ _ _ _ _ _ _   19. _____

Schedule 3 Statement of Property Accumulated with Prior Approval of Revenue Canada, Taxation

Note: If the Department has granted your organization more than one written approval for the accumulation of property, please

attach a statement of each approval using the following format.

Expiry date of the accumulation period stated in the written approval [| | |]

Day   Month   Year

Specific purpose for which the Department granted permission to accumulate property _____

_____

_____

Total accumulation to date (minus disbursements) at the end of the previous fiscal period_ _ _ _ _ _ _ _ _ _ _ _   1. _____

Amount accumulated, including income earned on the total property accumulated, in the fiscal period

just ended (report this amount on line 115 on page 2 of the return) _ _ _ _ _ _ _ _ _ _ _ _ _ _ _ _   2. _____

Total accumulation to date (add lines 1 and 2) _   3. _____

Minus

Disbursements for the specific purpose outlined above made during the fiscal period to which this return relates _ _ _ _   4. _____

Balance still to be disbursed _   5. _____

Please do not
use this area   [801] [ ][ ][ ][ ][ ]

12

THE GOODS AND SERVICES TAX

There are three ways non-profit organizations or corporations may find themselves involved in GST procedures:

(a) when they pay the GST on goods and services they purchase,

(b) when they apply (if eligible) to receive a rebate on GST they have paid, or

(c) when they sell goods and services to the public, charge, and remit the GST.

The issue is complicated for the non-profit society or corporation because organizations may be both a purchaser or customer and in many cases, a seller or retailer of goods and services.

For Revenue Canada purposes, charities (including most places of worship) and registered amateur athletic associations are designated "charities" rather than "non-profit" organizations. There are slightly different rules for non-profit organizations and for charities. The designation of non-profit includes organizations such as professional associations; service clubs; dining, recreation, or sporting clubs; and local boards of trade. Charities are organizations registered under the Income Tax Act that have a registered tax number and that give tax deductible receipts to donors.

a. PAYING THE GST ON GOODS AND SERVICES PURCHASED

Both non-profit societies and charities can expect their operating costs to increase by 7% calculated on purchases such as rent, utilities, insurance, office equipment, printing, renovations, and fees for such services as bookkeeping, lawyers' advice, plumbing, or carpentry. *You will likely be eligible for a rebate of 50% of the GST you pay on goods and services used in your non-taxable activities.* However, even if you are eligible for periodic rebates, plan for this additional expenditure or it could lead to cash flow problems.

b. CHARGING CUSTOMERS THE GST

The GST will not usually be charged on most of the goods and services charities provide, or on membership fees or donations received. The test used by Revenue Canada, Excise and Customs is whether or not your organization competes with commercial establishments. An organization is not considered in competition with commercial establishments (and does not have to charge the GST at all) if *any one* of the following apply.

(a) *Small suppliers' exemption:* Applicable if annual sales do not exceed $30 000. In such cases, the organization is known as a "small supplier" and need not charge the GST on taxable sales. You are not required to register with Revenue Canada, Excise and Customs. However, you may choose to register in order to claim input tax credits on purchases used in taxable activities.

If you earn more than $30 000 a year in activities that are deemed to compete with commercial establishments, you will have to register with Revenue Canada, Excise and

Customs, pay the GST on purchases, and charge and remit the GST on sales.

(b) *Volunteer exemption:* Applicable if functions are carried out substantially (90%) by volunteers. Volunteers are defined as people who are not paid a salary (but who may have expenses reimbursed). To determine this percentage, you need to keep track of the number of volunteers and volunteer hours in relation to that of paid staff.

(c) *Nominal consideration exemption:* Applicable if sales of goods and services recover only their purchase cost, or less.

(d) *Relief of poverty, suffering, or distress:* Applicable if food, drink, or short-term accommodation is supplied for the purpose of relieving poverty, suffering, or distress. Short-term accommodation is defined as 30 days or less.

If your society sells goods or services to the public that are considered to compete with commercial establishments, you have to charge the GST. Examples include a meal provided at a fundraising event, items sold in a gift shop, or a fitness course. However, on purchases related to these activities, you can recover *all* of the GST paid through an "input tax credit." The basic principle is that it is the final customer who pays the GST, not the retailer — whether commercial, non-profit, or charity. This principle covers the following situations.

(a) *Bingo and casinos:* You do not have to collect the GST on proceeds from bingo and casino nights nor charge the GST on admission, providing the event is operated substantially by volunteers and is held in a place not used primarily for gambling.

(b) *Sale of used or donated goods:* You need not charge the GST on sales of used or donated goods.

(c) *Small item sales:* You do not have to charge the GST on fundraising sales of small items that sell for less than $5.

In addition, note the following circumstances in which the GST is or is not charged.

(a) *Exempted services:* You *may not* charge the GST on fees for day care services or for supervised recreational programs (athletics, music, and arts and crafts) when these programs are primarily for children 14 years old or younger. The GST is not charged on recreational programs primarily for individuals with mental or physical disabilities. You are not required to collect the GST on services such as research, counselling, rehabilitation, education, and other social services.

(b) *Memberships:* Memberships in charitable organizations (or local chapters of Canadian parent organizations) are generally not taxable —

　(i)　if members do not receive any special benefits other than the right to vote at meetings and to receive a newsletter or other publication reporting on the group's activities or

　(ii)　if any discount received is insignificant in relation to the total cost of membership.

However, if the membership includes benefits (including discounts) such as an admission to a recreational complex or to professional performances, then the GST is charged on membership fees.

(c) *Donations, subsidies, and sponsorships:* There is no GST charged on donations, grants, subsidies, or sponsorships given to charities. When a commercial sponsor pays an amount in cash or in kind to a non-profit organization in return for promotional services, this amount is not taxed but is treated like a grant or donation. If a portion of a ticket sold is a donation to a charity and a portion is a purchase of a product or service, such as a fundraising dinner, the GST applies only to the purchase of the product or service.

c. INFORMING CUSTOMERS

Let your customers know whether or not the GST is applicable to goods for sale. If you must charge the GST, appropriate signs and notices are available free from Revenue Canada, Excise and Customs.

d. TO REGISTER OR NOT TO REGISTER

Determine if you need to register with Revenue Canada, Excise and Customs.

You cannot register if you are not involved in any taxable activities. That is, if you are involved only in GST-exempt activities. This is the case for most small charities.

And as of February, 1994 the following rule applies:

Charities in their first fiscal year or whose annual gross revenues do not exceed $175 000 in either of their last two fiscal years are not required to register.

You may, however, still need to register if your organization's sales of goods and services are over $30 000 a year. If this is the case, check to see if you qualify for the "over-riding exemption" which will apply if sales and services are done substantially (90%) by volunteers.

Under these circumstances, you are not required to charge the GST, so your customers or clients receive your goods or services for less.

Your organization will still be able to recover 50% of all GST paid on purchases, including goods purchased for resale. In order to deduct all GST paid on goods purchased for resale (in the form of a procedure called input tax credits) your organization must register with Revenue Canada, Excise and Customs and submit a return to claim such credits.

e. APPLYING FOR GST REBATES

1. Eligibility for rebates

As a registered charity, your organization is eligible for rebates whether or not you have registered with Revenue Canda for GST purposes. Both non-profit organizations and charities are eligible for a 50% rebate on GST paid on most purchases used in non-commercial, non-taxable activities. This includes general operating costs such as rent, utilities, office equipment, supplies, and professional services as well as items bought for resale.

Non-profit organizations such as colleges, that are funded 40% or more by any level of government, are eligible to receive a 50% rebate of the GST they pay for items bought to produce exempt income. The amount of the rebate is arrived at by first calculating the amount of GST paid on purchases used in exempt activites, and then calculating 50% of this amount.

Non-profit organizations and charities can claim a rebate whether or not they have registered with Revenue Canada, Excise and Customs, providing they are recognized by Revenue Canada as a charity or receive 40% of funding from government.

2. Qualifying as a claimant

There are seven categories of claimants, and each has a different rebate rate. A charity is defined as a registered charity or registered Canadian athletic association within the meaning of the Income Tax Act. Incorporating as a society or corporation without share capital under provincial legislation is not enough. You must apply to Revenue Canada to establish your status as a charity (see chaper 11).

3. Filing a return

Rebate applications are available at local offices of Revenue Canada, Excise and Customs. Complete the application (see Sample #52) and file for each fiscal quarter (every three months) or once a year for the whole fiscal year.

On your first application, leave the space for the GST Rebate Identification Number blank. You will be assigned a number by mail after your first rebate application has been processed and approved.

The address entered on the application must be the current legal address of the society at the time the application is submitted. If the address changes, notify your provincial Revenue Canada, Excise and Customs office.

Calculating the rebate is a matter of adding up all GST the organization has paid on all goods and services for the reporting period. If, on any of the invoices you paid, the GST was included in the price, calculate the 7% GST from the total charged before any provincial sales tax was added. For example, if an item, including GST, cost $620 (before provincial sales tax), multiplying by seven and then dividing by 107 gives you the total GST amount of $40.56.

Rebate forms are separate from return forms. If you do collect the GST, file your rebate claim along with your GST return. If you don't collect GST on any sales, file a rebate claim either quarterly of annually. The government will send a rebate within 21 days or pay you interest.

f. ADJUSTING BOOKKEEPING PROCEDURES

As an exempt charity, your major bookkeeping responsibility is to keep track of GST on purchased goods and services. Remember that financial records are subject to audits. Keep original invoices for at least six years.

READING AND RESOURCES

Appel, Robert. *The GST Handbook: A Practical Guide for Small Business.* North Vancouver, B.C.: Self-Counsel Press, 1990. $7.95.

A useful guide for those charities that operate businesses to support their charitable activities.

The following materials are available from Revenue Canada, Excise and Customs:

GST: Information for Non-Profit Organizations (1993)

Includes details on contracts signed before January, 1991, prepaid goods and services, rules regarding registering branches of organizations, dealing with refunds, sponsorships, and other details. A short form brochure is also available on the same subject.

GST: Basic Information for Charities (1994)

Includes details on determining whether large charities with several branches may register for GST, dealing with service contracts and leases, when annual memberships and subscriptions are subject to GST, rules related to gambling and sponsoring or operating games of chance, and a variety of transitional provisions. A short form is available.

GST: Completion Guide for: Non-registrant Public Service Bodies Rebate.

This is the essential guide for most charities that do not register but are eligible for rebates of GST paid in the course of their non-taxable activities. The guide includes the rebate application form and instructions for completing the form.

If your organization registers with Revenue Canada for GST purposes, obtain the following free guides from your local or provincial office of Revenue Canada, Excise and Customs office.

GST: Completion Guide and Form for: Registrant Public Service Bodies. This guide includes the tax rebate form for charities registered with Revenue Canada for GST purposes.

Quick Method of Accounting Guide and Election Form: 1993. This guide includes the election form for "quick method accounting."

GST: Guide to the GST Tax Return for Registrants. 1993. This guide includes a sample return form only. If you have registered, you will receive personalized forms by mail. If you are in the process of registering, ask for a set of forms called *Goods and Services Tax Return (Non-personalized).*

GST Signs: Guidelines and Order Form

Information lines

For information about how the GST affects your organization or charity, the following phone numbers and addresses for Revenue Canada Excise offices should put you in touch with someone who can answer your questions.

Newfoundland and Labrador
P.O. Box 5500
St. John's, NF   A1C 5W4
Tel: (709) 772-2851

Nova Scotia
P.O. Box 9306
Halifax, NS   B3K 5Z3
Phone: (902) 426-1975

Prince Edward Island
P.O. Box 1488
Charlottetown, PE   C1A 7N1
Tel: (902) 566-7272

New Brunswick
P.O. Box 1070
Moncton, NB   E1C 8P2
Tel: (506) 851-3727

Quebec
P.O. Box 2117, Postal Terminal
Quebec, PQ   G1K 7M9
Tel: (418) 648-5700

P.O. Box 6092, Station A
Montreal, PQ   H3C 3H3
Tel: (514) 283-6644

Regional Excise and GST Liaison Office
2nd Floor
325 Marais Street
Ville Vanier
Quebec, PQ   G1M 3R3

Regional Excise GST Liaison Office
400 Place d'Youville
8 étage
Montreal, PQ   H2Y 2C2

Ontario
P.O. Box 8257
Ottawa, ON   K1G 3H7
Tel: (613) 990-8584

375 University Avenue
9th Floor
Toronto, ON   M5G 2J5
Tel: (416) 954-0473

P.O. Box 638 Station B
London, ON   N6A 4Y4
Tel: (519) 645-4154

Manitoba
P.O. Box 1022
Winnipeg, MB   R3C 2W2
Tel: (204) 983-4525

Saskatchewan
P.O. Box 557
Regina, SK   S4P 3A4
Tel: (306) 780-7279

Northwest Territories
Room 902
4920 - 52nd Street
Yellowknife, NWT   X1A 3T1
Tel: (403) 920-6650

British Columbia/Yukon
P.O. Box 82110
Burnaby, BC   V5C 2J3
Tel: (604) 666-4664

301 - 1385 West 8th Avenue
P.O. Box 33860, Station D
Vancouver, B.C. V6J 5C9
Tel: (604) 775-5300

There are additional regional offices in most provinces. To check for the one nearest you, call toll-free 1-800-463-6737 except in Quebec where the toll-free number is 1-800-667-3232.

Hearing disability

If you are deaf or have a hearing disability, and you have access to a Telephone Device for the Deaf, you may telephone toll free: 1-800-465-5770.

Regular hours of telephone and counter service

Monday to Friday 8:00 a.m. to 5:00 p.m. (except holidays)

Other languages

Some excise offices offer help in languages other than English and French. Contact your excise office for more details.

SAMPLE #52
GST REBATE APPLICATION

Revenue Canada
Customs and Excise

Revenu Canada
Douanes et Accise

GOODS AND SERVICES TAX REBATE APPLICATION
FOR NON-REGISTRANT PUBLIC SERVICE BODIES

Mail to: GST Interim Processing Centre
Ottawa, Ontario
K1A 1J6

Cette formule est disponible en FRANÇAIS

For use by a Municipality, University, School Authority, Public College, Hospital Authority, Charity or Qualifying Non-profit Organization (as defined in sections 123 and 259 of the Excise Tax Act) that are not required to be registered for GST purposes and that satisfy the requirements of Part IX, section 259 or 260 of the Excise Tax Act.

• To complete this form, refer to the Completion Guide
• Please print or type

A – CLAIMANT IDENTIFICATION

GST Rebate Identification No. ▶ 2 4 6 8 0 2 4 6 8

Legal Name
Vulnerable Valley Environmental Society

Mailing Address (Number, Street and Apt. No. or P.O. Box No. or R.R. No.)
55 Sawmill Road

City	Province	Postal Code	Telephone No.
Anyville	B.C.	V0N 1C1	(604) 220-5768

Business Address (If different from mailing address)

City	Province	Postal Code	Telephone No.
			( )

Type of Claimant (Choose one only).

1) ☐ Municipality   4) ☐ Public College   7) ☐ Qualifying Non-profit Organization (See Funding Calculation, Section D, on reverse side of this form.)

2) ☐ University   5) ☐ Hospital Authority

3) ☐ School Authority   6) ☒ Charity (Provide Taxation Registration No.) 1 2 2 3 4 5 6 - 8 9

This Claim is Being Filed by ▶ ☒ Head Office/Parent   ☐ Branch/Division

Language Preference
Préférence linguistique ▶ ☒ English Anglais   ☐ French Français

B - CERTIFICATION

It is hereby certified that: 1) the information in this application is true, correct and complete in every respect;
2) the amount claimed has not been previously claimed; and
3) in addition to any documents submitted herewith, books, records and invoices are available for inspection.

Signature of an Authorized Signing Officer of the Public Service Body

Peter White

Name (Print)	Position or Rank of Officer	Date
Peter White	Treasurer	Y 9 1 M 0 7 D 1 0

Canadä

GST 191E (91/04)

190

C - REBATE OF GOODS AND SERVICES TAX CALCULATION FOR THE CLAIM PERIOD

• Claim Period of the Rebate Application   From | 9 Y - 0 M 4 0 D 1 | To | 9 Y - 0 M 6 3 D 1 |

Reconciliation of Total Goods and Services Tax Paid for the Claim Period (See lines 200 to 204 in Guide.)

Total Amount of GST Paid on All Purchases for the Claim Period	**200**	521	40
Deduct GST Paid on Purchases Exported by a Charity (amount to be recorded on line 216 below)	**201**		
GST Eligible for Rebate (Subtract line 201 from line 200.) Enter the amount on line 204 on the line applicable to the claimant type (line 205 to line 209).	**204**	521	40

Calculation of Rebate of Goods and Services Tax for the Claim Period (See lines 205 to 217 in Guide.)

Claimants who are more than one claimant type and are required to calculate their rebate using more than one rebate factor, should refer to the Special Rules for Public Service Bodies in the Completion Guide.

Claimant Type		GST Eligible for Rebate (from line 204)	Rebate Factor		
Charity or Qualifying Non-profit Organization	**205**	521 ¦ 40	X 0.50 =	**210**	260 ¦ 70
Municipality	**206**		X 0.5714 =	**211**	
University or Public College	**207**		X 0.67 =	**212**	
School Authority	**208**		X 0.68 =	**213**	
Hospital Authority	**209**		X 0.83 =	**214**	
Rebate Entitlement (Add lines 210 to 214 inclusive.)				**215**	260 ¦ 70
GST Paid on Purchases Exported by a Charity				**216**	
Total Rebate (Add lines 215 and 216.)				**217**	260 ¦ 70

D - NON-PROFIT ORGANIZATION GOVERNMENT FUNDING CALCULATION

If the type of claimant selected in Section A is a qualifying non-profit organization (box 7), this section must be completed annually.

1) Quarterly Filer: Complete funding information for the past two fiscal years in columns 2 and 3 and calculate the average percentage of government funding in column 4.
2) Annual Filer: Complete funding information in column 1. If line F in column 1 is less than 40%, provide the funding information in columns 2 and 3 and calculate the average percentage of government funding in column 4.

	(1) Current Fiscal Year End Y M D	(2) Last Fiscal Year End Y M D	(3) 2nd Last Fiscal Year End Y M D	(4) Add Financial Information in Columns 2 and 3
A) Total Annual Revenue	.00	.00	.00	.00
Annual Government Funding B) Federal	.00	.00	.00	.00
C) Provincial	.00	.00	.00	.00
D) Municipal	.00	.00	.00	.00
E) Total Government Funding (B+C+D)	.00	.00	.00	.00
F) Percentage of Government Funding ($\frac{E}{A}$ X 100)	%			%

NOTE: - The government funding threshold is met when the calculation on line F in column 1 or column 4 is at least 40%.
- Annual reports, including financial statements, must be filed annually by all claimants for each of the fiscal years reported above.

FOR DEPARTMENTAL USE ONLY
☐ Input Code ☐

This form is prescribed by the Minister of National Revenue under the Excise Tax Act.

13
EARLY DAYS:
PUBLICITY AND PUBLIC EDUCATION

a. INTRODUCING YOUR SOCIETY

Sharing the work related to your society goes beyond your own organization. Most societies have a social cause or concern, and part of the task is to inform the public about those concerns, and persuade and convince when you can. And because you are a member of a new group which has identified a need, you are involved in shifting the status quo — in making changes in your community.

To do this, you will need support from the community — from individuals, other groups, agencies, services, and perhaps some level of government. Publicizing your group, its goals, and ideals is a way to inform public opinion. This is particularly vital if advocacy is one of your goals. You need to gain support for your concerns; you also need new members, volunteers, and donations.

1. Reaching the public

It is important to let people know about the work and objectives of your society. The style your organization chooses in seeking publicity will be determined by its goals, values, and philosophies, as well as the publicity target.

For example, the Vulnerable Valley Environmental Society may demonstrate with placards at the B & M Sawmill gates. They will notify the press and other media. Their objective will be twofold: to embarrass B & M into changing its practices related to effluent in the river and to attract the attention of the public to their cause.

Simultaneously, or as an alternative action, the Vulnerable Valley Environmental Society president may write a series of articles for the community newspaper and another board member may arrange to be interviewed on local television. You will use different strategies at different times.

Keeping a high profile is the objective. Your methods should be carefully considered in order to achieve your chosen ends and a favorable public view of your group and its goals.

2. Credibility

In the course of publicizing your organization and explaining your purpose or mission, your group will become known as expert in the field. The parents who form a society for the learning disabled speak from personal experience and from study of the issues and solutions (e.g., new teaching techniques). The teachers' federation may look to such a group for support for new programs at budget time or as volunteers in the schools. The home and school association may want a speaker for their fall meeting, and the probation officer may ask a board member to sit on the advisory committee to a treatment home for young offenders.

3. Clarity of message

The problem of stream reclamation or starting a reading program can sound very technical and dry to the uninitiated. But your goal statement puts your purpose into ordinary words; it's worth repeating often and in as many forms as possible. In every article in every interview, it will be necessary to state as simply as possible what the problem is that you address and how you do it. "Nothing is too obvious" is a good guideline. Your objective is not to dazzle the public with your expertise, but to make your concern their concern and to gain the support you need, whether in votes, active participation, contributions of money, or attitude change.

b. STRATEGIES FOR GAINING SUPPORT

The new non-profit society must work particularly hard to inform the community about its existence and its goals. The following are some of the ways to increase public knowledge and in the process garner public support.

1. Publicity

Flyers, posters, balloons, brief radio messages, booths at fairs, parades, stunts, entertainment, demonstrations, media conferences, media releases, advertisements, articles, or opening announcements for a new service/office/facility.

2. Education

Workshops, conferences, speeches, talks, panels, articles, interviews, pamphlets, brochures, handouts, information sessions/days, debates, fact sheets, newsletters, creation of slides, tapes and videos, staff development days, information kits, or resource lists.

3. Lobbying and advocacy

Briefs to commissions and government, representations to councils, boards, formal contacts with aldermen, MPs, MLAs, and any related representatives, policy statements, draft policies, and legislation, letter writing campaigns, or laying charges in court.

4. Local networking

Identifying your group's constituency, joining interagency councils or forums, making presentations to relevant service or issue groups, affiliating with other groups with the same goals on local, provincial, national and international levels, fairs, resource networks, booths, and professional days.

5. Research

Needs surveys, incidence research, bibliographies, resource lists, evaluations and reviews, impact studies, data gathering and analyses, or profile reports.

6. Requesting help

Giving people an active role in volunteering or otherwise identifying themselves with your society and its goals, funding for projects, services in kind, contributions (token or substantial) from local services, and bequests.

In summary, strategies for gaining support include any activities which inform, involve, and engage others.

c. YOUR PUBLIC RELATIONS COMMITTEE

Public relations (PR) has got itself a bad name. In the corporate world, the PR department is increasingly becoming known as the communications department. In fact, the word "communicating" is the appropriate one for you because that is really the objective of a non-profit society. Not all factions in the community will necessarily think well of your goals and work towards them. Nevertheless, you want more people to become informed and persuaded. A PR committee (whether it is called "Education," "Advocacy," or "Publicity") is a good idea.

Members of this committee, and particularly the chairperson (who is probably also the designated spokesperson), should understand all aspects of the society and its work. He or she can develop a talent for stating clearly and simply what the society is all about and what its current tasks or projects are. Being able to write and speak well is important; being reachable at home and at work (with a good message-taking system in place) is essential.

Designate *one* person as spokesperson or contact for the society, but have a backup person available. The committee will meet regularly to develop strategy, but it must be clear who is responsible for meeting deadlines, getting press releases delivered to all media, and being on hand to answer questions and give interviews.

Following is a list of the usual tasks of a media committee:

(a) Maintaining a list of addresses and phone numbers of radio and TV stations and newspaper offices

(b) Identifying a contact person for each media outlet (for example, an interested reporter or city editor who will take special notice of your news release or event)

(c) Knowing media deadlines

(d) Knowing when free public service announcements are made on radio or printed in newspapers and how to access them

(e) Writing brief, effective media releases

(f) Speaking on radio and TV and being "a good interview" who will be asked back again

(g) Following up on media about your society. Why didn't the editor use your release? Did the film crew have enough notice and know exactly where to find your meeting or demonstration?

(h) Asking for feedback from the community. Did you see the story? What impression did it give?

(i) Keeping a roster of speakers about different aspects of the society's work to meet requests for participation at conferences and workshops

(j) Writing and doing layout for brochures, pamphlets, flyers, handouts, and posters

(k) Developing a file of photographs, fact sheets, statistics, biographies of society members and other key figures useful to such people as media

personnel, teachers developing curricula for schools and colleges, or documentary filmmakers

(l) Keeping files on past media, releases, clippings, posters, and so on

(m) Evaluating publicity and educational efforts

d. COST

In general, good publicity need not be expensive. The point is to have TV, radio, and newspapers meet the expense. You provide the news.

Brochures, pamphlets and flyers need not be glossy or professionally typeset. All of the materials described above can be typed on stencil and reproduced on colored paper or by any other inexpensive duplicating process.

Two folds on an 8½" x 14" piece of paper provide six surfaces for type, which is adequate space for text. A printed pamphlet with two folds on 8½" x 11" paper will provide similar space and leave one section free for mailing information.

Again, typesetting is not important, but a typewriter is an essential tool for the public relations committee. Records should be neatly typed and any material produced must be clear enough to copy (don't use really dark paper that a copy machine cannot read) (see chapter 4, Laying the Groundwork for Good Record Keeping).

If your group has no money for printing, production of a pamphlet is an ideal small project for service clubs or other local groups to undertake.

If you produce a resource list of interest to the public, ask the local newspaper to print it for you in a regular edition. It will have good distribution at no cost to you.

e. NETWORKING

Mutual aid is important for groups with small budgets and big goals. The lessons learned in one place can prevent repeating problems in other places.

Having a means of sharing is vital, so get on the mailing list of other organizations relevant to yours and join provincial and national groups with similar concerns both in your area and as non-profit organizations.

Networking for the non-profit society has several important purposes:

(a) *Giving information:* Who needs to know about your work? Where else can you find support? Who can make even more use of your materials (audiovisual or print)?

(b) *Getting information:* Who is active? What are they doing? How did they do it? How did it work?

(c) *Collaboration:* What have they got we can use? What have we got they can use? How can we join forces for more impact?

Keeping in touch with the national non-profit network will help you stay informed about new books, articles, conferences, and services. The **Reading and Resources** section includes some national organizations that support non-profit societies in general and several that support social service-related societies in particular. Any library will give you names and addresses of national organizations in other areas such as arts, heritage, environment, recreation, and so on.

READING AND RESOURCES

PUBLICATIONS

Kome, Penny. *Every Voice Counts: A Canadian Woman's Guide to Initiating Political Action.* Ottawa, 1989. Free. Available from:

Canadian Advisory Council on the
  Status of Women
9th Floor, 110 O'Connor Street
Box 1541, Station B
Ottawa, ON K1P 5R5
Tel: (613) 992-4975

MacLeod, Flora. *Transition House: How to Establish a Refuge for Battered Women.* United Way of the Lower Mainland, Vancouver, 1989. Available in French and English. Distributed by:

National Clearinghouse on Family
  Violence
Health and Welfare Canada
706 Brooke Claxton Building
Tunney's Pasture
Ottawa, ON K1A 1B5
Tel: 1-800-267-1291

ORGANIZATIONS

Canadian Council on Social Development:

The Council is a national, non-partisan, non-profit organization for research, policy analysis, and advocacy activities in the fields of housing, income security, personal social services, health, family violence, self-help/mutual aid, social planning, and citizen involvement. Membership includes receipt of a social policy magazine, *Perceptions,* and two bilingual newsletters *Initiative* (self-help/mutual aid) and *Vis A Vis* (family violence) as well as *Overview* (social policy) (published as *Perspectives* in French). Fee for an organization with an annual budget of less than $100 000 is $75 per year; individual memberships are $50 per year. Contact:

Canadian Council on
  Social Development
55 Parkdale
Box C.P. 3505, Station C
Ottawa, ON K1Y 4G1
Tel: (613) 728-1865

United Way/Centraide Canada

A national organization providing support services to member United Ways, including training, research, policy development, and consultation for allocations, fundraising, and management. Information available on where United Ways operate in Canada and how to form United Ways for co-ordinated co-operative campaigning. Contact:

United Way/Centraide Canada
Suite 600, 150 Kent Street
Ottawa, ON K1P 5P4
Tel: (613) 236-7041

Canadian Centre for Philanthropy

The centre is a registered charitable organization providing services, programs, and publications of interest to all Canadian organizations involved in charitable activity (foundations, operating charities, government, corporate, and professional advisers). Works to inform the public about the critical role philanthropy plays in the community and sponsors the Imagine Campaign, a national initiative of the centre to increase awareness about giving and about volunteering. Produces *Network* for associate members and sponsors an annual Conference on Philanthropy. Contact:

The Canadian Centre for Philanthropy
1329 Bay Street
Suite 200
Toronto, ON M5R 2C4
Tel: (416) 515-0764

National Voluntary Organizations

National Voluntary Organizations (NVO) is an information coalition of some 146 national organizations across Canada providing information on services and policies of special interest to non-profit societies. All publications are bilingual. Monthly bulletin, fact sheets, and special reports are available free. Contact:

National Voluntary Organizations
160 George Street
Suite 200
Ottawa, ON K1N 9M2
Te.: (613) 230-3080

Canadian Child Welfare Association

The Canadian Child Welfare Association is a national association of people who provide services to children at risk and teens in care.

Their newsletter is available three times a year, and provides information on resources in Canada, programs, policy, and major issues of concern to practitioners. There are individual and agency membership categories. Contact:

Canadian Child Welfare Association
3rd Floor, 55 Parkdale Avenue
Ottawa, ON K1Y 1E5
Tel: (613) 761-9243

Canadian Council on Children and Youth

The CCCY is a national voluntary organization which speaks on behalf of children and youth on issues affecting their interests.

Topics include sexual abuse, environmental pollutants, child poverty, children's rights, fair play, conflict with the law, and child care. *For Canada's Children* is produced by CCCY five times a year.

Membership is $25 per year and includes a newsletter subscription. Contact:

Canadian Council on Children
  and Youth
3rd Floor, 55 Parkdale Avenue
Ottawa, ON K1Y 1E5
Tel: (613) 722-0133

14

TRENDS AFFECTING THE VOLUNTARY SECTOR

The number of charities has more than doubled in the past decade. Operating a non-profit organization in Canada has become an increasingly complex task for staff and volunteers. Non-profit societies represent a young and lively sector in our country today. Why the growth? What new problems and challenges do they face?

a. GOVERNMENT POLICY PATTERNS

1. Restraint

Belt-tightening has been the order of the day in the eighties and "down sizing" has continued into the 1990s as federal and provincial debt grows and deficit budgets prevail. Government services have been cut back, staff reduced, vacant positions left unfilled, and whole services eliminated. Governments have reduced or eliminated community service grants or have held the line on contracts, hoping for lower cost, tightly controlled programs. Concerns voiced by the voluntary sector about the consequences of restraint include:

(a) reduction in quality of service

(b) poor working conditions and wages

(c) growth in the number of people who need service

(d) reversal of the trend to reduce poverty and income disparity

(e) pressure on voluntary social services to pick up the slack — many organizations have gone into debt rather than eliminate proven services that government contracts no longer cover adequately, or at all

(f) isolation of individuals who are no longer a part of a network or collegial group of service providers

(g) increased competition for reduced public and private funding

(h) lack of cross-sectoral, long-range planning and research

(i) increased demand for volunteer time to manage new or expanded non-profit societies.

2. Privatization

Governments, particularly provincial governments, increasingly contract for services with private sector, non-profit organizations and for-profit businesses. This policy shift reverses a traditional pattern in Canada, particularly in the social services field. Now, long-established services such as institutional care for the mentally or physically disabled are being turned over to the private sector. Care for the elderly, day care for children, and counselling services, for example, are increasingly operated by private companies for profit.

The trend toward privatization began in the early eighties and is now more than a decade old. The devolving of direct service responsibility seems likely to continue as governments move toward a decentralized, less structured mode in order to reduce deficits. Some specific effects are evident:

- The funding of non-profit organizations has shifted to contract-based relationships, on a program or project basis. Fewer organizations receive core funding from government sources.

- Advocacy oriented groups have an increasingly tough time finding support from government sources. Short-term projects or consultant-basis proposals suit the new government agenda.

- Funding is time-limited and results-oriented with an emphasis on manageable pieces more amenable to evaluation of results. Efficiency, productivity, and accountability are key.

- Fully funded services are more and more at risk because of competition from for-profit service providers. Time-consuming yearly negotiations sap the energy of non-profits, which operate with a leaner management structure than government and smaller, more local bases than franchised businesses.

- The "down loading" trend, with the federal government passing on responsibility to the provinces and the provinces to the municipalities puts more pressure on non-profits to fill service gaps funded from donations.

- Salary and benefit inequities continue in the social service sector and are tied to the decline in unionized positions. The house supervisor in a non-profit society funded institution for the disabled may earn half the salary of a supervisor who works for a government-funded institution providing the same service. The non-profit society worker also has less job security and fewer benefits.

- The voluntary sector is in danger of splitting into two camps — large organizations with a workable relationship with government and the capacity to deliver high-demand services efficiently and professionally, and smaller organizations that are more vulnerable because they depend on take-it-or-leave-it and short-term, project-specific funding.

3. Charities and their advocacy role

The broadened definition of political activity which non-profit societies may carry out without loss of status as a registered charity has been described in chapter 11.

Over the past few years, the non-profit voluntary sector effectively lobbied to convince policy-makers that non-profits have a legitimate role to play in advancing their special interests with politicians as well as within local communities.

However, charities still struggle with inconsistencies in the way that policy related to their charitable status is interpreted. They have traditionally defended the rights of minorities such as the disabled, the poor, and the homeless. While being active within their mandate on these issues and other newer concerns, such as the environment, they may risk losing charitable status.

For example, a non-profit environmental group has limited resources to spend to lobby against detrimental industrial expansion or for controls and standards that may protect the environment. Companies, on the other hand, can deduct their costs related to lobbying and advertising — money spent to publish their views and organize campaigns to support their ideas. Businesses have unlimited ability to use commercial advertising for political purposes and to deduct it as a business expense. Charities, who are players on the same field, are threatened with loss of their charitable status if they respond in kind. Equity in representing competing interests will be a continuing concern for Canadian non-profit organizations in the future.

The federal government is aware of these issues related to legislation and policy governing charities, their various privileges, and responsibilities. The government is committed to continuing consultation with the voluntary sector on these matters. The success of the consultative process will depend on the informed participation of Canadians across the county.

4. Charitable donations and their impact on government revenue

The percentage of tax payers claiming tax credits has risen in recent years. The amount of the average donation has dropped somewhat, but the number of people donating has increased. Older donors aged 55 to 64 years give the most. Despite the recession, taxpayers gave charities $3.1 billion in 1991, up 7% from the previous year. In 1993, personal tax credits reduced government revenue by $800 million. These trends must attract the attention of a government committed to deficit reduction and may result in re-evaluation of the charitable tax credit.

5. The GST and its impact on non-profit organizations

Whether or not a charity or non-profit is required to register with Revenue Canada, Excise and Customs, the GST costs organizations more in their rent, utilities, supplies, and furniture. If they are eligible for rebates, staff or volunteer time must be spent to keep abreast of and carry out bookkeeping and accounting procedures. Organizations that carry on businesses in order to support their charitable activities and earn more than $30 000 in doing so, must follow the installation and collection of the tax in detail.

6. Public gaming

At the provincial level, non-profit societies and corporations are increasingly concerned with policy related to public gaming (casinos, bingos, and lotteries). As money to support core expenses — rent, staff salaries, and utilities — becomes scarce, many organizations are relying on the funding available via their participation in government regulated public gaming.

Provinces vary as to the degree of control that is exercised and the level of training (if any) available for volunteers in terms of their responsibilities in running lotteries, bingos, and casinos. The future indicates continued growth in public gaming, pushed by government as an alternative means of funding charitable services and tolerated by volunteers who see few other options for obtaining the necessary funds to carry on their work.

b. ORGANIZATIONAL MANAGEMENT

1. Exploring new structures and styles

The challenge for the voluntary sector has been to improve management style and effectiveness without becoming bureaucratic (like government) or faceless (like big business). But management style and skill need to be tailored to the voluntary sector, not lifted from the private sector. At the same time, organizational management has become more complex, dealing with a range of codified requirements related to harassment, gender and racial equity, access to information, right to privacy, and fair employment practices. Some of the management ideas being practised in the voluntary sector include:

- non-hierarchical structures

- decentralized decision making

- team management of programs and service delivery

- involvement of volunteers as members of service and policy teams

- organizational flexibility such as rotation of staff and volunteers into various jobs to enhance personal skills and organizational overview

- adult learning approach to staff and volunteer development

- paid staff as fully participating members of the board of directors of the organization

2. Sophisticated fundraising

There is more competition for the volunteer dollar than ever before. Not only small societies but also hospitals, universities, private and public education facilities, and major non-profit agencies are all searching for new ways to tap corporate and private donations.

Societies now are more systematic in approaching governments, private foundations, corporate donors, and individuals. The tax gift has become a taxable dispensation; charity is a smart business move. People are being asked not only to give now, but to write wills that ensure charities will benefit in the future. Employee trust funds are being tapped. Volunteers are taking courses at local colleges and reading books on fundraising and proposal writing.

Organizations successful at attracting funds will become adept at tailoring donation programs for individuals and businesses. They will identify uncommitted donors, draw them into the vision of the organization, and keep their loyalty with clear communication about the organization's purpose, programs, needs, and accomplishments.

3. Doing more with less

The necessity to do the most with the available money has had some negative effects on wages, benefits, and quality of service in non-profit societies. It has also had some positive effects in the new emphasis on cost effectiveness, efficiency, better use of resources, more careful accounting, effective management, and the appropriate use of technology.

And non-profit societies are now working more closely together to share such resources, such as space, communications equipment, receptionists, vehicles, and joint bulk orders of supplies.

4. Entrepreneurship

The trend for government at all levels to contract out work is becoming more entrenched. And, while traditional employment sources such as forestry or mining are drying up, the growth of the social service sector is evident. Not only are the care-givers increasingly running owner-operated services rather than taking wages home, but also the planners, researchers, and evaluators are also working outside of government.

To fill the widening gap between available funds and service demands, many non-profit societies are starting and running businesses. With the new demand for new marketplace skills, some societies work on a profit-sharing basis with a private company. Others learn the ropes themselves and develop businesses, such as restaurants or second-hand shops, that employ their clients while financially supporting their services. Business activity does not contravene restrictions on non-profit societies, providing the business is secondary to charitable purposes and the money earned is used to support the same goals.

5. Using information technology

Non-profit societies are part of the technology revolution. In particular, agencies with high service demands (that operate social, health, recreational, and other services) are using the latest information technology to improve their flexibility and efficiency. Computers, fax machines, and photocopiers have moved from the "wish" list to the "need" list for effective operation. In the future, computer networking will increase, particularly in specialized areas and over long distances. Teleconferencing for decision making and information sharing is cheaper than long distance travel and has been adapted for use by people operating within the same organization over town or over the province and by organizations with a national mandate but a restricted budget.

c. VOLUNTARISM

1. Recognizing the economic value of volunteers

While volunteering is, by definition, an unpaid activity, there is growing recognition of the market value of such work and its contribution to the national economy. To demonstrate the point, the value of volunteer work, based on an average service sector wage, is currently estimated at $13 billion annually. And, while many people would be counted in both work and volunteer categories, there are 13 million people in the Canadian labour force and six million volunteers active across the country. For more information on volunteer activity in Canada, see the resource section of chapter 3.

2. Participation and empowerment

The non-profit sector is both a training ground and a major arena for participation by citizens. They acquire skills in the democratic process and can organize powerful advocacy groups to influence social policy. Voluntarism is a vehicle; it is a means of empowering people in important areas of their lives and bringing forward major concerns that do not have adequate acknowledgment from public bodies or private enterprise.

Non-profit volunteer activity is not so much charity, helping a bit but not changing much, as it is an effort to build new structures and alliances that are more responsive to the people they serve. A major challenge for the voluntary sector in the 1990s is finding an effective means to involve new Canadians in both service and advocacy organizations in ways that acknowledge and reflect the multicultural nature of our society.

3. Improving volunteer management

The management of volunteers has become professionalized. Management includes diverse skills: planning, priority setting, policy development, co-ordination, problem solving, program and individual evaluation, as well as hiring, training, scheduling, and supervising. Volunteer co-ordinators also need program administration skills and the ability to work within agencies and communities.

To meet the demand for better managed volunteer programs, there has been substantial growth in the number of courses offered across the country, ranging from a series of evenings at a local volunteer centre to full university certificate programs at the graduate level.

Well-run programs that operate with a volunteer component reflect the importance of proper care of the volunteer relationship in all its aspects. It requires attention to such issues as risk management, the awareness of responsibilities and liabilities of both service and policy volunteers.

Volunteers require training, supervision, support, and recognition. They need meaningful work, the opportunity to develop new skills, and innovative ways of becoming involved in relevant decision making in the organization.

Understanding motivation is a key to attracting and keeping dedicated volunteers. Most people want to help others, meet people, make use of their skills and experience, and do something worthwhile for their community. For others, volunteering also may be a step toward paid employment, a wind-down toward retirement from full employment, or a precursor to a whole new occupational direction. Whatever the motivation, volunteers have high expectations of their volunteer experience. They deserve the help necessary to make a meaningful and effective contribution.

d. VOLUNTARY SECTOR

The voluntary, or "third," or "independent" sector traditionally has occupied territory distinct from government and business. Privatization and other shifts in policy and practice has changed structures and relationships in the service sector. The following new opportunities have emerged:

- The "third sector" has grown dramatically in the past decade not only in size, but in influence. Increasingly called the "independent sector," it is one of the largest employers in the country, commanding substantial resources and economic influence in terms of employment, purchase and provision of service, and with the advantage of volunteer involvement at both service and policy levels.

- Non-profits hold increasing power in negotiations with government about contracts; they hold the key to economical, innovative, and well-informed alternatives in program delivery. Besides being experienced, they are seen to be more accountable and credible than the for-profit service sector.

- Non-profit services have the capacity to be more flexible in responding to community and client needs than the heavily bureaucratized government service. To maintain this flexibility and responsiveness, the sector is experimenting with new models of decision making, program management, and delivery.

- Knowledgeable about service needs and not driven by competitiveness, agencies are more likely to share facilities, training, and other resources as well as a locally planned approach to service delivery. In the process

of developing and sharing a point of view, newsletters, journals, conferences, and less formal meetings proliferate the voluntary sector.

- Cooperative action continues, displaying a strength unique to the non-profit sector. Collectively, in coalitions, alliances and partnerships, non-profit organizations have the capacity to influence the direction of public opinion and public policy.

Opportunities and changes also bring new challenges; the future of the voluntary sector depends on these challenges being met. Among the challenges facing the volutary sector are the following:

- With the need to gain credibility in the eyes of the public, government, and other funders, and to improve program efficiency and effect, the voluntary sector is moving toward professionalization. For many agencies, being expert in developing and delivering service is essential to survival. In addition, economies of scale and the tendency to combine resources with other groups has lead to larger organizations. The difference between government or private agencies and big, multi-service agencies will begin to blur and large organizations will risk taking on the classic characteristics of bureaucracy: inaccessible, depersonalized, centralized, rigid, and authoritarian. Increasingly there is financial and philosophical pressure to adopt marketplace practices, including fee for service. How sensitive and responsive to client needs (rather than funders' requests or marketplace demands) can service organizations afford to be?

- There is a growing consciousness that the mandate of the voluntary sector is not only to deliver services but to speak to injustice in society.

Responsibility goes beyond the provision of service to the promotion of empowerment of the people served. To support an advocacy role, organizations need to work continually to develop and maintain a strong membership base, a strong volunteer board and board control, client input, and evaluation of services. These goals need to be balanced with the need for professional control at both the program and management levels; organizations must work toward high standards of service and, at the same time, deal with the organizational complexity such service requires. If organizations become increasingly involved in providing service, will they lose sight of their advocacy mandate?

The voluntary sector has had a traditional and vital role in identifying need and advocating on behalf of social reform. Many organizations will continue in this direction, particularly those dedicated to advocacy and activism. Those whose mandates shift toward direct service need to safeguard the tradition of volunteer leadership. They need to keep in sight their responsibility to the broader social vision that the voluntary sector represents.

If you have enjoyed this book and would like to receive a free catalogue of all Self-Counsel titles, please write to:

Self-Counsel Press
1481 Charlotte Road
North Vancouver, B.C.
V7J 1H1